Praise for Mark Mathabane's
Kaffir Boy

"Mr. Mathabane confronts his experiences—from the most humiliating to the most hopeful—with candor, yet without bitterness."
—*The New York Times*

"I'd like to think that *Kaffir Boy* might acquire the same status that Richard Wright's *Black Boy* or Claude Brown's *Manchild in the Promised Land* had for earlier generations of American readers. It is in every way as important and as exciting a book—with the additional ...or of showing us the horrors of apartheid through the victim's ...es."—*The Washington Post*

"What television newscasts did to expose the horrors of the Vietnam War in the 1960s, books like *Kaffir Boy* may well do for the horrors of apartheid in the 1980s. . . . Mark Mathabane has given us a front-line perspective on an increasingly grim confrontation. . . . Yet, his story also proves that reason can prevail under the most wretched human conditions."—*Chicago Tribune*

"With relentless honesty, Mathabane observes apartheid's effects on families and communities. The people in his narrative are often illiterate victims of poverty and fear. Their system turns blacks against blacks. In *Kaffir Boy*, the reader is given a rare personal glimpse of the daily fear and hunger that are so devastating to the body and the soul."—*The Philadelphia Inquirer*

Kaffir Boy in America

[handwritten inscription] ...est Wishes

Mark

KAFFIR BOY
IN AMERICA

An Encounter with
Apartheid

MARK MATHABANE

COLLIER BOOKS
Macmillan Publishing Company
New York

Mathabane Books
1320 NW Frazier Court,
Portland,OR 97229

Library of Congress Cataloging-in-Publication Data
Mathabane, Mark.
    Kaffir boy in America: an encounter with apartheid/Mark
Mathabane.
        p.   cm.
    ISBN 0-02-034530-5
    1. Mathabane, Mark.   2. Blacks—United States—Biography.
3. Immigrants—United States—Biography.   4. South Africa—
Emigration and immigration.   I. Title.
E185.97.M38A3   1990
305.8′968073—dc20   89-25297   CIP

Mark Mathabane's books are available at special discounts for bulk purchases for
sales promotions, premiums, fund raising or educational use. For details, contact:

Special Sales
Mathabane Books
1320 NW Frazier Court,
Portland,OR 97229
mark@mathabane.com
www.mathabane.com

First Collier Books Edition 1990
First Mathabane Books Edition1998
Printed in the United States of America

To Magdaline, my mother,
for keeping hope alive,
and for teaching me to believe in myself

The word *Kaffir* is of Arabic origin. It means "infidel." In South Africa it is used pejoratively by whites to refer to blacks. It is the equivalent of the term *nigger*.

A few names in the book have been changed to protect the privacy of the individuals concerned.

Contents

Preface

After *Kaffir Boy*, a portrait of my childhood and youth in Alexandra, a notorious ghetto of South Africa, became a best-seller, I received scores of letters and telephone calls from readers across the world. All pointed out that the book revealed a truth about apartheid they had never known or thought existed. All expressed support, admiration, and love for me and my family, especially my mother, who was seen as a rare and beautiful woman of indomitable faith, courage, and love.

Kaffir Boy ended with my leaving South Africa in 1978 for America, on a tennis scholarship arranged by Stan Smith, the tennis professional. Most of the book's readers wanted to know the following: How has my life turned out in America? What has happened to my family, whom I left behind in the ghetto? How do I compare the black experience in America and in South Africa?

Kaffir Boy in America is an attempt to answer these questions.

I would like to thank my wife, Gail; my editor, Ned Chase, and his assistant, Charles Flowers; and my agents, Fifi Oscard and Kevin McShane, for their invaluable support, encouragement, patience, and advice during the writing of this book. A special thanks to all the readers of *Kaffir Boy* who, through the story of my family, have joined the black majority's struggle in South Africa for freedom with dignity.

North Carolina, 1989

He who domineers over you has only two eyes, only two hands, only one body, no more than is possessed by the least man. He has indeed nothing more than the power that you confer upon him to destroy you. Where has he acquired enough eyes to spy upon you if you do not provide them yourselves? How can he have so many arms to beat you with, if he doesn't borrow them from you? The feet that trample down your cities, where does he get them, if they're not your own? How does he have any power over you, except through you? What could he do to you if you yourselves did not connive with the thief who plunders you? If you were not accomplices of the murderer who kills you? If you were not traitors to yourselves?
—ÉTIENNE DE LA BOETIE, Discourse on Voluntary Servitude

No government can exist without compromise.
—EDMUND BURKE

I believe that man will not only endure; he will prevail. He is immortal not because he alone among creatures has an inexhaustible voice, but because he has a soul, a spirit capable of compassion and sacrifice and endurance.
—WILLIAM FAULKNER

When weakness claims indulgence it justifies the despotism of strength.
—MARY WOLLSTONECRAFT

Pleasure which must be enjoyed at the expense of another's pain can never be such as a worthy mind can fully delight in.
—SAMUEL JOHNSON

If all mankind minus one were of one opinion, and only one person were of a contrary opinion, mankind would be no more justified in silencing that one person, than he, if he had the power, would be justified in silencing mankind.
—JOHN STUART MILL

"You, my friend,—a citizen of the great and mighty and wise city of Athens,—are you not ashamed of heaping up the greatest amount of money and honor and reputation, and caring little about wisdom and truth and the greatest improvement of the soul, which you never regard or heed at all?"
—SOCRATES, The Apology

PART ONE

I LEAVE
SOUTH AFRICA

1

PARTING FROM MY FAMILY; WITNESSING A POLICE RAID; DOUBTS ABOUT LEAVING SOUTH AFRICA; DREAMING ABOUT LIFE IN AMERICA; PANIC AT THE AIRPORT

As the jalopy left the yard and rattled up the potholed street, I turned my head for a last look at my family, standing in a row in front of the shack, waving sadly in the pale morning mist. There was my mother, brother, and five sisters; my father had already left for his menial job under white bosses, who ignored his self-taught skills as a carpenter and underpaid him. I wanted to tell the driver to turn back but I didn't. My family vanished from sight. I wondered if I would ever see them again—alive. The year was 1978 and I was eighteen years old.

The jalopy lumbered through the narrow, garbage-strewn streets of Alexandra, a South African ghetto, along which ghostly figures of black men and women hurried to catch the black buses, droning in the distance, that would carry them to their places of toil in the white world. Suddenly, rounding a corner into Twelfth Avenue, we stumbled upon a convoy of police vans and trucks stationed alongside the street. A pass raid was in progress. Black men and women, some half-naked and others disheveled, were being hauled out of their shacks and flung into the vans and trucks, leaving behind children standing in tears in front of smashed and gaping doors. Panic seized us. The driver, a short, gaunt, middle-aged Venda man who lived in Alexandra illegally, quickly suggested we turn back and follow another route.

"No, they've already seen us, Nditwani," I said. "If we turn back they'll get suspicious. Drive through and let's keep our fingers crossed." We spoke in Venda, our native dialect. The name "Nditwani" meant "What are you doing to me?"

3

"What if they stop us?" Nditwani asked anxiously. "You may never get to America."

"I will," I said defiantly. "My papers are in order. My passbook has all the necessary stamps."

"But mine doesn't," Nditwani said. "Remember, I live in Alexandra illegally." The Peri-Urban authorities, white administrators who lorded over the ghetto, had repeatedly refused him a residential permit, insisting that he belonged and should return to the Venda homeland where he could not eke out a living.

"It's too late now," I said. We had already entered the police zone. "If we turn back we'll surely be stopped. Anyway, they seem to be having so much fun rounding up and humiliating their prisoners that they probably won't even notice us."

I said all this in a calm, determined voice. It was all bravado; in truth my heart throbbed with fear at the likelihood that we might be stopped, interrogated, and possibly arrested on some trumped-up charge. The jalopy slowly made its way past the police vans and trucks with barred windows. The short distance of a block seemed interminable. I prayed silently. Several black policemen in brown uniforms, armed with truncheons and *sjamboks* (rawhide whips with metal tips), threw brief glances at us but did not order the car to stop: they seemed preoccupied with rounding up the scores of men and women and ensuring that none escaped. Prisoners meant money in the form of bribes and arbitrary fines. At last we were through. Panic subsided.

"That was a close call," Nditwani said.

"Yes, very close," I replied with a sigh.

But my relief was short-lived. What if my home just a few blocks away were raided before the morning was over and my mother arrested? Where would she get the bail or bribe money, since she had insisted that I take every penny with me because "you need a little something to start you on your new life in America"? I boiled with impotent rage. Was I doing the right thing in leaving? Shouldn't I stay and fight it out like all the rest? My heart was torn.

"Don't leave," a voice pleaded inside me.

"Leave and save yourself," a second voice countered. "What's there to stay for?"

"Your family, the struggle," the first voice said.

"What about your freedom?" the second voice returned. "What about America? What about your dreams?"

I left. The instinct to survive, sharpened by years of living under the nightmare of police oppression, without freedom, without hope, told me that leaving was the right thing to do and that someday the reasons would be made clear. But guilt continued to torture my heart.

The jalopy finally left the ghetto and entered a wide, paved road—roads used mainly by whites were always paved—leading to Lombardy East, one of the white suburbs through which we had to pass to reach the main highway to the airport. The sun had now fully risen and burned off the mist covering a large tract of farmland to our left as we headed east. The farm belonged to a choleric Portuguese derisively known among blacks as Matariani. He was notorious for underpaying and overworking his laborers. From time to time Granny, my mother, and other women in the neighborhood, most without permits to live in Alexandra, toiled for him, planting and harvesting corn, beets, potatoes, and other crops. They were paid about three rands ($1.50) for a ten-hour day.

I sat stiffly alongside Nditwani, who now hummed a tune to himself. Since the police roadblock, the two of us had hardly exchanged a word. He seemed aware that I was grappling with a tormented conscience and thought it wise to live me alone. The backseat was crowded with my luggage of several cheap suitcases and a totebag, packed with all my worldly belongings.

As I stared at the luggage, there came flooding into my mind the strange coincidences which had led me, at the age of eleven, to make that terrifying yet auspicious trip to the white world of Rosebank, a wealthy suburb of Johannesburg, where I met the Smiths, Granny's employers, who did not fit the stereotypes I had grown up with. The Smiths treated their black servants with paternalistic generosity. They introduced me to books that changed my life and provided a ray of hope in a hopeless world. Later, when I began working for them at several menial jobs—sweeping driveways, shining shoes, cleaning the pool, washing cars, weeding the garden, and polishing brass and silver—they gave me my first tennis racket, a slightly warped Rod Laver autograph model, which led me to extraordinary adventures in the white tennis world of South Africa.

Then there was that purely accidental—or was it accidental?—meeting with Stan Smith, the American tennis professional, and his wife, Margie, during the South African Breweries Open in November 1977, in which Stan reached the semi-finals in singles and won the doubles with Bob Lutz. I was the only black player participating and I lost in the qualifying rounds to Abe Segal, a former Wimbledon doubles champion with Gordon Forbes. Stan and Margie, after hearing my life story of growing up destitute in the ghetto, and my burning desire to go to college in America, had befriended me and made possible the miracle of my being awarded a tennis scholarship by an American college. Everything had happened so quickly. Nothing in all my life had prepared me for this day. Was I truly leaving or was it all a dream?

"You're very lucky to be going to America, you know," Nditwani said, breaking the spell of my thoughts as we entered Lombardy East.

"Yes. Very, very lucky."

"Man, just look at all those nice houses," he said, pointing out the window. "White people sure live like kings and queens."

In the bright morning sun the elegant houses of white folks could be seen in all their splendor. Birds sang from budding and evergreen trees, heralding the early arrival of spring in the Southern Hemisphere. Nditwani, a self-taught mechanic who repaired jalopies for a living, was one of my biggest fans. He had followed my tennis and scholastic career with interest. Though poor, he occasionally gave me money to buy books and used tennis balls, usually in return for my washing his cars. I appreciated his generosity.

"Things just don't happen this way for a ghetto boy, you know," Nditwani said. "So many of us try to escape from this hell but we always fail. We're like those prisoners in the movie *Papillon*. Remember *Papillon*?"

We had both seen the movie, a favorite among males in the ghetto, several times at Kings, the local black cinema.

"Yes," I said. "I still can't believe they're letting me go."

"Well believe it, my friend," Nditwani said with pride. "Believe it because our African gods, the gods of our ancestors, are powerful. They made this miracle possible."

"Do you really believe in Midzimu, Nditwani?" I asked. The pantheon of Venda gods was known as Midzimu.

"Of course I do. Don't you?"

"This god business is very confusing," I said. "There are so many of them. I don't know which one to believe."

"Well, whatever you choose to believe," Nditwani said, "don't ever believe in the white man's god."

"But my mother believes in Jesus Christ," I said.

"I respect your old lady," Nditwani said. "She's a good woman. There's no kinder person in the yard. But I think she's wrong to believe in the god of people who oppress us."

"I, too, have my doubts about the Christian god," I said. "You know what, Nditwani? I'll put off believing in any god until I have enough proof which is the true god and which are phony."

"Suit yourself," Nditwani said. "But I still believe that the African gods gave you this chance. They're watching over you. So don't waste it, or they'll get mad. And make us proud, my friend. Let the world know about our sufferings and our struggle and our dreams. Learn as much as you can in America and come back and teach us. There's a desperate need in Alexandra for educated people like you, as you know."

"Yes, I will come back."

"Okay, now that I've said what had been oppressing my chest, let me get back to the road," Nditwani said. "We mustn't get lost on this very special day."

In the silence which ensued I pondered the strange fate which had decreed, against all odds, that I should survive the nightmares of my childhood—hunger, police raids and beatings, poverty, suffering, death—and at eighteen should leave my family, my friends, my home, everything and everyone I loved, to begin life anew in a strange land called America. Was there truly a purpose to my life after all?

My mother always insisted there was a purpose each time something unusual occurred to alter my fortunes. She had said so when I was granted the permit without which I could not have registered at the local tribal school; again when I took my first trip to the white world of Rosebank and met the Smiths, Granny's employers; and a third time when I met the Americans Stan and Margie who made my dream of going to America come true. She was also the one who prevented me from committing suicide at age ten by telling me, with tears streaming down her cheeks, as she took the knife away from my hand, that she loved me, that I was her only hope and if I died she would die, too, that I should cling to life and things would get better. She emphatically believed that an all-knowing and loving God had planned everything right from the start, and that mischievous and ungodly people had temporarily botched things in a futile attempt to prevent the inevitable.

I lacked my mother's kind of faith in God. When I was still a mere child apartheid had savagely robbed me of that innocence and trust without which such a faith is impossible, and had planted in my mind the seeds of a skepticism doomed to persist so long as I remained imprisoned under a system which maintained that the oppression and degradation of black people was God's law.

Yet my skepticism had begun to be shaken, especially when I realized that countless black youngsters in the ghetto, some of them more gifted than I, had ended up dead, imprisoned, exiled, or driven insane by frustration, bitterness, rage, and lack of opportunity. Others had become alcoholics, chronic gamblers, hardened criminals, drug addicts, unwed teen mothers, and prostitutes, or had yielded themselves up, after heroic but futile struggles, to the countless temptations in the ghetto that led only to self-destruction. And here I was, at eighteen, relatively unscathed by comparison, going to America on a tennis scholarship, the first South African black ever to do so.

What power had saved me? I wondered. My own efforts? Talent? The spirits of my ancestors? Luck? My mother's inflexible resolve to see me succeed? Or was there indeed a greater power, in the form of the Christian God my mother worshiped, a God who governed her life and actions and gave her an almost saintly serenity amid the hurricane troubles of ghetto life? Maybe someday, amid freedom, in a society where I could read and question without fear of persecution, I would get to the bottom of this question of my mother's Christian God.

The jalopy left Lombardy East and entered the sprawling white suburb of Edenvale. As we drove past ritzy houses with tennis courts, I remembered the times when I had played tennis illegally in some of them, in defiance of segregation laws. I played with enlightened white friends, one of whom, André Zietsman, had studied in America. My thoughts turned to that strange and fascinating country. I wondered what sort of future awaited me there. Would my dreams, half-formed and fantastic as they seemed, be given the opportunity to come true? Was America truly the land of freedom and opportunity even for black people, as André had told me, as the magazines and pamphlets I had read, from the American consulate in Johannesburg and the embassy in Pretoria, depicted it to be, and as the few black Americans I had seen, the successful athletes, singers, and entertainers, heralded it to be? Or was there racism and oppression lurking somewhere in

American society that André had overlooked, that the contents of these magazines and pamphlets, and the lives and utterances of these superstars, had not revealed?

As the various scenes of Edenvale—department stores, parks, schools, houses, bowling greens, athletic fields, billboards, neatly dressed white people, expensive cars, gas stations—glided past the car window through which I stared vacantly, I chided myself for thinking too much, for imagining things, for being too anxious. America *was* the land of freedom. Slavery had long been abolished and the legendary Dr. King had won black people their equal rights which had enabled them to perform wonders. There could be no apartheid in America.

I ran my eyes over the three Donnay tennis rackets on my lap, a gift from André. Along with books, they had been my salvation from a dead-end life, my passport to freedom. Maybe they would be my key to a new life of fame and fortune in America. Once in the Promised Land I hoped to pursue without restraints a dream I had cherished since I first heard of Arthur Ashe: to become a professional tennis player. Many people had advised me to abandon such a delusion, but here I was taking the first step toward making it a reality.

"You know," I said to Nditwani, as we finally entered the highway leading to Jan Smuts Airport. "I feel more powerful, more alive and full of hope armed with these rackets than I would if I were armed with guns. I know that sounds foolish. Particularly now, when guns are needed, and not tennis rackets, to fight back against white oppression. But that's how I feel."

"We all have to fight the struggle in our own way," Nditwani said, echoing words I had heard before and believed. "Some have to use guns. Others must become doctors and teachers and lawyers. Maybe you'll become our first Arthur Ashe—who knows. Then you can prove to white people that we, too, can succeed if given the chance."

"I want to make tons of money playing tennis," I said.

"Why?" he asked laughing.

"Because money means power," I said. "It's the only thing white people respect."

"How did you get so clever?"

"I have been learning the ways of white folks," I said.

We again lapsed into silence. Our conversation was in spurts.

Aside from my meditative mood, we had to be constantly on the lookout for the police, who under apartheid laws had the right to stop any vehicle driven by blacks and interrogate its occupants.

The silence brought into my mind thoughts about my family. The realization that I was leaving them filled me with guilt. Yet it fired my determination to succeed in America so I could alleviate their suffering, which I knew I could have done had I chosen to stay. And this knowledge added to the guilt.

As the eldest of seven children, and the first in the family to be educated, I would have been there to protect my siblings from the destructive elements of ghetto life, to insist on the importance of their education, and would have paid for their school fees, uniforms, and books. I would have been there to urge them—just like my mother and Granny had urged me—to set goals in life, to be ambitious, to believe in themselves, to have dreams. After all, I had against all odds completed my matriculation. With André's help, I had landed a banking job at Barclays Bank, with prospects of advancement and reward dizzying for a ghetto boy. I was paid five times the combined wage of my mother and father, though I had been on the job only a few months, and they had been drudges for white people for years.

But I had to leave. My mother understood that my yearning for freedom had made me leave. The others in my family did not. She had to help them understand. Yet I was mystified by how she had come to know the true meaning of freedom when she had spent her entire life under the stunting force of a triple oppression: as a woman, an illiterate, and a black. There was no doubt in my mind that I could never have survived the hell of ghetto life without her. Tears came to my eyes at the thought of her.

"We've made it, Mark," Nditwani shouted with joy, pointing to a sign which read JAN SMUTS AIRPORT, NEXT RIGHT. "I can hear the airplanes."

Once we reached the huge airport we had difficulty following the signs to the terminals. We were afraid of entering areas reserved for whites. We saw white policemen nearby but dreaded asking them for directions to the international departure terminal, lest they end up arresting us. So we kept going around in circles. Finally we spotted the sign INTERNATIONAL DEPARTURES. Nditwani dropped me and the bags alongside the curb.

"I can't risk parking the car and coming inside to see you off," he said.

"I understand," I said. Since his papers were not in order, any mishap like a parking ticket could have landed him in jail or had him deported to the tribal reserves. "Thanks very much, Nditwani, and good luck on the way back. You'd better tell the family that you did see my plane off or they'll die of worries."

"I will. The gods be with you," he said in Venda, a tear in his eye.

We embraced and he left.

As I lugged my heavy bags through the gigantic airport, white men and women gave me questioning looks, and some pointed at me amid whispers. The bunch of tennis rackets clutched under my arm apparently proclaimed me as the "black tennis star who was jetting to America," as one paper, the now-defunct *Rand Daily Mail*, had blazed the news of my imminent departure for the United States.

Armed white policemen in neat uniforms and shiny boots stood at various locations inside the terminal. They stared at me as I made my way from the British Airways ticket counter to the international departure lounge. Except for the forlorn-faced men and women engaged in menial jobs, I was the only black in sight. I remained cool and occasionally stared back at an exasperated policeman. I relished the giddying and unbelievable prospect that in a few hours I would be beyond their reach, their persecution, their sadism, their vindictiveness, clean out of the house of bondage of which they were the guards.

I wondered what they thought as they watched me leave. Did they know how ancient I felt at eighteen, how worn my soul had become? Did they know that I was leaving behind millions like me, who longed to breathe freedom in the land of their birth? Did they know that their ruthless enforcement of apartheid was embittering and destroying an entire generation, the hope and future of a people, the salvation of our beloved country?

If they did know, I wondered, was there a grain of humanity left in them to feel any remorse? I doubted it. For a moment I pitied them. But when I considered what they stood for they became targets of my rage, a rage whose intensity frightened me, but which I couldn't help feeling. I cursed them under my breath and exulted in the thought that though they had tried many times, though I still bore the invisible scars of their barbarity, they had not broken me; I had remained defiant to the end. I even had the impulse to yank out my passbook, tear it to shreds, and fling the pieces at their pink faces.

I reached the boarding area and was warmly welcomed by British

Airways stewardesses with beaming faces who addressed me as "Sir." Some of the white passengers continued gaping at me, as if I were some monkey escaped from the zoo. There were no BLACKS ONLY or WHITES ONLY signs in the departure lounge. I boarded the wide-bodied jumbo jet without incident. Once inside, I stowed my carry-on bags and rackets and took a seat next to the window. In the seat across the aisle from me sat an elderly silver-haired white man in a khaki suit. No one occupied the two seats between us. I scanned the half-full plane and saw two other blacks, seated separately and alone. They looked like foreigners. I longed to join either of them for companionship but was afraid.

I tried reading a magazine but could not concentrate. I kept thinking about the white policemen. The police are such an inseparable part of a black South African's reality that once they invade one's consciousness it takes forever to get rid of them. Suddenly I became acutely aware that in a few minutes I would be beyond their reach. With this realization my sense of reality wavered—doubts whirled in my mind that I would not be allowed to go. I wondered why the plane was taking so long to leave. Did the delay have something to do with my presence aboard? I recalled the problems I had experienced obtaining the passport. I expected momentarily to be dragged off the plane by agents of BOSS (Bureau of State Security) and told that I was not leaving for America after all, that something was wrong with my papers. I had heard of black people at the last minute being hauled off planes and flung into detention to prevent their leaving South Africa and telling the world the truth about black life under apartheid.

I began trembling uncontrollably and my clothes were drenched in a cold sweat. My eyes darted anxiously about the plane. Stricken with anxiety, I felt dizzy and faint. A sharp pain pierced my breastbone. I loosened my necktie, reached above my seat, and released a gush of oxygen. I took a couple of deep breaths. The elderly white man in the khaki suit leaned over and asked kindly, "Anything wrong?"

"Nothing, sir, nothing," I muttered. "I'll be fine. Too much excitement, I guess. I'm not used to flying."

"Don't worry," he said. "Once we're airborne you won't even know that we're flying. Keep taking those deep breaths and just relax."

"Thank you, sir."

I muttered a prayer under my breath. Slowly the plane left the gate. The stewardesses demonstrated how to use the safety equipment. We taxied down the runway. I scarcely believed it was happening. Tears came to my eyes. The strange symptoms gradually went away. I began to feel better. I sighed heavily several times. We were airborne. I was free at last.

2

FLIGHT TO NAIROBI; CONVERSATION WITH ENGLISH-SPEAKING WHITE SOUTH AFRICAN; FIRST GLIMPSE OF A COUNTRY RUN BY BLACKS

From Jan Smuts Airport we flew directly to Nairobi, Kenya, a trip lasting several hours. During the flight the old man in the khaki suit—his name was Phillip Knox—and I found occasion to talk. Phillip was an English-speaking South African from Lower Houghton, one of the wealthiest suburbs of Johannesburg. He had made his fortune in the diamond business, was now retired, and annually took safari trips to East Africa, where he indulged one of his favorite hobbies: shooting pictures of wildlife. Phillip was impressed to learn that I was headed for America on a tennis scholarship.

"Have you been to America before?" he asked.

"No, sir."

"You'll love it there. I've been to America several times. Too big and too wild for me."

I said nothing.

"You must be a very good player to have won a tennis scholarship."

"I was very lucky. I still have much to learn."

"Where did you learn to play the game?"

"In Alexandra."

"Ah, yes, I've heard of Alexandra," he said. "One of my boys"—at the pejorative word "boy" he caught himself—"one of my workers, I mean, his name is Amos," he said awkwardly, "used to live there."

I felt tempted to ask him if he had ever set foot in the ghetto, but his next remarks provided the answer.

"What sort of place is Alexandra, anyway?" he asked. "I

constantly read in the papers that there's lots of unrest and violence. I remember one time Amos couldn't come to work for days because students were burning buses."

I proceeded to explain that Alexandra was a one-square-mile ghetto with a population of over 100,000 black souls, most of whom lived in shacks made of pieces of plastic, rusted zinc, cardboard, and crumbling adobe bricks; that it had no electricity, no running water, no sewers, and only one paved road and one understaffed clinic; that many of its inhabitants lived there illegally, were unemployed, and being quarantined and desperate, preyed upon one another in the most violent ways; and that following the Soweto uprisings of 1976, in which scores of men, women, and children were killed by the police, the ghetto had been under military occupation.

"Good heavens," the old man exclaimed. "That many people in so small and terrible a place. How do you live?"

"We survive," I said laconically.

"No, this is wrong," he said, shaking his head. "I didn't know things were that bad. The bloody Afrikaners are mad."

I said nothing. English-speaking whites, despite their liberal tendencies and self-righteous blaming of Afrikaners for apartheid, also benefit from the system: they have their posh whites-only suburbs, their "boys" and "girls," they pay taxes which support the apartheid bureaucracy and military, and they vote in whites-only elections, thereby legitimizing the regime.

"Did you leave your family behind?" the old man asked.

"Yes."

"How many are there in your family?"

I told him four sisters, a brother, and both parents.

"Are they safe?"

"I hope so."

"How long will you be gone?"

"Four years."

"Are they provided for?"

"My father works."

"How much does he make?"

"Fifteen rands [about eight dollars] a week."

"Good heavens!" the old man cried. "How do you make it on that little money?"

"We manage somehow."

"Here's my card," he said, reaching into his coat pocket. "Next time you talk to them, give them my address and telephone number. Tell them to contact me whenever they need help."

"Thank you, sir," I said.

Our conversation was interrupted by stewardesses who served us breakfast. Following breakfast our conversation resumed briefly, touching on, as we flew over Zimbabwe (then Rhodesia), the raging bush war between the racist army of Ian Smith and the black liberation forces of Robert Mugabe and Joshua Nkomo known as the Patriotic Front.

"I pray to God war doesn't break out in South Africa," the old man said. "The whole country will be ruined."

"War is a terrible thing," I said. "It only breeds hatred and bloodshed."

"You're absolutely right," he said.

I soon left the old man to his maps and camera equipment to feast my eyes on the spectacular scenery below. It was a clear cloudless day. The landscape unveiled a breathtaking vista of snow-capped mountains, grassy plains, waterfalls, lakes, and rolling hills. We landed at Nairobi's Kenyatta International Airport in early afternoon. Having learned that the plane wouldn't be leaving for another two hours, I deplaned and wandered about the airport, hunting for souvenirs and catching my first glimpses of a country run by Africans. I was amazed to see around the airport, which teemed with white tourists, so many black people in positions of authority, confidently talking to whites, courteously giving them orders and instructions on what to do or where to go. And most whites obeyed without a single complaint. This was in stark contrast to the scenes of black subservience I had witnessed throughout South Africa. I was impressed.

At once I saw through the lie white South Africans are so fond of indulging in. They constantly say that blacks in the rest of Africa envy the lot of black South Africans, and that the whole of independent black Africa is run by corrupt, bloodthirsty lunatics like Idi Amin and Emperor Bokassa, who were proof that blacks were incapable of civilized and democratic self-government.

Without doubt many African countries are experiencing very serious problems with totalitarian rule, civil wars, corruption, and badly managed economies. All these problems must be exposed, criticized, and corrected. But critics of Africa often overlook the important fact that many of Africa's problems have their roots in colonialism with its bitter legacy. That terrible system of oppression and exploitation, which raped and plundered Africa for the comforts and progress of European and American societies, which erected artificial boundaries between black nations, thereby exacerbating tribal differences and fomenting internecine wars, which, in the name of progress and civilization, indiscriminately destroyed African cultures, and which created elite classes of blacks while depriving the majority of the necessary education and livelihood, has in many an African country left behind pernicious and despicable creatures, "black colonialists" I call them, who have learned and improved on all their former masters' tricks. Black tyrants throughout independent Africa, I feel, are no different from the white colonial overlords they have replaced. We in South Africa have similar pests in our midst. I mean those black people who, for an illusion of power and freedom, for crumbs from the white man's table, for the satisfaction of their ambition and avarice, allow themselves to be used as expendable instruments of oppression of their brethren by the apartheid system.

STOPOVER IN LONDON; FLIGHT TO ATLANTA, GEORGIA; SPECULATIONS ABOUT AMERICA SPARK FEELINGS OF INFERIORITY; WARNING FROM A BLACK MUSLIM; ARRIVAL IN AMERICA

From Nairobi we flew nonstop to Heathrow Airport, London, where I was booked on a flight to the United States. Throughout the long flight I kept to myself. I read magazines, watched the hilarious in-flight movie, *The In-Laws*, listened to pop music on earphones, was served a delicious dinner, perused the various documents needed to enter the United States to make sure they were in order, and slept. We landed at Heathrow in the early morning hours. Once I was on English soil South Africa and the problems of apartheid ceased to dominate my mind.

I was intimidated by the gigantic airport swarming with passengers from various countries. I was bewildered by the strange languages spoken by the persons I constantly bumped into as I wandered through the terminals. The confusion worsened as I tried to keep track of the voices booming over the loudspeakers about canceled, connecting, departing, and arriving flights, and paging various individuals. I feared getting lost. Luckily I was able to follow instructions, read signs, and ask directions. Everyone was helpful, including the police, who, unlike their South African counterparts, did not carry guns. I was glad that I had spent all those years reading English books, listening to the BBC and VOA (Voice of America) on shortwave radio, and speaking the language, despite being ridiculed by my father and some blacks as "an imitation white man."

I learned that my plane to Atlanta, Georgia, would be departing from Gatwick Airport instead of Heathrow. That meant I would arrive in America several hours late. While waiting to be transferred to Gatwick by shuttle bus, I removed from my totebag a dogeared booklet containing the American Constitution, the Bill of Rights, and that manifesto of revolutions, the Declaration of Independence, and once more read them. I almost knew the words by heart, especially the passages concerning individual liberties, equality, and the right and duty of an oppressed people to overthrow tyrannical governments. Along with the plethora of black American success stories I had read about in magazines like *Ebony*, *Jet*, and *Drum*, these three documents, which I obtained from the U.S. consulate in Johannesburg, formed the basis of my understanding of American society, of my implicit belief that America had long solved its racial problems and created a paradise for all of its citizens.

I was so completely under the spell of the words "We hold these truths to be self-evident, that all men are created equal, and endowed by their Creator with certain unalienable rights, that among these are Life, Liberty and the pursuit of Happiness . . ." that I had ignored the warning one of my uncles had given me before I left, after he had heard me recite the words and explain their sensational meaning to incredulous family members assembled around the brazier one evening.

"Such a society, my dear nephew," Uncle Cheeks had said in Tsonga, "can never exist on the surface of this world. Wherever black and white people live together, and whites have the power, then blacks must somehow be their slaves."

I remember dismissing his warning with "What do you know about America, Uncle Cheeks? You've never been there. Haven't you heard of Muhammad Ali, Diana Ross, Sidney Poitier, Arthur Ashe, and all those famous, rich, and powerful black Americans?"

And he had replied, "My dear nephew, take it from me, I may not know America, but I know the white beast. He is the same everywhere. His primary function, his greatest joy in life, is to keep the black man down and suffering."

Aware that Uncle Cheeks, like my father, had been repeatedly imprisoned, denied decent jobs, demeaned, and emasculated by white people, and that such bitter experiences had left him with an implacable hatred and suspicion of everything and everyone white, I had attributed his remarks to his impotent rage. I was far from being aware that the Declaration of Independence, the Constitution, and the Bill of Rights embodied the ideals Americans strove for, not the actual reality.

On the flight to America I sat alongside a middle-aged white couple from Arizona who, like many passengers on board, were returning home from a European vacation. We exchanged polite greetings but hardly talked. For much of the flight the happy couple was preoccupied with reminiscing over visits to Ireland, Scotland, and England, and admiring their many photos of castles, cathedrals, and other famous tourist sights. The two filled me with a longing to travel, and brought to mind one of my favorite books, *Around the World in Eighty Days*, by Jules Verne.

After several cups of orange juice and a hearty meal (the stewardess even gave me seconds), I watched a movie and then slept about an hour. I was awakened by the plane encountering turbulence over the Atlantic. I almost panicked as it bobbed up and down. After several minutes the ride smoothed out. I rose and went to the bathroom. On returning I noticed in the row of seats behind mine a bearded Black Muslim in white robes. He was asleep.

Back in my seat I took out the letter from Dr. Ronald Killion, the white tennis coach and a history professor at Limestone College. In it he congratulated me on having won the tennis scholarship, worth about $5,000, and provided me with the description of his friend, Dr. Charles Waller, a professor of English at the University of Georgia, who was to meet me in Atlanta. I also took out the Limestone College brochure and perused it again. The four-year, coeducational liberal arts college, founded in 1845, was located in Gaffney, South Carolina, a town of about 20,000. The college had close to five hundred students. The brochure stated that many of the South's most influential families used to send their children to be educated at Limestone College. The pictures of its stately buildings and verdant surroundings, the list of the various majors and courses offered, led me to think it one of the finest colleges in America. All this impressive information on Limestone bolstered the image I had of America as the richest, most powerful, sophisticated, and civilized society in the world.

When the pilot announced we were approaching the mainland, this image of America made me feel inferior for having been born and raised in a South African ghetto. I could not conceive of a more deprived origin. I imagined my competitors at Limestone to be brilliant students who had been taught to read and write while still infants, had been showered with toys and children's books and fed nutritious food that had fully developed their brain power and intelligence. I imagined them to have attended the best high schools and to be years ahead of me in terms of maturity, ability, and knowledge of the world.

I was convinced that apartheid and the tribal education of the ghettos had retarded my growth as a human being, and that I possessed none of the skills to function effectively, let alone succeed, in such a society. All of a sudden my dreams of acquiring a university degree, of conquering the tennis world as Arthur Ashe had done, of becoming rich and famous and independent of whites, seemed ridiculous.

How could I hope to accomplish all these miracles, I asked myself, when I had been born of illiterate parents whose lives were still ruled by superstition and antiquated tribal beliefs; when I had lived my entire life in a crowded and crumbling shack, without electricity or running water; when hunger had been a constant childhood companion; when I was a self-taught tennis player who had yet to master the basics of the sophisticated white man's game; when I had failed the mandatory course in Tsonga, my native tongue, because I had focused my energies instead on mastering English; when in my own country I was considered a fourth-class citizen, part of the dregs of society? What had deluded me into believing I could compete with Americans, who put men on the moon, let alone beat them, on their own turf, with the game played according to their complex Western rules? In America I expected to be judged according to my imperfections and background.

Because of my origins, I saw myself looked down upon by civilized Americans and derided for my ignorance of how things were done in their cosmopolitan world. I saw myself, in tennis, having to compete against college players of the caliber of Arthur Ashe and Jimmy Connors. I saw them drub me mercilessly, and the coach realize his mistake in awarding me a tennis scholarship without having seen me play, solely on the assumption that, because I had been discovered by the tennis star Stan Smith, I would turn out to be another Yannick Noah. (After being discovered by Arthur Ashe during a visit to Cameroon, Yannick Noah had gone on to become one of the best tennis players in the world.) I saw my tennis scholarship revoked and my ignominiously being sent back to South Africa as a failure.

I started wondering if I hadn't committed a terrible blunder in fleeing from problems and dangers and difficulties I knew, and to which in some measure I had become inured, to those I knew not. Had I remained in South Africa I was at least assured of living in splendid vassalage. After all, I had already climbed a few grades up the ladder of a lucrative banking career before I became intoxicated with wild ideas about freedom and tennis fame.

What could I do? There was no turning back. Atlanta was only a few minutes away; South Africa, thousands of miles. Besides, I had a one-way ticket.

What did I have going for me? I frantically asked myself.

Who or what could I turn to when the going got rough? I was alone in a foreign land, with no family or friends, no wise mother to give me sound advice. As for Stan and Margie Smith, they'd already done too much for me, and the last thing I wanted was to become dependent on them. Besides, would they allow me to become closely associated with them, given their celebrity status and my humble origins? I only had a few dollars to my name.

It became clear to me that I had nothing left to depend upon but my own determination to succeed; nothing left but faith that some greater power watched over me and would never forsake me as long as I tried; nothing left but the vague belief that though I was burdened with an apartheid childhood, though I may have to start from rock bottom in America, at least the scholarship gave me an opportunity, and with no apartheid laws to curb my ambition and prescribe my place in life, I would be free to work upon my handicaps, whatever they turned out to be. And given time I was confident I would succeed in something. To me this freedom and opportunity were worth everything, including all the self-doubt, the fears, the risks. Finally I consoled myself with the thought that, for all the qualifications, America, the Free World, was better than South Africa, the slave world.

The plane landed at Atlanta's International Airport the afternoon of September 17, 1978. I double-checked the name and description of Dr. Killion's friend who was to meet me. Shortly after the plane came to a standstill at the gate, and I was stashing Dr. Killion's letter into my totebag, I felt a tap on my shoulder, and turning met the steady and unsettling gaze of the Black Muslim.

"Are you from Africa?" he asked as he offered to help me with my luggage.

"Yes." I wondered how he could tell.

"A student?"

"Yes." We were aboard a jumbo jet, almost at the back of it. From the throng in front it was clear that it would be some time before we disembarked, so we fell into conversation. He asked if it was my first time in the United States and I replied that it was. He spoke in a thick American accent.

"Glad to meet you, brother," he said. We shook hands. "My name is Nkwame."

"I'm Mark," I said, somewhat intimidated by his aspect.

"Mark is not African," he said coolly. "What's your African name, brother?"

"Johannes."

"That isn't an African name either."

I was startled by this. How did he know I had an African name? I hardly used it myself because it was an unwritten rule among black youths raised in the ghettos to deny their tribal identity and affiliation, and that denial applied especially to names. But I didn't want to offend this persistent stranger, so I gave it to him. "Thanyani."

"What does it stand for?"

How did he know that my name stood for something? I wondered in amazement. My worst fears were confirmed. Black Americans did indeed possess the sophistication to see through any ruse an African puts up. Then and there I decided to tell nothing but the truth.

"The wise one," I said, and quickly added, "but the interpretation is not meant to be taken literally, sir."

We were now headed out of the plane. He carried my tennis rackets.

"The wise one, heh," he mused. "You Africans sure have a way with names. You know," he went on with great warmth, "one of my nephews is named after a famous African chief. Of the Mandingo tribe, I believe. Ever since I saw 'Roots' I have always wanted to know where my homeland is."

I found this statement baffling for I thought that as an American his homeland was America. I did not know about "Roots."

"Which black college in Atlanta will you be attending, Thanyani?" he asked. "You will be attending a black college, I hope?"

Black colleges? I stared at him. My mind conjured up images of the dismal tribal schools I hated and had left behind in the ghetto. My God, did such schools exist in America?

"No, sir," I stammered. "I won't be attending school in Atlanta. I'm headed for Limestone College in South Carolina."

"Is Limestone a black college?"

"No, sir," I said hastily.

"What a pity," he sighed. "You would be better off at a black college."

I continued staring at him.

He went on. "At a black college," he said with emphasis, "you can meet with your true brothers and sisters. There's so much you can teach them about the true Africa and the struggles of our people over there. And they have a lot to teach you about being black in America. And, you know, there are lots of black colleges in the South."

I nearly fainted at this revelation. Black schools in America? Was I hearing things or what? I almost blurted out that I had attended black schools all my life and wanted to have nothing to do with them. But instead I said, "Limestone College is supposed to be a good college, too, sir. It's integrated."

"That don't mean nothing," he snapped. "Integrated schools are the worst places for black folks. I thought you Africans would have enough brains to know that this integration business in America is a fraud. It ain't good for the black mind and culture. Integration, integration," he railed. "What good has integration done the black man? We've simply become more dependent on the white devil and forgotten how to do things for ourselves. Also, no matter how integrated we become, white folks won't accept us as equals. So why should we break our backs trying to mix with them, heh? To them we will always be niggers."

I was shaken by his outburst. I longed to be gone from him, especially since he had drawn me aside in the corridor leading toward customs. The Black Muslim must have realized that I was a complete stranger to him, that his bitter tone terrified and confused me, for he quickly recollected himself and smiled.

"Well, good luck in your studies, brother," he said handing me my rackets. "By the way, where in Africa did you say you were from? Nigeria?"

"No. South Africa."

"South what!" he said.

"South Africa," I repeated. "That place with all those terrible race problems. Where black people have no rights and are being murdered every day."

I expected my statement to shock him; instead he calmly said, "You will find a lot of South Africa in this country, brother. Keep your eyes wide open all the time. Never let down your guard or you're dead. And while you're up there in South Carolina, watch out for the Ku Klux Klan. That's their home. And don't you ever believe that integration nonsense."

He left. I wondered what he meant by his warning. I stumbled my way to customs. There was a long queue and when my turn came the white, somber-faced immigration official, with cropped reddish-brown hair, seemed transformed into an Afrikaner bureaucrat. I almost screamed. He demanded my passport. After inspecting it, he asked to see my plane ticket. I handed it to him.

"It's a one-way ticket," he said.

"Yes, sir. I couldn't afford a return ticket," I answered, wondering what could be wrong.

"Under the student visa regulations you're required to have a return ticket," he said icily. "Otherwise how will you get back home? You intend returning home after your studies, don't you?"

"Yes, sir."

"Then you ought to have a return ticket."

I remained silent.

"Do you have relatives or a guardian in America?"

I speedily handed him a letter from Stan Smith, along with several completed immigration forms indicating that he had pledged to be my legal guardian for the duration of my stay in the States. The immigration official inspected the documents, then left his cubicle and went to consult his superior. I trembled at the thought that I might be denied entry into the United States. But the one-way ticket, which created the impression that I was coming to America for good, was hardly my fault. Having had no money to purchase a ticket of my own, I had depended on the charity of white friends, and I was in no position to insist that they buy me a return ticket. The immigration official came back. He stamped my passport and welcomed me to the United States. I almost fell on my knees and kissed the hallowed ground.

"Welcome to America, Mark," a tall, lean-faced white man greeted me as I came out of customs. It was Dr. Waller.

His kind voice and smiling face, as he introduced himself and asked me if I had a good flight, raised my spirits. As we walked toward the baggage claim area I stared at everything about me with childlike wonder. I scarcely believed I had finally set foot in *the* America. I felt the difference between South Africa and America instantly. The air seemed pervaded with freedom and hope and opportunity. Every object seemed brighter, newer, more modern, fresher, the people appeared better dressed, more intelligent, richer, warmer, happier, and full of energy—despite the profound impersonality of the place.

"I would like to use the lavatory," I told Dr. Waller.

"There should be one over there." He pointed to a sign ahead which read RESTROOMS. "I'll wait for you at the newsstand over there."

When I reached the restroom I found it had the sign MEN in black and white on it. Just before I entered I instinctively scoured the walls to see if I had missed the other more important sign: BLACKS ONLY or WHITES ONLY, but there was none. I hesitated before entering: this freedom was too new, too strange, too unreal, and called for the utmost caution. Despite what I believed about America, there still lingered in the recesses of my mind the terror I had suffered in South Africa when I had inadvertently disobeyed the racial etiquette, like that time in Pretoria when I mistakenly boarded a white bus, and Granny had to grovel before the irate redneck driver, emphatically declare that it was an insanity "not of the normal kind" which had made me commit such a crime, and to appease him proceeded to wipe, with her lovely tribal dress, the steps where I had trod. In such moments of doubt such traumas made me mistrust my instincts. I saw a lanky black American with a mammoth Afro enter and I followed. I relieved myself next to a white man and he didn't die.

The black American washed his hands and began combing his Afro. I gazed at his hair with wonder. In South Africa blacks adored Afros and often incurred great expense cultivating that curious hairdo, in imitation of black Americans. Those who succeeded in giving their naturally crinkly, nappy, and matted hair, which they loathed, that buoyant "American" look were showered with praise and considered handsome and "glamorous," as were those who successfully gave it the permanent wave or jerry-curl, and bleached their faces white with special creams which affected the pigmentation.

I remember how Uncle Pietrus, on my father's side, a tall, athletic, handsome man who earned slave wages, was never without creams such as Ambi to bleach his face, and regularly wore a meticulously combed Afro greased with Brylcreem. Many in the neighborhood considered him the paragon of manly beauty, and women were swept away by his "American" looks.

From time to time he proudly told me stories of how, in the center of Johannesburg, whites who encountered black men and women with bleached faces, Afros, or straightened hair, and clad in the latest fashion from America, often mistook them for black Americans and treated them as honorary whites. A reasonable American accent made the masquerade almost foolproof. So for many blacks there were these incentives to resemble black Americans, to adopt their mannerisms and life-styles. And the so-called Coloureds (mixed race), with their naturally lighter skin and straightened hair, not only frequently took advantage of this deception but often passed for whites. But they were rarely secure in their false identity. And in their desperation to elude discovery and humiliation at being subjected to fraudulent race-determining tests like the pencil test (where the authorities run a pencil through one's hair: if the pencil slides smoothly through, one gets classified white; if it gets tangled, that's "positive" proof of being black), they often adopted racist attitudes toward blacks more virulent than those of the most racist whites.

I had sense enough to disdain the practice of whitening one's skin. I considered it pathetic and demeaning to blacks. As for the companies which manufactured these popular creams, they are insidiously catering to a demand created by over three hundred years of white oppression and domination. During that traumatic time the black man's culture and values were decimated in the name of civilization, and the white man's culture and values, trumpeted as superior, became the standards of intelligence, excellence, and beauty.

I left the bathroom and rejoined Dr. Waller at the newsstand. I found him reading a magazine.

"There's so much to read here," I said, running my eyes over the newspapers, magazines, and books. Interestingly, almost all had white faces on the cover, just as in South Africa.

"Yes," replied Dr. Waller.

I was shocked to see pornography magazines, which are banned in South Africa, prominently displayed. The puritan and Calvinistic religion of the Afrikaners sought to purge South African society of "influences of the devil" and "materials subversive to the state and public morals" by routinely banning and censoring not only books by writers who challenged the status quo, but also publications like *Playboy*.

"So many black people fly in America," I said.

"A plane is like a car to many Americans," said Dr. Waller.

"To many of my people cars are what planes are to Americans."

At the baggage-claim area I saw black and white people constantly rubbing shoulders, animatedly talking to one another, and no one seemed to mind. There were no ubiquitous armed policemen.

"There truly is no apartheid here," I said to myself. "This is indeed the Promised Land."

I felt so happy and relieved that for the first time the tension that went with being black in South Africa left me. I became a new person.

DR. KILLION; RECEPTION AT LIMESTONE COL-
LEGE; THE ONSET OF CULTURE SHOCK

The long drive along Interstate 85 to Limestone College in Gaffney, South Carolina, lasted several hours. We arrived around evening. I spent the night at Dr. Killion's house. Though exhausted by the long journey, I was up at the crack of dawn, to the surprise of Dr. Killion and Dr. Waller, as they thought I would still be asleep. I told them that in South Africa, because of police raids, blacks seldom had the luxury of sleeping late.

"Well, thank God you made it to America," Dr. Killion said. "No more police raids. We're civilized over here."

The nightmare of these unannounced, almost daily raids—which were to haunt me for a long time after my arrival in America, make me wary of policemen, make me jump at the sound of sirens, at sudden bright light—was typified by one which occurred when I was five years old. My three-year-old sister Florah and I were sleeping on pieces of cardboard, under the kitchen table. My parents, along with my brother George, one year old, were asleep in the other room, on the only bed in the shack, a secondhand twin bed whose legs were propped up by bricks. The police came a little after midnight, amid blaring sirens, barking dogs, and blinding flashlights. After smashing the windows and door of the shack, they terrorized Florah and me for failing to open the door on time. We had delayed in order to give our parents time to hide. The police broke down the bedroom door, stormed in, dragged my father, who was naked, from under the bed, and interrogated him in the middle of the room. My mother had hid herself inside our tiny wardrobe. My parents' crime was that they did not possess a permit allowing them to live together as husband and wife.

Dr. Killion was a middle-aged, energetic man with a velvety voice, thick eyebrows, and a Mongolian nose. He grew up poor in Steger, Illinois. His grandparents had been serfs to the Junkers (privileged, landowning aristocracy) in Prussia. His mother, Mary, a woman of strong will and faith, was a major influence in his life. She was an elementary school teacher in her early years, and raised her three sons in the Lutheran tradition. For thirty-nine years his immigrant father, Daniel, labored in the Gould-National battery factory. The hardships undergone by his father, alongside whom he often worked while in high school and at college, taught Dr. Killion the importance of acquiring an education to avoid a similar fate. This he did by graduating from St. John's College in Kansas, then attending Concordia Seminary in St. Louis, before going to Columbia University in New York, where he obtained a master of arts degree in American history and was one of the first recipients of an E.D.D. (Doctor of Education and College Teaching) degree. The E.D.D. program resulted from protests by students in the sixties against professors who knew their subjects but couldn't teach. The E.D.D. was designed to produce professors who knew their subjects and *could* teach.

Before coming to Limestone, Dr. Killion had been a fellow at the University of Georgia, where he wrote two books: *A Treasury of Georgia Folklore* (most of which was black folklore), and *Slavery Time: When I Chillun' Time on Master's Plantation*, which won the Abingdon Award for Southern Fiction. An avowed liberal in one of the most conservative states in the country, Dr. Killion cared deeply about social issues and helped found the United Black Students Association, a black-consciousness group on campus. There were no black professors at Limestone.

During breakfast Dr. Killion informed me that the fall semester had already begun and that I had missed orientation. The problems I had encountered in getting my passport had delayed my departure from South Africa. Limestone had reopened the week after Labor Day and I was about two weeks late. After breakfast Dr. Killion and I left for the college.

When I first saw Limestone College, with its small, picturesque campus dotted with old dogwood and oak trees, and situated by a serene quarry, whose sloping banks, covered with kudzu ivy, gave the water an emerald color, I thought I had arrived at the dream college. I knew of no school for black students in the whole of South Africa with such lovely facilities. Only wealthy whites attended such schools. Yet, by American standards, Limestone was a tiny and poor liberal arts college. I looked forward to the best four years of my life, despite persistent anxieties about how I would be treated, how I would perform, how I would be judged.

My first day on campus was spent moving into Eunice Ford Hall, the male dormitory, meeting various teachers and administrators, and registering for courses. Everyone was friendly and helpful. I was struck by the large number of black students; they were about 34 percent of the student population. One of the first friends I made was David Mark Bomar, a black freshman from the nearby town of Spartanburg. David acted as my guide for much of the day. A recipient of the South Carolina Press Association Award Scholarship, which paid his tuition and board, David's ambition was to become a journalist, but since Limestone had no journalism major, he chose English. He was on the staff of *The Candelabra* (yearbook), *The Lantern* (college paper), and *The Shield* (literary magazine), and was treasurer of the freshman class, of which Dr. Killion was adviser. A stocky eighteen-year-old with short black hair and genteel manners, David impressed me with his sensitivity and intelligence, and his confidence before whites.

My assigned roommate, Harold, a black, was a senior and a former member of the basketball team, The Limestone Saints. He was out when I moved in.

"I hope we can be friends," David said in a euphonious Southern accent, as he helped me unpack.

"I hope so, too."

"Dr. Killion told me that you're a very good writer," David said. "Maybe you should join the school paper."

"I would very much like to," I said. "But I'm afraid tennis may take up much of my time."

"If there's anything you need, let me know," David said as he was leaving. "I'll be going home this weekend. When I return we'll get together."

"Thank you."

I was surprised by how large my room was. It was almost the size of our fifteen- by fifteen-foot house back in Alexandra, which at any given time was home for about a dozen people. I had no linen; I was given a set of towels and sheets by a kind white associate professor of music theory, Janet DuBois, a friend of Dr. Killion's. Janet also provided the tennis team with food treats during trips. She was shocked when I told her that at home my family shared a single facecloth.

Everything I saw throughout that lovely September day filled me with awe: the size of the college library, the gym and athletic fields, the private study rooms, the many offices for teachers and their easy accessibility, the variety of expensive cars belonging to students who had not reached their twentieth birthdays, the spacious and well-kept grounds, a fountain with a seven-stick candelabra signifying the seven liberal arts, the neat classrooms oversupplied with desks, the cafeteria with more food than I had ever seen in my life.

During lunch I ate my first hamburger and hated it. The meat tasted rubbery.

That evening after dinner in the student center, I came face-to-face with the amazing variety of programs on American television. I was overwhelmed, and it was not long before I became addicted to television. In South Africa television had just been introduced in 1976. It was dull and was on only a few hours a day. The apartheid regime ran it, and mostly whites owned television sets. So it can be imagined with what gusto I devoured soap operas, commercials, talk shows, and old movies, as well as football, basketball, and baseball, sports I hardly understood and whose rules I learned only from watching. My favorite shows were "The Three Stooges," "Gunsmoke," "Sherlock Holmes," "M.A.S.H.," "Star Trek," and Tarzan movies which came on Saturday mornings.

Later that evening I finally met my roommate. Harold was tall and sinewy, with a small face and a full set of even teeth, which made me conscious of my missing front tooth, the result of being struck with a brick by thugs. Harold dressed well and seemed sophisticated. He was amused by my accent.

"I must teach you how to speak like a Southerner," he said.

"No way," I said. "My English is fine. I'm not interested in mutilating the English language."

Throughout the evening a procession of Harold's friends, all of them black, came. I was on display. Most had never seen a live African. He introduced me as "Mark, a student from Africa." This appellation displeased me because the types of questions I was asked gave me the impression that many of them associated Africa with jungles, tribes, and missionary work.

When Harold discovered that I was fascinated by television, he gave me permission to use his small black-and-white set whenever I wanted.

"Thank you, Harold."

"Remember, now, I may ask you to do me some favors some day," he said.

"I'll remember," I said, wondering what he meant.

A day or so after I moved in, I was visited by Phillip, a sophomore who was trying out for the tennis team. Phillip was white, came from a large Southern town, and had an exaggerated opinion of my tennis ability, because I was friends with Stan Smith and was the only player on the team with a full tennis scholarship. After chatting awhile I asked him, "Do black and white students get along well?"

"Yes, they do," he replied.

"Are they ever allowed to be roommates?"

Since arriving at the college, I had noticed that black and white students largely kept apart. My idea of an integrated college was one in which black and white students lived, ate, studied, worked, and socialized together. That way they could get to know each other better and become accustomed to and tolerant of whatever differences existed between them.

"The college doesn't prevent mixing," Phillip said, somewhat surprised at my question. "But there's very little of it."

"Why?" I asked.

"It's hard to say," said Phillip, groping for words. "It's just that way, I guess. Blacks prefer rooming with blacks and whites with whites. If a black student and a white student want to room together they can. But that seldom happens. Each seems happy among their own people and friends."

This answer had an unsettling and familiar ring to it. It reminded me of some of the vague apologies for apartheid I had heard from the lips of certain whites in South Africa, but I didn't express my opinion. I dreaded the consequences of being wrong.

"Why did you ask that question?" Phillip said. His voice sounded pained. "Do you think this is a racist school or something?"

"No, not at all," I said hurriedly. "I'm just curious, that's all," I added, suddenly feeling guilty of some unknown wrong. I detected bewilderment in Phillip's face. It seemed as if with my questions I had ventured into a forbidden zone. Though my convictions and curiosity had pressed me to ask him the questions, my instincts cautioned me that it would be foolhardy for me to offend a white American, especially since I had just arrived. So I felt compelled to explain myself thoroughly to avoid any misunderstanding of what I had uttered.

"You see, Phillip," I began. "I'm new to this country. I'm trying to learn as quickly as I can about the way things operate. I'm bound to make mistakes, and to ask silly questions, just as I think I may already have done."

"No, that's all right," Phillip said. "You can ask me anything. I'm not offended."

"Thank you," I said. "I'm glad to hear that. I must confess that I'm still in a state of shock, still confused and overwhelmed, by the enormous differences between your society and mine. America is like another planet to me. Another galaxy. For instance, I can't even begin to comprehend the amount of freedom I have as a human being over here.

"In just these few days I've experienced more genuine freedom, more warmth and understanding from white people than I have ever known in my entire life in South Africa. The simple fact that Dr. Killion let me sleep in his guest room; the simple fact that you're in this room with me, laughing and joking with me; the simple fact that I have caring white teachers—all these things are wonders to me. In my country things just aren't done that way. Black people are expected to know their place."

A look of amazement swept Phillip's face as I spoke. It was hard to tell whether he was shocked by my revelations or struck by my passion and clarity. I had noticed since my arrival that white people were surprised by my ability to express myself clearly and confidently, and had complimented me effusively, as if they did not expect a black man to be fluent in English.

I went on. "You know, Phillip, blacks in my country seldom talk back to a white man. They usually just listen and obey. Blacks and whites seldom meet as equals. Our everyday relationships are those of master and servant. Our society is based on laws forbidding the races to mix in any manner whatsoever. We have separate schools, separate residential places, separate buses, and even separate graveyards. A black person who breaks any of the apartheid laws can be imprisoned or killed."

There was an uneasy silence when I finished my speech. I didn't know what to make of Phillip's reaction, as he still wore the same amazed expression. I wondered, too, if he truly could relate to what I had just said. Finally he spoke.

"What's happening to your people is terrible," Phillip said, genuinely touched. "To be honest with you, I had never heard of your country's problems till today. I can't even say I fully understand what you've just told me. I hardly know much about Africa. So I hope you won't mind if I ask a silly question: What exactly is apartheid?"

I could hardly believe my ears. Phillip, an American, a college student, the product of what I thought the best educational system in the world, did not know what apartheid was. What on earth was being taught in American schools? Was Phillip feigning ignorance to make me feel at ease, to ingratiate himself to me, or was his lack of knowledge real? Had I overestimated the intelligence of American students? I thought I was the one who had received an inferior education.

I described the basic features of apartheid. I could tell that Phillip was having difficulties conceiving of such a society. And yet he was born and bred in the South, the very South which I was soon to discover had, not too long ago, resisted changes in an apartheid system of its own and still practiced it in subtle forms.

"I hope my answers didn't give you the impression that there's apartheid in this school just because blacks and whites don't room together," Phillip said, almost apologetically. "Far from it. Blacks in America have the same rights as white people. They got their rights a long time ago, when Martin Luther King marched for them. But like I said, it's just that blacks prefer being with other blacks and whites with whites. You'll find the same situation at other schools. Even in my high school and town they did that. They seem happier that way. I wish they would mix some, but you can't force people to change their ways if they don't want to."

I thought I was hearing things. Though Phillip's face bore an expression of sincerity, though he had expressed genuine repugnance at apartheid, though for all I knew his assertions about black-white relations in America could well be true, I could not be rid of the feeling that he was giving me the same justifications, the same rationalizations for segregation I had heard from the mouths of whites in South Africa.

On the other hand, wasn't I enrolled in an integrated school? Wasn't Gaffney supposed to be an integrated town and America ruled by the egalitarian creed? And, despite my misgivings, neither Phillip, Dr. Killion, Dr. Waller, Dr. Jack Early (the president of the college), nor any of the numerous white people I had met since arriving in America had treated me like a Kaffir, so how could apartheid possibly exist with such omissions? The whole matter was too confusing. I must definitely be overreacting.

Phillip mentioned something about my calling on him if I needed any help. "And let's hit a few balls together sometime," he added.

I thanked him and he left. For a while I lay in bed, staring at the ceiling, pondering the significance of what Phillip had said. My conclusions were contradictory. I needed more proof, more evidence. Phillip's ignorance about South Africa turned out to be shared by over half the students I talked to, blacks and whites. Some of them didn't even know where South Africa was.

On Saturday Dr. Killion invited the tennis team over to his house for dinner. It was quite an affair. The entire team, some eight students, attended. I was the only black. Dr. Killion's house, a two-story Cape Cod cottage, was situated in a pretty section of town, had a garden filled with flowers, shrubs, and trees, and was surrounded by a well-kept lawn. It was tastefully furnished in the country style, to suit the needs of a fastidious bachelor.

Dr. Killion was a fine cook and a gracious host. Having never before sat for dinner with so many white people I was self-conscious throughout the evening. I was awkward with my knife and fork. But I enjoyed myself and surprised everyone with my hearty appetite. After dinner we watched television and talked, and my relationship with Stan Smith was probed.

"How did you meet Stan?" asked Scott Smith, a bearded senior and the number-one player on last year's team.

"Oh, by accident," I said. "I was the only black player entered in this professional tournament held in Johannesburg. I lost in the qualifying rounds and while wandering about the courts one afternoon, I saw Stan hitting against Bob Lutz. Stan was my hero, so I leaned against the fence and watched. To my surprise, he invited me to join them. After hitting we talked. And there began our friendship."

"You must be a very good player to hit against the likes of Stan Smith," said Butch Klopfer, a tall, soft-spoken junior transfer from Central Florida Community College in Ocala.

Before I could answer, Dr. Killion said, "Well, we'll find that out at tomorrow's practice session, won't we?"

"I'm not that very good," I confessed. "I only started playing the game four years ago. I still have a lot to work on."

"Don't be modest, now," said Rick Wisher, a junior with a high-pitched voice and a face resembling Robert Redford's. Rick was fond of teasing my accent. "Anyone who plays in professional tournaments must be good."

"I hope we'll be competition enough for you," said Mark Freiherr, a stocky, playful junior with a mop of black curly hair.

Throughout the evening I was bombarded with questions about tennis. I had the uneasy feeling that because I had been discovered by a tennis legend, and had participated in several professional tournaments in South Africa, everyone took me for a rising tennis star who would bring great honor to their program and school. Would I meet their expectations? What if I disappointed them, as I feared I would?

The first interteam matches were held on a hot Sunday afternoon. Since my arrival, aside from hitting a few balls against Rick Wisher and Mark Freiherr, I had had little practice. I still hadn't fully recovered from several injuries (torn left arm muscle and sprained ankle) I had sustained during tournaments in South Africa, which affected my ground strokes and limited my mobility. I was under enormous pressure to do well. Scott was the first player I took on. A crowd of spectators, including a group of black students, gathered around the shaded court, whose badly maintained surface had grass growing in cracks. We played the best of three and Scott handily won in two straight sets.

"You need to work more on your backhand," Dr. Killion said, a bit disappointed at my poor performance.

"It's always been my weaker stroke, coach," I said. "But I'm ready to practice very hard."

"I'm glad to hear that," Dr. Killion said. "I have invested a lot of money in you, you know. Even Scott doesn't receive half the scholarship money I have given you."

I later learned that my full tennis scholarship came from personal contributions by Dr. Killion, Dr. Waller, and several of their friends. I was deeply touched by their altruism, especially since Dr. Killion made about $14,000 a year. He and his friends presumably saw the scholarship as a means of building a winning team while at the same time helping a destitute black South African.

This is how I came to get the money. After I met Stan in 1977 and told him of my eagerness to study in America, he contacted George Toley, his former tennis coach at the University of Southern California. It turned out that George Toley had already given out all his tennis scholarships. So during the NCAA tournament in Athens, Georgia, George Toley approached Dan Magill, tennis coach at the University of Georgia and a good friend of Dr. Killion's, to see if he could help. He, too, had no scholarships left. Shortly thereafter Dr. Killion approached Dan Magill in search of some recruiting leads, and was given my name. He immediately called Stan's office in Washington, D.C., and was directed to Stan, who was playing a tournament in Stowe, Vermont. The two arranged to meet in Atlanta to discuss my situation. From their meeting came the scholarship offer, which snatched me from the jaws of detention by the police, who were rounding up participants in the student rebellion of 1976. Such are the unpredictable happenings, the unforeseen circumstances, that shape our lives.

I reacted with astonishment the first time I saw students drinking liquor and smoking marijuana in the dormitories. Back in Alexandra, any student caught drinking or smoking as much as a cigarette faced expulsion. Drinking parties were a regular feature on campus, and my roommate and several members of the tennis team were among students who frequently smoked marijuana. One afternoon, returning from the library, I was overpowered as I entered the room by the harsh smell of the drug. I looked around and saw Harold lying on his bed, staring dreamily at the ceiling. Lionel Richie's hit song "Three Times a Lady" was playing on a cheap stereo I had just bought. I complained to Harold about the offensive smell. He looked at me with glazed eyes, emitted a series of short laughs, and then flippantly cracked a joke about "reefer" being good for me.

"You should try it," he said.

"No, thank you. I have no interest in smoking that dangerous stuff," I said. "I haven't even smoked a cigarette in my life."

Harold laughed.

"Are you planning on becoming a preacher or something?" Harold sometimes teased me for having enrolled in a religion course, Faith, Knowledge and Selfhood, and for having joined the Religious Life Committee, instead of one of the many fraternities. My interest in religion was largely an attempt to explore my own spirituality and the basis and validity of Christianity.

"No."

"Then relax and have some fun," he said.

"What fun is there in drugs?" I asked. I had seen glue and benzene, popular drugs in the ghetto, wreck many young and promising lives. Luckily, hard drugs like cocaine, heroin, and crack were then unheard of.

"A special kind of fun," Harold said, looking me over with glazed eyes, as if to say, "What a fool this African is."

"I don't drink and I don't smoke," I said. "And I'm happy that way. Whatever fun I need I get from books and tennis."

Because I didn't drink and didn't smoke, I was unable to become one of the boys. That troubled me. I was anxious to make friends, to be liked. But I was unwilling to pay any price for friendship, for popularity. I wondered if, in America, among strange people and strange customs, where much was so new and alluring, where there was so much freedom that to many it became license, I could muster enough willpower to resist the temptations and the pressures to conform.

I had survived ghetto life in a large measure through willpower. When I was growing up I didn't mind being unpopular or being called a fool for not doing the "in-thing." As a teenager I was ostracized, harassed, and called a coward for quitting a street gang; in high school I was called a bookworm and accused of trying to be white for doing my homework on time, speaking proper English, getting high marks on tests, dressing neatly, constantly asking teachers questions and volunteering answers, playing tennis, and for my love of reading. Many times the burden of being different was unbearable. I remember one time, after I decided to quit the "Thirteenth Avenue Tomahawks" gang, following a bloody street battle in which a boy alongside me had his eye gouged out by a stone from a slingshot, my mother said to me, with a sigh of relief: "You had two paths to choose from, just like every black boy in Alexandra: to become a *tsotsi* [gangster, mugger, hoodlum], or not to become a *tsotsi*. You chose the difficult way out. From now on the going will be rough, for your *tsotsi* friends will try everything to make you change your mind. I hope you will remain firm in your decision. If you do, chances are you'll live to be old enough not to regret it." She turned out to be right.

But what would be the cost of noncomformity in America?

5   Worsening culture shock; Dr. Bassett; corporal punishment

My culture shock worsened with each day. My mind never stopped comparing my new world with my old. For instance, I still had a hard time believing that I now lived in a place with electricity, running water, showers, flush toilets, paved roads; that I now had a bed of my own (back home after I graduated from sleeping on the floor I began sharing a single bed with two siblings); that, even as a foreigner, I had more rights under American law than I had had in the country of my birth; and that I attended school with whites and received the same education.

I was awed by the degree of personal freedom I had. I could associate with anyone regardless of race or creed. I could go anywhere and say anything I wanted, without fear of persecution or imprisonment. I was amazed at the number of American newspapers and at how they printed so many stories critical of their government and society. I was jubilant to read that the United Nations Security Council had finally adopted Resolution 435, detailing a plan for Namibian independence and a withdrawal of South African forces.

The blacks of Namibia, Africa's last colony, were oppressed by the same apartheid machinery as the blacks of South Africa. Maybe, I thought, this powerful UN body will finally bring an end to apartheid.

There were times when the differences between my life in America and South Africa were so stark that I really thought the world around me a dream from which I would awaken and discover that I hadn't left the ghetto of Alexandra. But along with the immeasurable joy I felt at being free and treated like a human being, I had a difficult time mentally and emotionally adjusting to almost everything. I even had a hard time entering a car and crossing the road. In South Africa cars have steering wheels on the right side, and traffic flow is the reverse of America.

Each time I was overwhelmed by culture shock, I would go wandering by myself in the nearby woods, or read poems, particularly existentialist ones such as "In Memoriam," by Tennyson, or escape into the make-believe world of television movies and soap operas. No one, including Dr. Killion, knew much about my background, about the nightmares and pain I had endured, about the guilt I felt at having left my family behind, suffering. I sought to hide these facts of my former life, doubtful if anyone would understand, wondering how I would be judged.

Yet from time to time the memories of my former life resurfaced and made me weep, especially when I recalled that for my family nothing had changed: they were still trapped. I wondered how long I could continue grappling with such ambivalence, how long I could endure the pressures of adjusting to two such starkly different worlds.

Immersion in my school work alleviated some of the stress. Professor Killion, head of the social sciences department, was my academic adviser. All my previous education had been without proper guidance and my reading, though extensive, haphazard. Teachers praised my command of the English language. But overall my high school education under apartheid had been weak in crucial areas. My first semester courses were Mathematics; Elementary American Business, in which we studied basic accounting; Faith, Knowledge and Self-hood, a quasi-existentialist course; World Civilization; and Expository Prose. The last three became my favorite courses.

In several classes I found myself competing with freshmen who had scored impressively on SAT and ACT tests. I never took any such tests, and had I been required to, I doubt if I would have done well. Many of these students came from middle-class homes, owned cars, and took much for granted. To many, college was a place to have a good time. They were shocked that I couldn't drive and came from a home without electricity, running water, a stereo, or a television set. They assumed that the rest of the world was as fortunate as America.

Some of these students paraded their sophistication and material superiority. They displayed a vanity and selfishness which violated my simple values and depressed me with feelings of inferiority, for I knew that I could never be like them, and would never be accepted into their cliques. The material world of instant gratification, easy success, and hedonistic pleasures seemed to be the source of their trivial values and brittle identities. Yet grades meant a great deal to these students. At exam time they memorized, sweated, crammed, and obtained A's, then quickly forgot almost everything. Limestone had scores of disciplined and responsible students like David Bomar, but for me the spotlight was on those popular ones with whom I compared myself.

I found the subjects and teaching methods baffling. The Southern drawl of some teachers constantly bewildered me. Though I was fluent in English, there were times when I thought in Tsonga and had to translate; after all, English was my fifth language. I was attentive in class, handed assignments in on time, yet I got C's and D's on quizzes. I began doubting my own intelligence and seriously questioned my ability to make it through college. Had I set my sights too high? What would happen to my scholarship if I flunked my courses? Each time I imagined myself a failure I would recall my mother's words of encouragement: "Continue working hard and things will get better. As long as you're learning something, it's worth it."

Despite initially low grades I felt I was learning something more important than what was contained in textbooks and required on tests. Learning to me meant more than just memorizing facts and regurgitating them during exams. Each new day, each new experience at Limestone taught me important lessons about American society and its values, about the abuses of freedom and the way people can take things for granted through isolation and lack of perspective. Teachers praised my eagerness to learn. I took careful notes and sought to make the lessons part of my own knowledge of things, part of my thinking and feeling and acting. Everything was so new that sometimes I accepted things without criticism. My experiences with the totalitarian educational system in the ghetto schools sometimes made it difficult for me to distinguish fact from opinion when teachers spoke. To buttress my confidence I constantly asked questions and volunteered answers. Sometimes I was wildly wrong and would be laughed at by some students, but teachers encouraged my curiosity. They were surprised by my politeness, respect, discipline, and drive. I was called a model student, despite my grades.

"Grades may be important," I repeatedly told myself, "but they aren't everything."

Such is even more the case today. Studies show that students may know facts and get good grades but cannot think. Experience has taught me that effective learning takes place when, from books, observation, and the informed opinions of others brought out by a serious discussion of the issues, one is able to strengthen one's opinions, to fortify one's reason against prejudice, superstition, and error, to sharpen one's sensibilities, to enlarge and deepen one's understanding of the world and of life, and above all, to keep one's mind ever open to the acceptance of new truths and the discarding of old and useless ones.

One day I stopped by the office of one of my professors. Dr. Fred Bassett, an easygoing, bearded, middle-aged man with a scholarly air about him, taught religion and philosophy and was chairman of the humanities division. He was keenly interested in black issues. Dr. Bassett grew up in Roanoke, a small town in Alabama, and after graduating from Samford University in Birmingham, he got his Ph.D. in religion at Emory University in Atlanta. Dr. Bassett's challenging course, Faith, Knowledge and Selfhood, which I enjoyed enormously, sought to integrate insights from theology, philosophy, psychology, and sociology around the theme of self-actualization, by looking at the role played by faith and knowledge in the self-directed person. Dr. Bassett and I often avidly discussed each day's lesson after class.

I found him seated behind a table cluttered with books and papers. I handed him my paper with a politeness that seemed to baffle him.

"What kinds of teachers did you have in the ghetto, Mark?" Dr. Bassett asked.

I replied that because of the segregated education system, all our teachers were black. "And few of them," I added, "were qualified. Particularly in the lower grades."

Dr. Bassett seemed intrigued. He invited me to sit down and began questioning me about the education system in South Africa. I launched into a long explanation of apartheid education. I told him that racial segregation in South African society was so complete that the quality of education a child received depended strictly upon his race. Whites had the best schools, where, as part of the curriculum, they were indoctrinated about the necessity for racial purity; the divine mission of the white race in South Africa; the need to keep blacks subservient; and the Afrikaners' version of Christianity, which maintained, among other absurdities, that integration and equality were communist ideas which could be combated effectively only by a complete obedience to authority, a deep religious faith, and a literal interpretation of the Bible. One such interpretation claimed that the Old Testament story of the Tower of Babel (Genesis 11:1–9) was divine proof for segregation.

Dr. Bassett leaned back in his chair and shook his head in disbelief. "And what was education like for those who weren't white?" he asked.

"Each nonwhite group has its own separate school system," I said. "The education of the Indians and Coloureds, who were classified by the authorities as second- and third-class citizens respectively, was in many ways better than black education. It tended to reinforce their feelings of superiority over blacks, who were regarded as fourth-class citizens. And it made most Indians and Coloureds identify more with the values of the dominant white group."

"This is fascinating," Dr. Bassett said, and glanced at his wristwatch. "Have you had lunch?"

"No."

"Why don't you join me for a bite at the cafeteria?"

As we walked across campus amid trees bursting in autumn colors, Dr. Bassett asked, "And what was education like for the blacks?"

"Black education was by all standards the worst," I said. "We have few schools. They are chronically understaffed, overcrowded, and underfunded. For every ten dollars spent on white education, black education receives a single dollar. Everything taught in black schools is set down by white administrators who followed segregationist concepts. In the sixties there was an Afrikaner named Dr. H. F. Verwoerd. He was the minister of native affairs. He later became prime minister and was assassinated in Parliament. In an infamous manifesto on what a black child should be taught, he stated that since blacks were by law restricted to menial and low-skilled jobs, there was no need to teach a black child anything but what was needed to perform those jobs. He asked, 'What's the use of teaching a black child mathematics when he can't use it in practice?' "

"Did Verwoerd really believe that?" Dr. Bassett asked.

"Yes, he did," I replied, "and so did most whites."

"And how did black teachers respond?"

"Some protested and were fired," I said. "Most black teachers, however, feared losing their jobs, so they taught whatever the white bureaucrats told them to teach."

We had now reached the cafeteria overlooking Limestone Lake. We got our lunches, sat down at a table by the window, and continued our discussion.

"The high school teachers I had were very strict," I said. "They tolerated no insubordination from students. We were whipped with canes and switches for getting our homework wrong or for giving the wrong answers during oral quizzes."

"You mean you were physically beaten for getting homework wrong?" Dr. Bassett asked incredulously.

"Yes. And we were also whipped for arriving late at school, for being unkempt, for making noise during class, for being disrespectful to teachers, and for wearing the wrong uniform."

On Mondays, Wednesdays, and Fridays boys wore black shorts, white shirts, and the school tie; girls wore black gym dresses and white shirts. On Tuesdays and Thursdays boys wore khaki pants and shirts, and girls wore tunics. Uniform inspection was carried out by teachers during assembly in the morning, when all classes gathered to begin the day with hymns, the Lord's Prayer, and announcements for the day. When assembly was dismissed, those without uniforms were marched to the principal's office to be caned.

"Amazing. Corporal punishment is against the law in America."

"Really?" I reacted with surprise. "In South Africa parents would give the teacher a medal for whipping their child. Teachers are seen as an extension of parental authority. If students aren't whipped here when they misbehave, how do they learn? How do they become disciplined?" I asked.

"It's their responsibility to make the effort," Dr. Bassett said. "It is hoped that they will make the right choices without coercion."

"Maybe so," I said. "But I doubt it. During my years in lower primary school it was often the fear of punishment that made me study and do my homework instead of run around the streets. It took some time but I finally learned that if I was disciplined, respectful, and responsible, teachers and my parents would have little reason to punish me. Students have it very easy here."

"Tell that to the class sometime," Dr. Bassett said with a laugh.

Though now I wouldn't go so far as to advocate corporal punishment, having learned of its abuses, I nevertheless believe that some effective means ought to be found to enforce discipline and curb the anarchy, laziness, and disrespect toward teachers in many an American school. For parents and teachers to expect unruly and lazy students to become disciplined and responsible of their own volition is naïve, especially in a society where right and wrong are often relative, where freedom is often taken to mean license, to mean "doing what you please."

6

PEER PRESSURE; DATING WITHOUT SEX; THE EX-
PLOITATION OF BLACK ATHLETES; THE REM-
NANTS OF JIM CROW

In about a month or so the novelty of television had worn off. I could no longer watch more than two hours of it without feeling restless, my senses numbed. Then I would reach for a book. I was still awed by the power of television, but many of its programs, I had discovered, with their excessive violence, sex, fantasy, and commercials, corrupted the feelings and fostered superficial thinking. I made it a rule to watch mainly news and programs on public television. I especially enjoyed programs on nature, since my mother's stories had awakened in me a deep sensibility toward the natural world, and ghettos were such wastelands. Having learned how to use the library effectively, I now spent more time there, doing homework or research, or reading *The New York Times*, the *Atlanta Constitution*, *Time*, *Newsweek*, *The Washington Post*, and other major newspapers and magazines to acquaint myself with events taking place in America and around the world. The violence and rioting and killings in South Africa continued to make headlines. Black students were being detained and tortured. Many were fleeing into exile. I wondered how my family was faring. I had written them several letters but received no reply. Were they still alive?

My eighteenth birthday, which fell on October 18, 1978, found me still a virgin. I was hardly bothered by this, even though I was at an age when most young adults had already had their first sexual experience; also, I attended a school where many students were products of the sexual revolution. Condoms and the Pill were still enigmas to me.

At first no one knew that I was a virgin. But the gossip of a small college campus soon had it that because I had never been seen with a woman, there must be something wrong with me. I experienced intense peer pressure to become sexually active but I clung to my beliefs, mainly because my attitude toward sex lacked the sophistication that came with years of casually indulging in the act. I saw sex in a more innocent and wholesome light. My attitude was based on my convictions of what it meant to be a woman and how a woman ought to be treated by men. Having grown up in an environment where women had earned my respect as individuals with feelings and minds of their own and yet were frequently abused by men, as my mother was by my father, and granny by her husband, who abandoned her for another woman, I could not see myself treating my girlfriend or wife simply as a sexual or childbearing object. Moreover, to me sex was inconceivable without love. And though I was still inexperienced, and was not a moralist or puritan, common sense told me that sex bereft of feelings was just a sordid, animalistic act, hardly different from what dogs did when in heat.

Fortunately I befriended several black women students with whom sex was not the underpinning of a relationship. We had a wonderful time playing tennis, going out to dinner, discussing poetry, African culture, black American history, and other stimulating topics. It was ironic that, despite my strict morals, I ended up dating three of the most beautiful women on campus.

Valerie Hines, a tall, intelligent, vivacious senior from Florence, South Carolina, was a former fourth runner-up in the Miss Black U.S.A. contest. She was a friend of Dr. Killion's, majored in theatre, and was a member of the United Black Students. Valerie is now a model in New York City.

Sandra Naomi Tate, an outgoing, lithe, bright-eyed sophomore with full-bodied black hair and a charming smile, was a native of Gaffney and a finalist in the Miss Limestone beauty contest. She was a member of the Student-Faculty Senate and was also active in various other campus groups.

And Patrice Paula Abrams was an ebullient and talented freshman from Union, South Carolina. She majored in music education and theatre and was secretary of the freshman class, a staff member of the college paper, and a tennis enthusiast. Patrice was also extremely beautiful; by the time she graduated in 1982, she had won the Miss Limestone beauty contest, and had been runner-up in the Miss Black America pageant. She now teaches dance in Middlesex, England.

It obviously surprised many male students that I dated these "gorgeous and sexy women," as they were described, without going to bed with them. I usually answered that there was more to a woman than her body. The jealousy of some black male students, who were galled that an African succeeded where they had failed, led them to begin spreading rumors that I was a homosexual. They pointed to the following as "proof" of my "effeminacy": open expression of my feelings, love of poetry, refusal to sleep with women on a whim, tennis playing, mellifluous voice; and to my friendship with David, whose euphonious voice, polite manners, sensitivity, and intelligence were also considered signs of latent homosexuality. Apparently men in the America of this era were supposed to be unfeeling, rough, tough, and dumb; and, alas, women often copied and preferred them. This image of men as "macho" is idolized in movies, on television, in advertising, and on the sports field. Throughout my sojourn in America, by insisting on the femininity and masculinity of the human character, I have sought to debunk this false and harmful image, which I consider a great hindrance to creativity and self-actualization.

The truth of the matter was that David disdained the practice of competing with other boys to see who could bed the most girls. He had a girlfriend at another school and was faithful to her. He refused to play the stereotypical role of the black student; he partied little, was not a fanatic about sports, and was not cliquish—in the cafeteria he sat wherever and with whomever he wanted. Some black students accused him of seeking to be white; some white students disliked him for not being black enough to justify their prejudices. Aware that he could not please everyone, David had decided to please himself. I admired David for his individuality.

David and I became steadfast friends. He was among the most dedicated, ambitious, and disciplined students at Limestone, and we had much in common. We often studied together, encouraged each other to do well, and shared our dreams about the future. Like my mother, David's mother taught him to regard education as a powerful weapon of hope. And Mrs. Dorothy T. Lewis, his second-grade teacher, inspired in David a love for books and for poetry. Though he congratulated me on having won a full tennis scholarship, David warned me that many black student athletes were exploited by colleges and universities.

"Is that the case at Limestone, too?" I asked.

"Not as far as I know," he replied.

"How exactly are black athletes exploited?"

"Did you know that at most large schools sports is a multimillion dollar business?" David asked.

"No, I didn't know that."

"Yes. And many black athletes," he went on, "especially in big-time sports like football and basketball, often have poor grades when they enroll in college."

"How come?"

"Well, the reasons vary," David said. "Some athletes come from backgrounds where an education was never emphasized. Others spent all their time in high school playing sports, hoping to make it to the pros. Once these students arrive at these big universities, their education is seldom top priority. They are simply money-making machines for the colleges. They are encouraged to take easy courses so they can stay eligible to compete in sports. But these courses hardly prepare them for any useful career."

I later discovered that these courses, variously referred to as "jock courses" or "keep-'em-eligible courses," were mainly in the physical education and communications fields.

"But don't the athletes realize when they're being exploited?" I asked.

"Unfortunately most don't," David said. "How can they when they're treated like kings? As long as they're useful they're given anything they want: cars, women, money, even grades. But the minute they become useless, let's say by breaking a limb or something, they are discarded like junk. Seldom is any effort made to prepare them for the real life out there. And the fools, always dreaming of making the pros, often go along with their own exploitation." I later learned that of all black athletes in collegiate sports, only

1.6 percent ended up as pros. And between 65 and 75 percent never graduated from college.

"Sometimes I wish I had gone to Princeton," I said. "One of the brochures they sent me stated that all members of the tennis team graduated and held prestigious jobs as lawyers, accountants, scientists, and so forth."

"You mean you had an offer to attend Princeton University and you turned it down?" David cried. "The Ivy League university up North?"

"Yes," I replied, surprised at his sudden excitement.

"Why in the world did you do that?"

"The school wanted me to come a year later but I couldn't remain in South Africa any longer. The Pretoria regime was arresting all students who participated in the Soweto protests of 1976. So I accepted the offer from Limestone." David Benjamin, the tennis coach at Princeton, had officially informed me in a letter that I had a firm offer of a full scholarship to Princeton based on need, beginning in the fall of 1979.

"You were a fool to pass up Princeton for Limestone," David declared. "What did you hope to find in the South?"

"Isn't there opportunity down here just as up North?" I asked. To me all America, including the South, had seemed a Promised Land while I lived in South Africa; also, I had thought that all American universities and colleges were of the same caliber.

"There's little future here for the black man," David said. "Blacks are still in the clutches of white racists, many of whom are still fighting the civil war and have never forgiven black people for having caused it."

"Well, if things get bad I'll transfer to Princeton," I said, little realizing then how difficult that would be.

"I'm also thinking of transferring next semester," he said.

Several black students at Limestone eager to educate me on black life in the South, from time to time drove me to nearby towns like Greenville, Union, Spartanburg, and Anderson. Most were members of United Black Students (UBS), a black-consciousness group on campus with about thirty active members. Dr. Frank Shelton, a liberal associate professor of English and a friend of Dr. Killion's, was UBS's adviser. As I noted earlier, there were no black professors at Limestone.

I regularly discussed black American history with members of UBS, among them Jerome McCray, a religion major, student government president, and coordinator of the Religious Life Committee; Valerie Hines; Costa Preshia, a freshman from East Jacksonville, Florida; and Willie Wilson, a powerfully built senior majoring in physical education and health. Willie was also manager of the basketball team and a friend of Harold, my roommate. Willie's candor, outgoing nature, and easy laughter made him a sort of confidant.

These students' knowledge of the history of the civil rights movement afforded me a valuable window into the black experience in the South. Up until then I knew little about the history of segregation and slavery in the South. I was shocked at the similarities between apartheid and the old era of Jim Crow: the segregated schools, water fountains, eating areas, entrances to buildings, bathrooms, residential areas, buses; blacks having to use the back door when entering a white man's home, stepping aside in the street to let a white man pass; department stores refusing to let blacks try on shoes and clothing; racist all-white juries, and so forth. That shock turned to anger and disillusionment at discovering that even today almost every town we visited had roughly two sections, one for blacks and the other for whites.

"How is residential segregation still possible?" I asked Willie one evening. He had stopped by my room for a chat. "I thought Jim Crow laws had long been abolished."

"The laws may be gone, Mark," Willie replied, "but the attitudes are still there. And these attitudes have subtle ways of carrying out what the laws did."

"Then did Dr. King, Malcolm X, and all your other freedom fighters die in vain?" I asked.

"There are some of us who think they did," Willie replied.

I had a strange feeling of *déjà vu* whenever I saw the white sections of Southern towns with their beautiful and expensive houses, well-maintained tree-lined streets, large department stores, well-kept parks, swimming pools, and golf courses. The sight of the whites who lived in these luxury homes and exuded the same confidence and security and health of whites in South Africa made me wonder how they could champion freedom and equality and democracy around the world without extending the same to their fellow black citizens.

Though in Gaffney residential segregation was more along class than racial lines, there still were white churches and black churches.

In fact I discovered that 11:00 A.M. Sunday was the most segregated hour in America. Whites attended the First Baptist Church and blacks the Bethel Baptist Church. Again there were no laws forbidding integration during worship, yet the two races seemingly kept apart as if separated by invisible walls.

I attended the Bethel Baptist Church for some time. Its pastor, the Reverend J. W. Saunders, a short, portly light-skinned man, ever jovial, had written me a warm welcome letter while I was in South Africa. The church was located on Floyd Baker Boulevard, an area of modest but well-kept homes belonging to hard-working middle-class blacks and whites. Despite such proximity, the two races existed in different social worlds.

I was invited to several homes of members of the Bethel Baptist Church. Everyone was hospitable; I was showered with love and attention. During almost weekly Sunday invitations to brunch and dinner I was introduced to a variety of "soul food," including fried chicken, grits, greens, catfish, and chitlings. Reverend Saunders gave me clothing from his massive wardrobe, adding to the winter shoes, pants, and shirts Dr. Killion had bought me. I was now fortified against what everyone warned would be a winter unlike any other I had been through in temperate South Africa.

Everyone I met at the Bethel Baptist Church was eager to know more about South Africa and apartheid, and shared my concern over the well-being of my family. Weekly prayers were said in their behalf in church. Despite having grown up amid terrible poverty and degradation during the years of Jim Crow, many of these blacks, following the gains of the civil rights movement, had quietly gone about getting unionized and better-paying jobs. They were a proud people. They spontaneously took care of each other within their small, closely knit community. Had I confined myself to this relatively comfortable world, the world of the black middle class, I most likely would have been happy and content; my adjustment to America would have had fewer bumps and shocks.

But my curiosity led me to parts of Gaffney and other Southern towns where the majority of blacks, the poorest, lived. These areas were almost like forbidden zones. Even middle-class blacks kept away from them. They formed a crowded world of tiny, run-down tenements and projects, shoddily paved roads, overturned scrapped cars, garbage scattered around, and black men full of despair sitting in clusters along the roadside, drinking and boisterously talking their sorrows away. Many inhabitants of these blighted areas were on welfare. Normal family life was almost nonexistent. Here children bore children. Just as in Alexandra, where poor blacks had been quarantined without hope and without opportunity, crime and alcoholism were rife in these sections of Southern towns.

I discovered that a good number of the black students I had encountered at Limestone, and had believed to be from stable middle-class homes, were actually products of these terrible places and circumstances. Some had been abandoned by their fathers; others never knew who their fathers were and had been raised by their mothers or grandmothers or aunts, who in their strength and love resembled in many ways the black women of South Africa. Yet many of these students did not appreciate their sacrifices. Some took education for granted; some dissipated money and time and energy on parties, clothes, jewelry, and cars; some often gave up easily when confronted by obstacles erected by white racism. Overall, the behavior of many of these students reinforced the stereotypes many whites had of blacks as unambitious, immoral, unthrifty, living for the moment, and happy-go-lucky.

But it was when I was taken to the rural areas of South and North Carolina that I came face-to-face with the true horrors of black poverty in America. I saw shacks without running water or indoor plumbing. Adults and children worked all day long in the fields, picking tobacco and other crops, almost like slaves in the antebellum South. Hunger, poverty, neglect, and disease were rampant. Malnourished children ran around barefoot and in rags, their eyes full of pain and confusion and lost innocence and hope. This was not Alexandra. This was not Ethiopia. These children and their parents were American citizens. How could this be in America?

7   NO LETTERS FROM HOME; GROWING DEPRESSION;
I FAIL TO MAKE TENNIS TEAM; STRAINED RELA-
TIONSHIP WITH TENNIS COACH AND TEAMMATES;
DISILLUSIONMENT WITH LIMESTONE COLLEGE

Daily I brooded over the nature of American racism and the state of black life in the South, and over the safety of my family, who still had not replied to any of my letters since I arrived in the U.S. I later learned that the letters never reached them. Most likely they were intercepted by the authorities to intimidate me into not speaking out against apartheid. Such tactics are a known part of the Pretoria regime's psychological warfare against dissidents. Whenever I received letters from home it was because they had been mailed from white post offices instead of black ones, where the mail was strictly monitored by the government.

Every newspaper I read reported escalating violence and repression in South Africa. My depression and homesickness increased. My inability to adjust effectively to the American culture worsened matters. I gradually withdrew into myself, became antisocial and uncommunicative.

My tennis game was negatively affected by my mood. When I looked for advice from Dr. Killion on how to improve my game, little was forthcoming. It turned out that he was more of a manager and organizer than a tennis coach, a phenomenon typical of many college tennis programs, where the coaches expected recruited players to possess already the necessary technical skills. I also discovered that Limestone's tennis program was run on a shoestring budget. I had expected a well-funded top-rate tennis program, complete with floodlit courts, ball machines, and sophisticated training equipment, under which program I could work on becoming a pro. I regretted having passed up the Princeton offer. My relationship with Dr. Killion and the tennis team deteriorated as I became more withdrawn. During a round-robin tournament to determine a potential lineup, I lost all but one of my matches and I failed to make the top six. I was crushed.

"You know, Mark, some players are wondering what's wrong with you," Dr. Killion said to me one afternoon. "You used to be so outgoing. Now you always keep to yourself."

"I don't drink, coach, and I don't smoke," I replied. "And I don't like parties. And they are always doing all that. So it's understandable why I shouldn't be with them often."

"They think you're too proud," Dr. Killion said. "Some think that because you know Stan you look down on them."

"That's not true," I said. "You know, coach, some of them don't even want to practice with me." The top players, once they had defeated me in challenge matches, seldom practiced with me but only among themselves.

"Is that why you're always playing with that high school kid?"
Dr. Killion asked.

"Yes." I had befriended Kevin Covington, a thin, soft-spoken
senior and top player at the local high school. Kevin, who was white,
was essentially a loner like myself. He neither drank nor smoked and
came from a deeply religious family. He and I practiced almost daily at
the city courts, and I was able to work on the various weaknesses of
my game, notably the backhand and volley.

"Remember that you're in college now, not high school," Dr.
Killion said. "Be more of a team player."

"I'll try."

I was in the habit of doing odd jobs for Dr. Killion to earn some
pocket money. One day he asked me to wash his car, a two-tone
Dodge Magnum. He gave me a bucket, rags, sponge, and several
S.O.S. steel-wool pads. I washed the car with the soapy sponge but
still it had streaks of dirt. Eager to leave it spotlessly clean, I scrubbed
the body with the S.O.S. steel-wool pads.

Dr. Killion gasped when he saw the job I had done. "What did
you do to my poor car?"

"Anything wrong?" I asked.

"Anything wrong? Look at all those scratches."

"I'm sorry."

"What did you do to it?"

"I only used steel-wool pads to remove the stubborn dirt."

"Scrubbed my car with steel-wool pads? Who told you to use
steel-wool pads on cars?"

"I've always washed cars that way in South Africa."

"But this is not South Africa."

"I'm sorry."

"My poor car is ruined," he lamented.

"I'm sorry."

The episode seemed funny but in my depressed state it accen-
tuated the feeling I had that everything in my life was going wrong. I
tried reaching Stan but he was out of the country. My depression and
withdrawal increased. In the cafeteria I often sat alone and brooded. I
longed to go back home.

One evening I received a call from Stan.

"I hear there are problems between you and the team," he said.

"I'm afraid we don't get along too well," I said.

"What's wrong?"

"Well, for one they have a different life-style from mine," I said. "They like having a good time. They drink and some smoke pot. I tend to take things a bit seriously. Maybe too seriously. Also, I'm worried about the safety of my family. I wrote them several letters but have received no reply. Added to all that, the tennis program at Limestone isn't much of a tennis program. There's little money, the courts are worn out, and I hardly get any instruction. So I don't know how to go about working on the weaknesses in my game."

"Have you discussed things with the coach?"

"Yes, a little," I said. "But I sometimes get the feeling that people misunderstand me. When I keep to myself, when I don't act like one of the boys, they say I'm aloof and proud. I guess I need a little more time to adjust to things."

"You must try communicating with the coach," Stan said.

"I'll try."

I tried to communicate with the coach but our relationship continued downhill. In fairness to Dr. Killion, he couldn't devote much time to my problems because he was saddled with a ton of responsibilities. He taught five classes so he could have more time to spend with the tennis team in the spring, was chairman of the social sciences department, served on the Academic Council, and was sponsor of the freshman class. His stewardship of the tennis program, for which he was paid nothing, was an act of love. As for the rest of the tennis team, I felt that some players had already made up their minds about me. They construed my withdrawal, seriousness, and reluctance to attend their wild parties to mean I looked down on them. Our racial and cultural differences also worsened the misconceptions; after all, these were white students who had trouble enough understanding and relating to black Americans. Toward the end of November, Stan and I again talked.

"I'm considering transferring to another school," I said to Stan.

"Are things that bad?"

"I'm afraid so."

"Which school did you have in mind?"

I reminded Stan of the offer I had received from Princeton University while I was still in South Africa.

"Does the offer still stand?" he asked.

"I don't know. I'll contact the coach and find out."

Accordingly I called David Benjamin, the tennis coach at Princeton, and expressed my desire to transfer to his school. He was sympathetic but replied that Princeton didn't accept midyear transfers.

"What if I came as a sophomore?"

"The problem with that is you would have to be red-shirted for a year."

"What does that mean?"

"It means that you won't play any matches for the school for a year."

"Why?"

He explained to me the NCAA eligibility rules.

"I'm willing to sit out," I said. "All I want is the opportunity to attend Princeton. I'm unhappy here."

"There's another problem," the coach said. "If you came to Princeton you would have to pay your way through college."

"What about the scholarship Princeton promised me while I was in South Africa?"

"Unfortunately transfer students aren't eligible," the coach said.

Tuition at Princeton then was about $10,000 (now it is almost $20,000). There was no way I could ask Stan to pay that kind of money, and I had no way of supporting myself. What could I do?

One afternoon I discussed with Butch Klopfer, the junior transfer from Central Florida Community College, my intention to transfer to another school. Butch was one of the few players on the team who from time to time practiced with me. He told me of the fine tennis program at his alma mater and of the availability of scholarships. He gave me the name of his former coach, Mel Carpenter.

"Give him a call and find out what he says," Butch said.

I called Mel Carpenter and inquired about his tennis program and the possibility of my transferring to his school. He sounded excited at the idea. He told me that he ran one of the best tennis programs in Florida, and requested that I send him my transcripts, which I did. I also contacted the tennis coach at St. Louis University. I came across the name of the school while reading the sports pages; its soccer team, "the Billikens," was a national powerhouse, having won several NCAA Division I titles. I had been one of the better junior soccer players in Alexandra. I therefore felt that it would be to my advantage, if I transferred, also to consider schools which offered both sports, particularly because it had become clear to me that Americans were on the average better collegiate tennis players, having grown up playing the game and participating in tournaments. For me, soccer—the most popular game in the ghettos of South Africa, along with boxing, and the least expensive to play—was the more natural sport. I grew up playing soccer in the dusty streets and vacant lots of Alexandra; on the other hand, I was nearly fourteen, an old man by tennis standards, when I first picked up a racket.

At the college level the tennis season is in the spring, and the soccer season in the fall. The tennis coach at St. Louis University expressed an interest in me and we promised to talk again after the Christmas holidays. I sat for exams uncertain of my future. Stan and Margie invited me to spend Christmas at their home on Hilton Head Island, South Carolina. They rented a small plane to fly me to Hilton Head Island. I was deeply touched by their generosity.

Dr. Killion drove me to the nearby municipal airport. The pilot of the two-seater plane was a casually dressed white Southerner with a scruffy beard. As the plane rose into the clear mellow afternoon sky a transformation came over me. I became so absorbed in contemplating the wonders of nature that I gained a new perspective on the troubles and pain of my first four months in America. In the far west, mountains reared their summits into the hazy blue sky. High above, the winter sun continued its unerring course across the heavens, scattering its rays of life over all creation as it went. And below, the open fields, meadows, woods, lakes, and the winding rivers which fed them radiated pastoral freshness, tranquillity, and simplicity. By comparison the cities and towns over which we flew appeared like deformities on the otherwise pristine face of nature.

Occasionally powerful winds tossed the plane about like a feather, as if to remind me of nature's power and man's mortality. On the final approach to Hilton Head, as the plane flew low along the smooth crescent South Carolina shore and the shimmering blue ocean, past a string of islands whose verdure made it seem like summer, I remember saying to myself, "How lucky I am to be alive and able to see and feel all this!"

From that day onward, in nature I was to find hope, comfort, and healing for the pain caused by separation from loved ones, grief over the death of relatives and friends, disappointment, despair, weariness, and exile from the land of my birth. I was to also find great joy. I was to understand why so many poets, so many sensitive spirits, young and old, celebrated and worshiped nature—and why William

Wordsworth, whose poems became a constant companion, a sort of therapy against the problems and cares of modern life, could have said:

> *. . . Nature never did betray*
> *The heart that loved her; 'tis her privilege,*
> *Through all the years of this our life, to lead*
> *From joy to joy; for she can so inform*
> *The mind that is within us, so impress*
> *With quietness and beauty, and so feed*
> *With lofty thoughts, that neither evil tongues,*
> *Rash judgments, nor the sneers of selfish men,*
> *Nor greetings where no kindness is, nor all*
> *The dreary intercourse of daily life,*
> *Shall e'er prevail against us, or disturb*
> *Our cheerful faith, that all which we behold*
> *Is full of blessings.*

8

VISITING THE SMITHS ON HILTON HEAD ISLAND; STAN'S ADVICE; I'M OUSTED FROM TENNIS TEAM; I WITHDRAW FROM LIMESTONE COLLEGE

Hilton Head Island at the time was reputed to be one of America's finest and most exclusive resort communities. I imagined Stan and Margie as living in a mansion, surrounded by all the trappings of wealth and success. After all, Stan was a celebrity, one of the best tennis players in the world, the 1971 U.S. Open and 1972 Wimbledon champion, and a millionaire with an annual six-figure income from tournament winnings and endorsements. He and Margie could afford almost any life-style they chose. What I found out surprised me and deepened my respect for Stan and Margie.

Their home was an unpretentious two-story apartment in Harbour Town. Unlike the homes of many celebrities, it had no high fence, video cameras, or vicious dogs to keep away the paparazzi, and was tastefully furnished but by no means ostentatious. The only sign that it was the home of Stan Smith were the many trophies, plaques, and pictures chronicling his illustrious career. His phone number was listed. He and Margie had friends from all walks of life. There was no caviar on their dinner table; just the regular American fare. They had no entourage of bodyguards, no bevy of servants, drove no Rolls-Royce, wore nothing spectacular, and went to the local Grace Community Church on Sunday.

Stan and Margie put me up in a condominium they owned at Shipyard Plantation. The Atlantic Ocean was about half a mile away, and I regularly took walks on the beach or watched the sunset. Since I could not drive, Stan would often pick me up for meals over at their place. One evening, as we drove along a winding road lined with trees whose overarching branches were draped in Spanish moss, headed for Harbour Town, we discussed my situation at Limestone. Stan felt that my difficulty adjusting to American culture, the pressure I felt to do well in the classroom and on the tennis court, and the constant worrying over the well-being of my family were largely responsible for my estranged relationship with the coach and tennis team.

"Remember, it'll take some time before you're well adjusted to things," Stan said. "In the meantime, relax and do your best."

Stan was pleased to hear that despite my problems, I had ended up with a 3.11 grade-point average for the semester: two A's, two B's, and a C.

Late one night, as Stan was driving me home, I said to him, "You know, Stan, this vacation and my talks with you have made me realize that I have many friends at Limestone and in the Gaffney black community. If I can straighten out my relationship with Dr. Killion and the tennis team, things are bound to improve."

"I think you're right," Stan said.

Wherever we went on the opulent island, Stan and Margie introduced me as their friend. There was no trace of condescension in their words or attitude. What a contrast they made to the other moneyed, hoity-toity inhabitants of the island! They were like a breath of fresh air in a stuffy hut. They introduced me to their close friends Reginald and Ellen Bray, with whom we spent Christmas Eve opening presents, the first time I had ever opened Christmas presents in my life.

Stan and I practiced regularly on the clay courts at Sea Pines. I could rally okay with him in practice but his game experience was superior to mine. Stan was an excellent teacher and my game improved tremendously from the pointers he gave me. I acquired a new left-hander's spin serve. My backhand, hit with top spin, was more controlled and powerful, and my volleys were crisper with a compact swing similar to a karate chop. I made so much progress that I was confident I could make the Limestone tennis team in the spring.

To relax, Stan and I watched football games, particularly the Rose Bowl in Pasadena, Stan's hometown. Stan always rooted for his alma mater's team, the University of Southern California "Trojans." Toward the end of my stay he gave me a bagful of used Adidas tennis shorts, shirts, sweaters, socks, wristbands, and a warm-up Stan wore as part of the victorious U.S. Davis Cup team. The items became my prized possessions, for they had been worn by Stan Smith.

I returned to Limestone well rested. Stan telephoned Dr. Killion about my intention to stay at Limestone and work things out with the team. It turned out that Dr. Killion, who had been away over the Christmas holidays, had during that time learned from Butch Klopfer that I was planning to transfer to Central Florida Community College. He was surprised by my change of mind, especially since I had even requested that my transcripts be sent to Central Florida. He said he would have to discuss the matter with the tennis team. A few days later Dr. Killion told me that the players had unanimously decided that I not be allowed on the team. I was shocked.

"Why?"

"They feel you're not a team player," he said.

That evening I talked to Stan. He, too, had heard from Dr. Killion the news of my rejection by the team.

"Since I'm not a member of the tennis team, does that mean my tennis scholarship will be withdrawn?" I asked.

"It appears that way," Stan said.

I was thunderstruck.

"If you still want to attend Limestone," Stan went on, "I'm willing to pay for your tuition, room, and board."

"Thanks, Stan," I said. "But I don't wish to remain in a place where I'm not wanted. I think the best thing to do is to go ahead and transfer to Central Florida Community College."

Stan and I called Mel Carpenter but to my surprise he told us that he could not use me on his team. I wondered at the sudden change. It turned out that when I first contacted Mel Carpenter, he called Butch Klopfer and asked how good a player I was. When Mel Carpenter learned that I wasn't the sensational player he assumed I was because I had been discovered by Stan, he apparently lost interest in me.

What would I do now? I recalled the tennis coach at St. Louis

University expressing interest in me. I told Stan about my exchange with the coach and added, "I hope he, too, hasn't been told that I'm a lousy player."

"We'll find out," Stan said.

In a conference call, Stan, myself, and the tennis coach at St. Louis University discussed the possibility of my transferring there for the spring semester on such short notice. The tennis coach was still interested in me. Even this late, he said, I could still be admitted if I sent my transcripts right away. Regarding scholarship money for the spring semester, there was none left as it was the middle of the year. Stan pledged to pay my tuition, room, and board for the spring, and the tennis coach promised me a partial scholarship in the fall.

"I also heard that St. Louis University has one of the best soccer teams in the nation," I said to the coach.

"Yes," he replied. "We've won several NCAA titles. Are you also a soccer player?"

"Yes," I said. "I was one of the best junior players in our area."

"I'll talk to the soccer coach," the tennis coach said. "If you're good enough to make his team, I'm sure he'll give you a partial soccer scholarship."

After the discussion with the tennis coach I immediately contacted the registrar's office at Limestone College and requested that my transcripts be sent to St. Louis University.

Stan warned me about midwestern winters and was surprised to learn that I had never seen snow. He told me to contact Margaret Van Milder, his secretary at the Pro Serve offices in Washington, about travel arrangements to St. Louis and an allowance for emergencies.

"Margie and I will be out of the country for several months," he said; he had tournaments to play in Europe. "Should you need anything, contact Margaret."

I was quite overwhelmed by his generosity. I promised him that I would make every attempt to stand on my own feet as soon as possible.

"As long as you do well in school," Stan said, "and you're happy, Margie and I are satisfied. Don't forget you're still new to America and it will take time for you to adjust. Expect a few bumps here and there."

Since the spring semester hadn't yet begun at Limestone, I couldn't bid farewell to David, Valerie, Sandra, and my other friends. On the seventeenth of January, 1979, shortly before I left for St.

Louis, Kevin Covington's parents invited me to dinner at their home, where they gave me, as a token of their friendship, a Bible, with the following inscription:

"May the Lord fill you each day with His love, peace, hope, faith, trust, health, joy, wisdom, strength, holiness and as such, you will Be His Witness."

Before I conclude my experiences at Limestone College, I will say a few more things about David Bomar. I mentioned somewhere in the preceding chapters that David and I had considered transferring to other colleges. After I left for St. Louis University, he applied and was accepted at Wofford College, in Spartanburg. But when the college refused to accept all his freshman credits, he remained at Limestone. He became editor of the yearbook, the college paper, and the literary magazine. As a senior, he was chosen as the McGill Scholar in South Carolina. The late Ralph McGill was the publisher of the *Atlanta Constitution*, and the awards from his trust fund are given to deserving students (B average or better) in their third or fourth year of college, from a Southern background, who have shown a proficiency in journalism.

In 1981, David graduated summa cum laude in three instead of the normal four years, and was named valedictorian. He went on to receive his M.A. in English from Bowling Green State University in nine months instead of the normal two years. David now teaches English at Byrnes High School in Duncan, South Carolina. He was twice voted teacher of the year, and in 1981 the U.S. Jaycees named him an Outstanding Young Man of America in recognition of his leadership ability and service to the community.

A telling example of David's idealism and individuality— qualities which first attracted me to him—is the following excerpt from an editorial he wrote in *The Lantern* on March 11, 1981:

> Limestone is not what I expected it to be, a strict, academically challenging and fulfilling little school. So why didn't I leave? I stayed at Limestone for four reasons: (1) I didn't want to run away from a problem; (2) I felt I could contribute to the school as a student leader; (3) I enjoy challenge; and (4) I found among the English faculty professors interested in my advancement in my chosen field as well as my worth as a person.
>
> For my purposes, with the exception of studies in English language and literature, learning at Limestone has been a result of self-motivation and my own curiosity and enthusiasm.

My time at Limestone College has been a growth experience. As I prepare to leave, however, I am still unsure of why I came. What matters are the contributions I have made, and the opportunities I have been afforded to emerge self-realized and to consistently be myself.

PART TWO

LIFE IN THE MIDWEST AND THE NORTHEAST

St. Louis University; the Blounts; attending a revival meeting; useless surgery; no scholarship

St. Louis was another world when I arrived in the middle of winter in 1979. I found the city digging out of a blizzard. Temperatures were below freezing. The days and nights were raw. My teeth chattered all the time. I went out and bought a pair of insulated boots, a heavy coat, and long johns. Walking along iced streets proved hazardous; I fell a couple of times. The tennis coach, a heavyset white man with a baby face, had high expectations of me, which I feared I would disappoint, just as I had disappointed Dr. Killion's at Limestone.

St. Louis University, a coeducational Jesuit school, had about five thousand students. I attended lectures in halls which contained multitudes. Unaccustomed to American mass education and still having much to adjust to, I needed the personal attention possible only at a small college. I knew none of my teachers personally; I was simply a name, a number. It soon became evident that I would never be happy in such a place.

My only solace was that I befriended Lee Blount, the top tennis player and only black on the six-man squad. He was an excellent serve and volley player and had played in a couple of the satellite tournaments, which were the testing ground for future professionals. I played against him several times and he always won, largely because of his greater match experience.

Lee's parents owned a large brick house on Delmar Boulevard, in the predominantly white and upper-middle-class suburb of University City. He often invited me to his home. His parents—his father was a doctor and his mother a housewife—were in the early stages of a

65

protracted and painful divorce, and the children—Lee, Colette, Kay, and Melissa—suffered. They were divided over which parent to choose or to blame. Witnessing their pain led me to wonder what marriage meant to Americans, since three in five marriages were said to end in divorce. Did people marry out of loneliness, for sex, or because it was the socially acceptable thing to do?

Among black South Africans of my parents' generation divorces were rare; marriage meant commitment. Not because marriages were perfect matches, with husbands and wives enjoying the same rights and sharing responsibilities. On the contrary: in most tribal marriages the husband was given near despotic powers over his wife by the practice of *lobola*, under which he bought his wife by paying with cattle or money. A wife so bought literally became her husband's possession, to do with as he pleased. Needless to say, bought wives easily became beasts of burden and often suffered terrible abuses, silently. My own mother, purchased by my father for several scrawny cattle, a couple of which I'm told died immediately following the nuptials, was frequently beaten by him for trifles such as answering back during arguments or not cooking. Though my mother would have been justified in divorcing my father, she stayed with him, partly because of the social stigma which attaches to divorced women (they're considered "damaged merchandise" and tribal men are unwilling to marry them); partly because, actuated by her Christian beliefs, she loved my father and felt a responsibility toward him; and partly—and this, according to my mother, was the overriding factor—for the sake of us children. The presence of both parents had a positive psychological effect on us children growing up.

Lee's fourth sister, Renée Blount, was a talented but struggling tennis professional, one of a handful of blacks on the women's tour. She had won several important satellite tournaments but was unable to break into the big time. She could not afford the expense of a full-time coach, tennis equipment, or the cost of traveling to major tournaments to play against the best. Lee, though he from time to time considered playing tennis professionally, had dedicated his life to Jesus Christ. He prayed constantly and read the Scriptures daily. He always wore a smile, greeted strangers in the streets with "God bless you," harbored no malice toward anybody, shared whatever he had with the destitute, and went to revival meetings in various cities across the country. He reminded me very much of my mother. He sensed that I was of wavering faith and thus set himself the goal of having me accept Jesus Christ as my Lord and Savior.

One time he took me to Busch Stadium, where one of his favorite white televangelists was conducting a mammoth revival meeting entitled "Jesus Ministry and Miracle Service." Thousands of Americans turned out to witness a mortal like themselves, who claimed to have divine powers, perform tricks which he called miracles. On a platform resembling a rock-'n'-roll stage, surrounded by a robed, all-white choir and a band, the televangelist strutted around, microphone in hand. He wore a gray suit, a thick diamond ring, and a gold watch; his carefully coiffed hair glistened under the bright lights. All the time the congregation chanted like participants in a witchcraft ceremony.

The televangelist's rhetoric was that of a shrewd businessman, and his gestures those of a consummate con man. He knew how to exploit people's fears and feelings of inadequacy. He boastfully compared himself to Jesus Christ and the Apostles. He cited various passages in the Bible to support faith in miracles. He began his healing ceremony. A long line of the sick stretched before him. He "cured" victims of cancer, kidney stones, heart diseases, gout, blindness, varicose veins, diabetes, and so on, by giving them a gentle shove on the forehead. The individuals so struck fell backward stiffly into the hands of the televangelist's attendants. Several people grabbed microphones and testified that the televangelist had snatched terminally ill spouses and relatives from the jaws of death. It was all such a sham. Yet thousands believed and gave thousands of dollars in pledges. The entire hoax was no different from some of those performed by quacks I had denounced back in South Africa. As Lee and I left the stadium I said to him, "You didn't believe all that nonsense about curing the sick and raising the dead, did you?"

Lee broke into one of his beatific smiles and said, "Mark, the Bible says miracles do happen. God often works in mysterious ways, you know."

"Those were no miracles, Lee," I countered.

"Then how were all those believers cured?"

"Come on, now, Lee," I said. "That was all staged. That televangelist is no magician and you know it. How could a human being like you and me perform the medically impossible?"

"Jesus and the Apostles did it," Lee said, smiling. "Nothing is impossible when you have faith."

I shook my head. I knew I would get nowhere arguing with Lee. He was one of those millions of Americans of sincere but blind faith, cunningly preyed upon by charlatans cloaked in religious garb. As Lee and I drove home I wondered how civilized Americans could be thus deceived, since I had believed that being civilized meant being free from superstition. Apparently there is a thin line between superstition and faith.

My roommate at the university was a thin, dark-haired, soft-spoken, ascetic Iranian student named Mahmud, who abhorred the Shah and longed for the forces of "the Iman," as the Ayatollah Khomeini was called, to come to power and establish an Islamic millennium of freedom, peace, and prosperity. The two of us shared a cubicle in a huge high-rise dormitory where sex and alcohol were rampant. Neither of us did any of that, so we stayed away from the wild college parties. Meals were served at a large downstairs cafeteria. I was accustomed to the South African diet of *pap* (porridge made from cornmeal), greens, and brown bread, which, though meager, was low in cholesterol and fat and high in roughage; my stomach still had trouble digesting the fat, grease, and preservatives which were in almost everything: hamburger, french fries, pizza, eggs, bacon, sausages, fried chicken. Also, I was constantly bothered by the amount of food that was thrown away daily, for I knew that back home people were dying for crumbs. One afternoon I went to the cafeteria and ordered a lunch of soup and salad. The soup was so oily, dark, and gooey that my body shivered at the thought of eating the slimy stuff, but since I was hungry, I ate. The next thing I knew I was back in the room, which was very hot, curled up in bed, my stomach wracked with pain. I thought I was going to die.

Mahmud came back from a class and saw the predicament I was in.

"What's wrong?"

"I don't know. It's this pain in my lower stomach."

"Maybe you have a ruptured appendix," Mahmud said fearfully. "How long have you been this way?"

"About fifteen minutes. I thought the pain would go away if I lay down but it's gotten worse."

He dialed the infirmary but no one was in. He dialed the emergency room at the St. Louis University Medical Center, located a mile or so from the campus, and was told that ambulances were only reserved for emergencies.

"But this is an emergency!" he said.

He was asked to describe my symptoms, which he did, in awkward English with a heavy Iranian accent. He put his hand over the phone and asked me if I could walk.

"I can try."

I was driven to the medical center emergency room in a borrowed student car. Mahmud went back shortly after I was admitted; he had an important exam that afternoon. I was alone. I was asked several questions by the white nurse. Did I have any insurance? No. How would I pay for the bill? I gave her my student ID and Stan Smith's address and telephone number in Washington, D.C. Two white doctors—they looked like interns—came to my bedside in the emergency room. I told them that the pain in my stomach was becoming unbearable, that it had spread to my groin and legs. In my frightened state the pain felt worse.

"We may have to operate," one of the doctors said after examining me and talking to his colleague. He was short, with dark brown hair and a youthful face. His colleague was tall and had a reddish beard.

"What's wrong?" I asked.

"We don't know exactly at this time," the young-looking doctor said. "But it looks like you may have a twisted spermatic cord."

"What's that?"

He explained. A spermatic cord connects each testicle to the internal reproductive organs. If this cord becomes twisted, the blood supply to the testicle is cut off. If the condition is not treated promptly, the cells in the testicle die from lack of oxygen and vital nutrients, then disintegrate and invite bacterial infection, which can cause an abscess in the testicle. The symptoms of a twisted spermatic cord are intense pain in the central abdomen or groin area. These sensations, however, can also be caused by a severe stomach ache.

"The pain began shortly after I ate lunch," I told the doctors.

"It's possible you may have a bad stomach ache," the bearded doctor said. "But we have to make sure."

The young looking doctor again examined me. So did his bearded colleague. By now the pain was unbearable. My entire abdomen and groin seemed on fire. When he touched my testicles, I winced.

"It looks like a twisted spermatic cord to me," the young-looking doctor told his bearded companion. The two stepped outside for several minutes and then came back.

"We're going to have to perform exploratory surgery on you, Mr. Mathabane," the young-looking doctor said.

My face became rigid with fear.

"Don't worry, it's a relatively safe procedure," he said reassuringly.

Ever trusting of American doctors—aren't they supposed to be the best in the world?—and terrified by the pain, I did not press the issue or seek a second opinion. I signed the consent forms.

I was prepared for the operating room. I recall the anesthesiologist instructing me to breathe deeply while I stared at a bright light above me. I went to sleep.

An hour or so later I awoke from general anesthesia in the recovery room. Still groggy, I felt a dull ache in my groin, and when I looked down I gasped. My groin was wound up in heavy bandages. For a minute I thought I had been castrated. I panicked. I rang for a nurse. She came immediately.

"Where are my testicles?" I demanded.

"They're on you. Aren't they?"

"I don't know. What happened? Why the heavy bandages?" I fired questions at the nurse.

"Easy now, Mr. Mathabane. Everything is all right. The surgery went well. Doctors found nothing wrong with your spermatic cord."

"Nothing?"

"Yes. Nothing, Mr. Mathabane. You're fine. You'll soon be going home."

It turned out that I was, after all, the victim of a severe stomach ache. Couldn't the doctors have conclusively determined that without the surgery? What if I had died on the operating table? I was released the next day. The medical bill came and I owed the hospital about a thousand dollars. I had no medical insurance. The bill was sent to Stan and he paid it. On hindsight, he should have refused to pay for the unnecessary surgery, which forced me to miss several important classes. Worse, the doctors told me not to participate in sports for at least a month. But I had that important scholarship to qualify for, so I ignored the doctor's advice and attended tennis and indoor soccer practice. My wound reopened and became infected. The period of convalescence lengthened and it was almost spring before I was once again healthy. By that time I had missed so many classes that I feared I might not pass any of my courses. When I approached the soccer coach and asked him what he thought of my chances of making the fall team, he replied, "You're a good player, all right. But even if you make the team, I'm afraid I can't give you any scholarship."

"Why not? The tennis coach promised that you would."

"The tennis coach runs his program his way. I run my program my way. My scholarships are reserved for American talent." He was Brazilian. He explained to me that the practice by many colleges and universities of recruiting foreign soccer stars was detrimental to American soccer, which was still in its infancy. He was especially critical of schools like the University of Alabama, A & M, Clemson, and the University of San Francisco, perennial soccer powerhouses which relied heavily on Africans and South American players.

I was flabbergasted. I argued no further. Though the coach's explanation had some merit, I still considered his treatment of me unfair. Didn't he know that for poor Africans and South Americans, the only way of escaping the ghetto, of getting a decent education in America, was by excelling in sports? Most financial aid programs were for American citizens. If I didn't have Stan's financial support, I would have long been sent back home by the Immigration and Naturalization Service (INS).

Now that a partial soccer scholarship was out I wondered how I would afford tuition and board next semester. Would Stan continue his support of me? A few weeks following this encounter with the soccer coach, the tennis coach called me to his office.

"Mark, are you happy here?" he asked.

"I can't give an unqualified 'yes' as I have had some bad times."

"If you had your choice, would you continue attending St. Louis University?"

"I don't know what you mean."

"Well, I hate to say this," the coach hemmed. "But I've looked at my budget for next year and I don't think there will be any scholarship money for you. I thought there would be something left after I'd recruited a couple of players, but I was mistaken."

I was speechless.

"Given the facts, do you still intend to stay?"

"I don't have anywhere else to go, coach," I said.

"Well, you can stay here if you want," he said. "I'll be glad to have you try out for the team. But Stan would have to pay your entire bill."

Anguish distorted my face and the coach saw my pain.

"I'm sorry. But there's nothing I can do."

"I understand."

"It will be a hefty bill," he said. "Therefore, I'd recommend that you consider transferring to a smaller school, where the tuition would be lower and you'd have a better chance of making the team."

I left his office devastated. David's words about black athletes being exploited and discarded when they are no longer needed came back to haunt me. Because I had missed practice due to an injury, because under the NCAA eligibility rules I was expected to sit out a year, and because I was not a sensational tennis player, the coach apparently thought that his money would be better spent on new recruits who were healthy and could play for him right away. He and I had discussed the NCAA eligibility rules before, and he had said my sitting out a year would be no problem, so he shouldn't have strung me on.

For weeks I was buried in the deepest melancholy and self-reproach. Why me? Why me?

During that time I received a letter from home, the first since I came to America, informing me that my father had lost his job and that several members of the family were ill. There was no money for medical care. My siblings were having difficulty staying in school for lack of money to buy books and pay school fees. The letter ended by asking me if I had made enough money in America to send some home. My mother requested that I convey to the Smiths her eternal gratitude for what they had done for me. "Every night I pray for their continued health and happiness," she said. "And child, I hope you have found a good family to take care of you. And a good church."

I again thought of returning home. I concluded that I had been deceived about the glories of life in America. I now actually longed for the familiar world of apartheid, where at least I knew what I was fighting against, rather than being ambushed at every turn. As I wandered along the streets of St. Louis, and visited from time to time the notorious black world of East St. Louis, with its poverty, projects, hopelessness, crime, violence, neglect, and decay, I became more disillusioned about America. What did this great American freedom mean? How could a foreigner hope to fare any better, when many American citizens led such inhuman and desperate lives?

The spring semester of 1979, marking the end of my freshman year, was almost over and I had not yet made up my mind about what to do with my future. There was another crackdown by the Pretoria regime on black students; many were killed, detained, and tortured, and others fled the country to escape arrest. I could not see myself returning home under such conditions.

I heard of a small Franciscan liberal arts college across the Mississippi River in Quincy, Illinois, which had one of the finest soccer teams in the NAIA. I wrote the soccer coach, Jack McKenzie, and expressed my desire to transfer if only he would promise to give me some financial aid if I made the team. He wrote back a cordial letter informing me that he would be delighted to give me a tryout, and that Frank Longo, the tennis coach at Quincy, was his assistant, so something could be worked out with him. I finally mustered enough courage to call Stan and discuss with him my plans.

"If that's what you want to do," Stan said, "I'm prepared to give you a chance."

"This is the last time I'll transfer," I promised. "This time I'll make it. I will win a scholarship."

"Good luck. And take care of yourself."

I transferred to Quincy College in the fall of 1979, my third college in just a year.

10

I ENROLL AT QUINCY COLLEGE; ATTEMPTS AT CONFORMITY; FRIENDSHIP WITH MARK ROOM, AN AFRIKANER

At Quincy changes began taking place in my life which were to leave a permanent imprint. The school, founded in 1860, was predominantly white and had about two thousand students. The few blacks came mostly from black ghettos in Illinois and, though toughened by street life, many were awed by white authority. I made myself the promise that I would try to fit in, to please everybody, since at the two previous schools being a maverick had brought me nothing but trouble. I made a determined effort to suppress my individuality, to be pliant, to conform to accepted rules of behavior and do the bidding of white superiors without overt complaint. Yet there were times when, like the narrator in Matthew Arnold's poem "A Summer Night," I did not know whether "to pray/Still to be what I am, or yield, and be/Like all the other men I see."

A conformist attitude made me popular with coaches, teammates, and students. I attended parties where I danced and gossiped all night long. I acted the part of a jock when I was with members of the soccer team, who always sat apart in the cafeteria. In certain classes I was the studious scholar who wrote fine essays, posed provocative questions to teachers, and handed in all assignments on time. In others I was laid-back and happy-go-lucky.

I joined the tennis team, quickly rose through the ranks, and became captain, along with being the number-one player in both singles and doubles. I convincingly won matches against players from MacMurray College, Knox College, Sangamon State University, Greenville College, Blackburn College, and other Illinois schools. I had no trouble finding dates because I now enjoyed being flattered and having my fake machismo stroked. Whenever I talked with Stan I always told him how happy I was at Quincy. I informed him that I had won a partial tennis scholarship and that the soccer coach had promised me some money if I made the team next year.

"Sounds like you've finally found a home," Stan said.

"I've lost all my inhibitions," I replied. "If you saw me now, you would think I was born in this country. I have adjusted very well. I even know slang and I can boogie. I really dig it here."

"I'm happy for you," Stan said. "And keep up the good work. I've just received your grades for the semester and you have a couple of A's." I did well in the following courses: Accounting, Fiction, Development of a Christian Conscience (Theology), International Economics, and Rhetoric.

In the summer of 1979 Stan paid for me to accompany the soccer team to Scotland. We played several matches against youth teams in Glasgow and Edinburgh. Though younger, they handled the ball like professionals and completely outplayed and out-hustled us. I met the lord mayor of Glasgow and visited an ancient castle overlooking a loch, a trip which made the historical novels of Sir Walter Scott come alive. I also visited the cottage where a famous Scottish poet I admired, Robert Burns, was born.

On the Quincy College soccer team I had made several friends, among them an Afrikaner named Mark Room. He was a junior from Pretoria and had been in the military defending apartheid. White soldiers, mostly two-year conscripts barely out of high school, were used primarily to occupy and patrol ghettos during periods of black unrest. The fighting on the border with Angola was done mainly by black soldiers, chiefly Namibians and Angolan rebels, the latter followers of Jonas Savimbi. Because few whites were ever killed, the South African army had acquired a reputation for invincibility, and the white community considered it an act of patriotic duty to serve "on the border." Angola had yet to become South Africa's Vietnam.

Mark Room and I sometimes discussed the different worlds from which we came.

"When you were growing up in Pretoria, did you ever believe that apartheid was wrong?" I asked him one time as we left the cafeteria.

"No," he replied. "We were taught in school that blacks were not as human as we are, so we needed to be separated from them. God, we were told, wanted things that way. Also, we had black servants who seemed very happy."

"Did you ever visit where they lived to see things for yourself?"

"No."

"Why not?"

"Because there was no need to. Anyway, whites were forbidden by law to enter the townships."

"When did your views on apartheid change?"

"When I was in the military."

"What happened?"

"I didn't feel that it was right for soldiers to kill schoolchildren."

"Did you kill any yourself?"

"No. But I had friends who did. And many suffered terrible guilt."

"Why didn't you resign?" I asked. Among white soldiers there was a small but growing number of conscientious objectors. They were persecuted by the regime and reviled and regarded as traitors by the white community.

"I believe apartheid is wrong," Mark said, "but I had a duty to my country."

"Even if you are told to do something that you know to be wrong?"

"It's not as easy as you think."

"Where do most whites think apartheid will lead them?" I asked.

"Most whites believe one hundred percent in the system," Mark replied. "They believe God created it. But strangely enough, they're also afraid."

"Afraid of what?"

"Afraid of blacks and of losing everything they've got."

"But blacks only want justice and equal opportunity. We aren't interested in making whites slaves."

"Whites don't believe that," Mark said. "They believe that blacks, once free, will give whites a taste of their own medicine."

"Do you believe that?"

"Basically I don't believe it. But there are times when I do. Just look at the rest of Africa. What's happened after blacks took over is hardly reassuring for whites."

I explained to Mark that I didn't think the same would necessarily occur in South Africa.

"What makes you so sure?"

"If apartheid is ended peacefully," I said, "I believe blacks and whites can arrive at a compromise on how to live together. The key is peaceful change. I have this theory that whenever people are forced to win their liberation through the barrel of a gun, they seldom feel the responsibility to share equally with those whom they have defeated."

During the course of our acquaintance I learned a great deal from Mark about the attitudes of white South Africans. I learned that even Afrikaners were not monolithic, that there were a few among them who truly believed that apartheid was wrong and were groping for ways to oppose and change the system.

MY MOTHER'S INSANITY; ITS EFFECTS ON ME; I DISCOVER BLACK AMERICAN WRITERS; THEIR INSPIRATION; POEM ABOUT AFRICA

One day in the fall of 1979 a letter arrived from home informing me that my mother had gone insane. The letter, written by my sister Florah in Tsonga, described in detail my mother's wrenching ordeal as a raving lunatic. The description broke my heart and brought tears to my eyes. Some mornings she got up and went to the entrance to the yard where she sat all day picking up stray pieces of paper and pretending to read them aloud, even though she could not read. She would talk to herself, about how pretty and kind she was. She would accost strangers and greet them with familiarity or suspiciously scan their faces. She refused to wash. Sometimes she spent entire afternoons staring into vacancy, or imploring God to come down from heaven and destroy the world because it was full of pain and evil-hearted people. Sometimes she suspected members of the family of seeking to poison her, and refused to eat anything, and would curl up like a child in the womb to sleep.

The family immediately suspected witchcraft. But plans to find a witch doctor to cure her had been postponed for lack of money. My unemployed father, instead of looking for piece jobs, attempted to drown in alcohol the pain of having a mad wife. The more delay in finding the cause of my mother's lunacy, the less hope for recovery. In her dementia, the letter went on, my mother often spoke of me. She blessed me and urged me to study hard and take care of my siblings.

The letter left me in shock for days. My mother, my own dear mother, mad? How could it be? Oh, the unbearable pain she must be enduring! Who was now taking care of the family, since she was the only breadwinner? Was her condition irreversible? How could anyone have done such a thing to her, a human being so loving, so giving, so without malice, always eager to help others and often forgetful of her own needs? What could I do to help her? How would the family stay alive? What was I doing having fun in America while my family was going through hell?

I sat down and wrote a rambling, emotional reply, in which I promised that I would take care of her no matter what. Though I didn't believe in witchcraft, I promised her that I would find the witches and bring them to justice, that I would not rest till she was well, that I would come home immediately if she wanted me to. I sent the letter by Express Mail, but again, as with all the others, I received no reply. I feared that the letter had been intercepted by the authorities, who were notorious for intercepting letters to loved ones by dissidents who criticized apartheid. There had been renewed violence and repression in the ghettos and anything was possible.

Reluctant to discuss my problems with anyone, I retreated into a shell and grieved. Finally I reached the conclusion that I should stop pleasing others and wasting my time; I should banish fear from my mind and do what my conscience told me was right. Life was too short and there was much to be done; plans for the future had to be made, weapons had to be acquired with which to fight for survival, with which to help my family. I once again adopted my former attitude of a noncomformist. I stayed away from wild parties and no longer hung out with the boys. Instead I spent most of my time in the library. It was at this time that I stumbled upon a different kind of black literature.

In the library one afternoon, having completed my homework, I began browsing among the bookshelves. I came upon a paperback copy of *Black Boy*, Richard Wright's searing autobiography. My attention was arrested by the title and by the following defiant words on the back cover of the book: "The white South said that it knew 'niggers,' and I was what the white South called 'nigger.' Well, the white South had never known me—never known what I thought, what I felt."

I mentally replaced "white South" with "white South Africa," and "nigger" with "Kaffir," and was intrigued by how Richard Wright's feelings mirrored my own. I immediately sat down in a chair by the window and began reading the book. I was overwhelmed; I could not put the book down. I even missed my economics class because I was so engrossed. When the library closed I was three-quarters of the way through the book. Bleary-eyed, I went back to my room and read the rest.

The next day I went back to the library and asked the head librarian—a good-natured Franciscan priest with white hair and a charming smile—if the library had more books by black authors. He guided me to the treasure. I checked out Richard Wright's *Native Son*, Eldridge Cleaver's *Soul on Ice*, W. E. B. Du Bois's *Souls of Black Folks*, *The Autobiography of Malcolm X*, Franz Fanon's *The Wretched of the Earth*, Claude Brown's *Manchild in the Promised Land*, James Baldwin's *The Fire Next Time* and *Notes of a Native Son*, Maya Angelou's *I Know Why the Caged Bird Sings*, James Weldon Johnson's *The Autobiography of an Ex-Colored Man*, and the autobiography and incendiary speeches of Frederick Douglass. I devoured the books with relish.

After this momentous discovery I knew that my life would never be the same. Here were black men and women, rebels in their own right, who had felt, thought, and suffered deeply, who had grown up under conditions that had threatened to destroy their very souls; here they were, baring their bleeding hearts on paper, using words as weapons, plunging into realms of experience I had never before thought reachable, and wrestling with fate itself in an heroic attempt to make the incomprehensible—man's inhumanity to man—comprehensible. Most astonishing was that these men and women had written about what I felt and thought, what I had been through as a black man, what I desired, what I dreamed about, and what I refused to compromise.

"These are soul mates," I said to myself, "these are my true brothers and sisters." Where had they been all those years when I was lost in the wilderness, feeling so alone, wondering why I was being misunderstood by the world, why I seemed so at odds with complacent reality? I had to learn to write like them, to purge myself of what they had purged themselves of so eloquently. Here was a way through which I could finally understand myself, perform the duty I'd pledged to my countrymen and to my mother.

Inspired by these black writers, I bought myself a pair of notebooks and sat down one evening and began to write. I chose as a topic an issue of which I had only superficial knowledge, but one which appealed to my fancy. Words came very easily to the pen, but when I paused to evaluate what I had written and compared it to the masters I was determined to emulate, I found my effort ridiculous. The language was verbose, the ideas vague and incoherent. What was I doing wrong? Maybe I needed some expert advice. One day Mr. Allan, my English teacher, asked us to write a short story.

My story—a vivid, fictional description of Africa—was considered the best by Mr. Allan, who was a hard-to-please but excellent critic and teacher of English. He was stingy with A's, no matter how well the job done. I received an A for my essay; my previous assignments had merited C's and B-minuses.

I carefully analyzed the essay to determine what exactly had so impressed the scrupulous teacher. I came up with the following answer: to write well, write about what you know, for experience is the best teacher, and writing is a means of self-expression.

Flushed with confidence from writing the essay, I jotted down ideas for more essays and possibly novels. I filled notebooks with descriptions and characters and plots. Maybe writing is my calling in life, I thought. Determined to hone my skills, I went back to my favorite writers for tips on how to go about the arduous task of learning how to move the world with the right word and the right accent. Every one of the writers I admired had been a voracious reader of books. I was already one. They had felt deeply. I felt deeply, too. They possessed an inborn obsession to share with the rest of humanity, through the written word, their innermost feelings, their vision of life, its agony and ecstacy, its manifold pains and sorrows and joys, its loves and hatreds—all of which they had extracted by looking deeply and with compassion into the human heart.

Such a temperament I believed I still lacked because I had yet to acquire a sound liberal arts education. The college library had an impressive record collection of Shakespeare's plays; the dramas of Sophocles, Euripides, and Aristophanes; the *Dialogues* of Plato; the poems of Milton; and the plays of Dryden and Goldsmith, read by such giants of the stage as Paul Robeson, Claire Bloom, Sir Laurence Olivier, Anthony Quayle, Richard Burton, Sir John Gielgud, and Paul Scofield, among others. I checked out these records at the rate of three a day, and listened to them over and over again. The head librarian expressed pleasure at seeing me madly in love with Shakespeare and soon I was being talked about.

I took an English course with Professor Ann Klein. She instantly detected my enthusiastic love for poetry and helped me improve my taste and understanding of Keats, Shelley, Wordsworth, Coleridge, and Byron. Whereas heretofore my enjoyment of classical music had been visceral, I enrolled in a piano class out of a belief that the best way to understand classical music was to play an instrument.

Other subjects I now enjoyed were economics and philosophy. In the latter, taught by the easygoing, amiable Father Lucan, I was introduced to the brilliant ideas and provocative arguments for greater liberty, toleration, and individuality by Locke, Rousseau, and John Stuart Mill. The notably eclectic course Personal and Moral Life merely mentioned in passing their great ideas, but I went out in search of the complete works and read them avidly. I was fascinated by Rousseau's *The Social Contract*, especially his famous assertion "Man is born free, and everywhere he is in chains. One thinks himself the master of others and still remains a greater slave than they." But I found some of his arguments elliptical and contradictory. Mill and Locke became my favorite philosophers. I was amazed to discover, with repeated readings of their seminal works, that they basically confirmed what I had believed instinctively about the nature of freedom, individuality, and natural and civil rights. Locke's "Treatise on Toleration," his "Second Essay on Government," and Mill's *On*

Liberty and *The Subjection of Women* left a decisive influence on my mind. This immersion in books alleviated the stress of constantly worrying about the condition of my mother and family.

Once again my love affair with the world of books landed me in trouble. I now walked about with a mind pregnant with thoughts inspired by reading. I longed to live only in the world of the imagination and ideas because physical reality suddenly seemed artificial, cold, dead. I became absentminded. Some of the black students on campus wondered why I no longer came to their parties, why I occasionally sat alone in the cafeteria, deep in thought.

"He's too proud," someone said.

"He's trying to be white," another said.

"He thinks he is better than us."

"He's stir-crazy."

They never understood my need for solitude, that "to fly from, need not be to hate, mankind." They never understood why I found great pleasure in watching squirrels racing up and down trees, in walking down to the Mississippi River and spending the afternoon staring at its murky waters, at the falling autumn leaves along its banks, at clouds sailing across the sky, and at the sleepy town of Hannibal on the other side, where Mark Twain was born. They never understood why I loved memorizing poetry, why I used quotations from books to illustrate a point, or why I urged them to become more politically active on campus so they could better protect their interests and make their presence felt as blacks. I tried establishing ties of solidarity with them, given our common experiences growing up in the ghetto, but we kept drifting apart because of our divergent attitudes. I was eager to fight, to protest, as black Americans had done in the 1960s, during those unforgettable days of Martin Luther King, Jr., Malcolm X, and Stokely Carmichael's misunderstood credo of Black Power. They were eager to accommodate, to live for the moment, to make their peace with the status quo, to wallow in apathy and self-pity. At times it appeared that I had come to America a generation too late. In fairness to many of these black students, they were concerned that an activist attitude might lose them their athletic scholarships or financial aid.

In celebration of black history month, in February 1980, I wrote the following poem, entitled "Longing for My Roots." It was a nostalgic poem, inspired by thoughts of home and of my ailing mother.

when I was a little child
living amidst innocence among
the chaste hills
and the pure forests and purer
streams
i never for a single moment paused
to think
that there might come a
time
when all i would have to live with
was to be just a memory

all the enchanting silhouettes of
the africa
i used to so lovingly know
all the natural beauty of her
beasts
the magnificent plumage of her
wild birds
the blithesomeness of her
black people
the eternal feeling of freedom
among singing titihoyes
the rivers that seem to eddy whirl
their courses
through hills and plains

all the everlasting elegance of
the springbok
the gentle tip-tappering of
summer's rain
the haunting murmur of
the windsong
the thundering of hooves
upon the serengeti

all that i am now without
all that boundless joy
i once so much cherished
i have prematurely left behind
to die and to decay

★ ★ ★

yet an african still am i
a proud man as such
i am black (soot black)
a handsome black warrior as such
i am still the proud possessor
of that undaunted spirit
reminiscent of endless freedom
among the misty hills
where the zebra used to cry
with ecstatic joy

i still remember the kraal
the grassy citadel of
my forefathers
i still can smell
the scent of fresh cowdung
and in hours of solitude
i still can hear
the bewitching sound of cowhide drums
and see through the haze of time
valiant, plumed warriors
as they leap and fall
while others
fall
never to leap again

even now
far, far away from home
oceans of water away
i still can see the misty hills
i can still hear mama's voice
echoing through the valley of
a thousand hills
calling me to come home
for supper around the fireside

I showed the poem to several black students. Some of them, apparently ignorant or ashamed of their heritage as African-Americans, regarded it as confirmation of Africa's primitiveness. But I was proud of it. I knew that Africa, despite its many and serious problems, despite the Western tendency to stereotype it, remained a place of immense natural and cultural beauty, and that its diverse, proud, brave, resilient, and beautiful peoples are descended from some of the oldest civilizations on earth, which have made valuable contributions to literature, art, music, dance, science, religion, and other fields of human endeavor.

12 I'M KICKED OFF THE QUINCY SOCCER TEAM; SUMMER AT NICK BOLLETTIERI'S TENNIS CAMP; TEACHING TENNIS TO DISADVANTAGED BLACK KIDS; MORE BAD NEWS FROM HOME

I landed a job as a tennis coach at the local indoor club where the tennis team practiced in the winter. I quickly won recognition as one of the best coaches in town, and well-to-do white parents brought their children to the sessions I conducted. My success and association with the club made some people jealous. Accusations of being aloof and proud were flung at me by several members of the soccer team. Some of them privately complained to the coach that I was a divisive influence on the team. This charge was partly made because I was casually critical in conversation of the special treatment soccer players received, and of their sense of self-importance as "Quincy's star athletes." And I no longer sat at the "soccer team's table" in the cafeteria but often mingled with other students. One day Coach McKenzie called me to his office and told me that he no longer wanted me on his team.

"Why?" I asked.

"You don't fit into my plans for next season," he said.

"In what way, coach?"

"Your style of play and attitude are incompatible with the rest of the team's. You dribble too much. The team's style is touch and go. That's why we won all those national titles."

"I can adapt my style of play," I said.

"And you sometimes don't show up at practice."

"It's because I'm also on the tennis team."

"I think both of us would be better off if you left the team," the coach said with finality.

Since the tennis coach was also the assistant soccer coach, I feared for a time that my tennis scholarship might be in jeopardy. But Frank Longo turned out to be independent of Coach McKenzie. After I had talked to him he assured me that my tennis scholarship was secure. He even counseled me not to do or say anything that would worsen my relationship with Coach McKenzie. But I just could not keep my mouth shut. Shortly thereafter, senior Mark Miller, myself, and several other teammates complained (in vain) to the athletics director that it was unfair for the soccer and basketball programs to receive disproportionately more financial support than the tennis program, and that the tennis courts shouldn't be used as parking lots during basketball games. The athletics director, who was also the basketball coach, was stung by the criticisms, and tensions between me and Coach McKenzie mounted, as it was assumed that I was the instigator of the complaints.

I was relieved when summer holidays came. Through the help of Stan Smith and Arthur Ashe I was offered a job as a tennis instructor at the Nick Bollettieri tennis camp in Sarasota, Florida. The camp was known worldwide as the breeding ground of future tennis professionals. Having endured a bitter midwestern winter, with blizzards and knee-deep snow, I looked forward to sunning myself in Florida, while at the same time earning some money and improving my tennis. But that was not to be.

When I arrived in Florida I discovered that Nick Bollettieri ran his tennis factory like a dictator. He brooked no opposition to his teaching methods. The adolescent boys and girls whose parents paid thousands of dollars to have him mold them into tennis stars were put through the most grueling and strictest tennis programs I had ever witnessed: they lived, ate, talked, slept, and dreamed tennis.

It seemed that Nick had been under the impression that I was another Yannick Noah in the making. After he found out that I had neither the talent nor the fanaticism of his whiz kids, but reluctant to offend Ashe and Stan by sending me packing, he decided not to employ me as a coach. Instead, I picked up balls, cleaned up rooms, swept courts, and, at twenty, was generally treated like the twelve-, thirteen-, and fifteen-year-olds with whom I lived. I felt humiliated, but with no alternative I stayed in Florida. My payment for the long summer, which included working at Nick's other tennis camp in Beaver Dam, Wisconsin, was in the form of occasionally taking tennis lessons with the rest of his pupils. Apparently I should have considered myself lucky just to be at Nick's exclusive tennis camp. I admit I was no seasoned coach, but I felt I could have added something to his program as an instructor. For instance, I observed that most of his star pupils were weak serve and volley players because Nick overemphasized the baseline game. Today it's the well-rounded players who become champions. Also, I knew a few things about conditioning and the mental part of tennis. In Nick's stable of tennis thoroughbreds were future pros Kathy Horvath, Jimmy Arias, Pablo Arraya, and Carling Bassett (Seguso), daughter of a wealthy Canadian industrialist who owned a brewery and the Tampa Bay Buccaneers professional football team. Nick is currently the coach of Andre Agassi, America's newest tennis sensation.

Watching the devotion of these talented youngsters, their sacrifice of adolescence for that long shot at tennis superstardom, and the physical, emotional, and psychological problems many experienced at the expense of their overall development as human beings finally convinced me that a tennis career definitely was not for me.

Except for Rodney Harmon, an outgoing, lanky eighteen-year-old with a two-fisted backhand, there were no blacks among the dozens of teenagers who were being groomed as future tennis champions. Rodney, a native of Richmond, Virginia, Arthur Ashe's hometown, was lucky to have won sponsorship from some foundation. However, he valued an education and had accepted a full tennis scholarship to the University of Tennessee, while many of his white peers bypassed college for the professional circuit. In America, just as in South Africa, tennis was essentially a white man's sport. To make it in the game one needed to have money to pay for expensive lessons, to travel to tournaments all over the country and overseas, to purchase rackets, shoes, tennis balls, and track suits, and to pay for coaches. Talent alone is not enough. I also realized that in America, just as in South Africa, there were many talented black youngsters doomed to perish in the caldron of ghetto life, the world never having witnessed and benefited from their abilities, simply because they were born in the wrong place.

I returned to Quincy in the fall of 1980 determined to coach black youngsters who lived in the black section of town. I contacted the local public school and offered to give free lessons to any youngster eager to learn the game. Scores of black youngsters flocked to the college courts on the first day. Their enthusiasm overwhelmed me. There was a shortage of rackets, so the youngsters took turns receiving instructions on the basics of the game. Toward the end of the session I gathered the youngsters and told them about the difficult life led by children in South Africa, and how tennis had made a difference in my life.

"Tennis can do the same for you," I said.

But aware that many black children often had unrealistic expectations about sports, I was quick to emphasize the importance of an education.

"For many of you, the only way to college may be through sports," I said. "Play sports, enjoy sports, but remember that an education is the most important thing. We can't all be professional boxers, baseball, basketball, football, and tennis players. But armed with knowledge, many of you *can* become doctors, teachers, lawyers, and legislators and do a lot more good for your communities and country. And remember, even superstar athletes need an education because they can't go on playing sports all their lives."

I had the sense many of the kids got my message. I have been told that I have a way of speaking to youngsters which leads to understanding. I think the secret is that I always treat them as friends, and with gentle firmness I try to convince them that what I want them to do is something I have done, enjoyed, and benefited from.

Because of the ardor of the youngsters, I extended the lessons to twice a week, and solicited donations of old rackets from the community, since most of the children could not afford to purchase any. I requested help from Stan; he sent me tennis balls and several rackets. Many of these children reminded me of the black boys and girls whom I had coached in the ghettos of South Africa. They reminded me of myself, and I knew that I was making an impression on them that probably would form for some the seed of hope in the future, and instill in them a determination to triumph over the obstacles of ghetto life. I was never more happy than when I encouraged youngsters to keep trying regardless of the obstacles, to believe in themselves and in their dreams, no matter what others might say.

Despite the tennis clinics, terrible news from home made my life at Quincy increasingly miserable. A letter from my sister Florah informed me that various means to cure my mother of her insanity had been tried and failed. Out of desperation Granny had taken her to my aunt, Granny's firstborn, who lived in Giyani, the homeland of the Shangaans in the Northern Transvaal. I knew Aunt Queen only slightly. I met her once or twice when I was a teenager. She was said to be a powerful *isangoma* (medicine woman) with an impressive track record for curing insanity. My sister Florah had been forced to leave school and now worked as a cashier at a supermarket on the outskirts of Alexandra. She was pregnant and unmarried. My other siblings were in and out of school depending on the political situation in the ghettos, and on their ability to afford school fees, books, and uniforms. As for my father, there was little hope that he would ever again be employed. Unemployment had worsened his alcoholism. To feed his disease he had sold several items of furniture my mother had bought while she worked. He routinely abused my siblings for refusing to give him food money so he could buy more alcohol. The nightmare days of constant hunger had returned. Two of my siblings, Maria and Merriam, had left home and were now living with Granny on Seventeenth Avenue. Granny's tiny shack was already over-crowded with Uncle Piet's ever-increasing family. Granny had re-garded Uncle Piet as her last hope, but he had become addicted to horse-racing. It was thought that he, too, had been bewitched.

Without assistance from any quarter, Granny, though aged and tired and longing for rest, was forced to scrounge around for pennies to keep two families alive and pay for my mother's treatments. Granny's health was failing but she kept plodding on, uncomplaining.

The letter went on to relate that conditions in Alexandra had deteriorated. More houses were being demolished by the authorities in the upper parts of Alexandra to make way for a new development of decent subsidized homes known as Phase I. These were to be inhabited by black professionals like teachers and nurses. Those poor blacks whose shacks were razed simply rebuilt them in the lower parts of the ghetto, leading to an overcrowding which defied the imagination. The population of roughly half of one square mile had mushroomed to about 150,000 souls. Desperation, violence, crime, witchcraft accusations, and murders had increased. Phillip Moloi, a bosom friend, roughly my age, from my days at Bovet Community School, was said to have been stabbed to death in a *shebeen* (speakeasy) following a trivial quarrel. After matriculating, Phillip had become a habitual drunkard from frustration and lack of opportunity. Another friend, Thomas Nkosi, who throughout high school had been my chief rival and a brilliant science student, and who teachers predicted would have important achievements, had gone mad following a stint at a medical school in one of the homelands. His parents believed he had been bewitched, but less superstitious minds blamed frustration and pent-up rage against the apartheid system. At twenty-two, he was now a notorious car thief and an incurable drunkard.

The letter left me numb. I felt intolerable guilt for having left my family to suffer. Had I remained home and worked at Barclays Bank, perhaps all this wouldn't have happened: my mother would not have gone insane; I could have bought my family a decent home in Tembisa, Soweto, or Phase I; my presence would have intimidated my father and probably curbed his alcoholism and abuse; Florah would still be in school; my earnings and example would have kept the family together, given them hope, uplifted them from the pit of hopelessness into which they now had sunk.

Why, why had I left? What had I accomplished since coming to America? If I were to return home tomorrow what could I show to justify my two-year absence? What was so great about America anyway, since in many places I saw the effects of the racist attitudes, insensitivity, hatred, intolerance, greed, and selfishness I thought I had left behind in South Africa? Many black Americans, whom as a group I had idolized while in the ghetto and thought rich, were actually destitute and suffering. They lived in ghettos ravaged by crime, teen pregnancy, gang wars, alcoholism, police brutality, illiteracy, and hopelessness, in much the same way as the Sowetos and the Alexandras. Why not go back home?

I did not go home. My rage and disillusionment passed. In their place emerged an icy determination to take advantage of the educational opportunities in America, to get that college degree so that I could go back home with something to justify my having left in the first place. American college degrees gave one the Midas touch. Armed with one I would be able to write my ticket to a splendid career. As what? A tennis career was out: the stint at Nick Bollettieri's tennis academy had settled that. Despite my love for writing I still lacked the confidence to believe that I could pursue that as a career. My economics professor, Dr. Faisal Rahman, had urged me to pursue a business career upon graduation since I had a knack for economic issues. I would follow his advice.

I made several resolutions which I vowed never to break for as long as I remained in America. I would never waste my time trying to please others. I would never conform to the American way of life, with its emphasis on materialism and self-centeredness, no matter the pressure and penalties. I would never allow any white man, any coach, to treat and exploit me as if I were a nigger, a Kaffir.

I knew that if I persisted in my nonconformist attitude it would only be a matter of time before I would have to leave Quincy. Where to this time? To another college? Or back home? My fate was in Stan's hands.

A month before Christmas I received an invitation from Stan and Margie to come and spend the holidays on Hilton Head Island, making it the third Christmas in a row. They now considered me part of the family. To show my gratitude I often ran errands for them, babysat their firstborn, Ramsey, and did various household chores. Before I left for Hilton Head, I contacted Dick Jamieson, the athletics director and soccer coach at Dowling College on Long Island, New York. I had picked Dowling from a random list of liberal arts colleges on the East Coast which had both tennis and soccer programs.

It was a desperate move on my part. Dick Jamieson's response was encouraging. If I intended to enroll at Dowling in the spring, two months away, I should immediately send over my transcripts. We would, he added, discuss scholarships once I got there, and he had assessed my athletic abilities. He was certain I would get something.

The time came for me to divulge to Stan my plans for transferring from Quincy to Dowling College. I wondered what his reaction would be. The transfer would be my third. Stan had borne all the cost of my restlessness; he had spent nearly $20,000 on tuition, books, clothes, airplane tickets, and a monthly allowance of about $150. He'd be bound to conclude that I was spoiled. I could hear him saying: "Mark, this is the final straw. I've had enough of your troubles. Why don't you go home? Here's a one-way ticket."

TRANSFER TO DOWLING COLLEGE; SIXTIES STUDENTS COMPARED TO THOSE OF THE EIGHTIES; I QUIT THE SOCCER TEAM; STAN AND MARGIE SMITH'S BACKGROUNDS

"I thought you were happy at Quincy," Stan said. We were in his Mercedes. He had picked me up at the condominium in Shipyard and we were headed for a threesome practice session with Ian Goolagong, the younger brother of tennis champion Evonne Goolagong Cawley. Evonne, an Australian aborigine, her British-born husband, Roger, and their daughter, Kelly, lived on Port Royal Plantation. They had brought Ian, nineteen, from Australia to attend college in America. It was a warm, sunny winter afternoon.

"Things have changed," I said. "The tension between me and the soccer coach has become intolerable."

"Remember, you can't keep transferring to other schools and hope to graduate," Stan said. "There comes a time when you have to stay in one place. If problems arise, try to resolve them instead of running away from them because the same problems may resurface elsewhere."

"I understand that," I said. "And I have tried adopting that attitude. But it has led nowhere. One minute I think I've adjusted to the American way of doing things, the next minute something happens to disprove that."

"At times you have to look at yourself critically to find out if you may not be part of the problem. You must learn to bend a little."

"I accept my share of the blame," I said. "And I'm always willing to meet people halfway. But I see little hope that that would change things for the better at Quincy. The soccer coach has already made up his mind about me. He no longer wants me on his team."

"But you're still on the tennis team, aren't you?" Stan asked.

"Yes. But the tennis program is in bad shape. And our budget is being cut while soccer and basketball are having increases."

"So what do you want to do?"

I told him about my acceptance at Dowling College.

"I hope this is the last transfer," he said.

"I promise this will be the last."

During the flight to the East Coast I prayed that things would work out at Dowling. I was deeply troubled by the fact that I had already caused Stan too much trouble and expense, and I was anxious to complete my studies and do something positive with my life.

My suspicion that the South African government was monitoring my actions, and that the regime most likely had more informants in New York because of the large community of black South African exiles there, led me to consider another name change. Just as in South Africa, when I had to take on the name of Mark in order to elude the police during the Soweto protests of 1976 and the brutal crackdowns which followed, I now added Pierre to my list of names. Ordinary Americans, who have lived all their lives in freedom and safety, immune to the persecutory devices of totalitarian regimes, may wonder why I changed my name so many times. But if you have lived in South Africa, Chile, the Soviet Union, or other totalitarian societies, where your every action, and sometimes it even seems like your every thought, somehow ends up being known by the ubiquitous state police, such changes may be a matter of life and death, to you or your loved ones. I enrolled at Dowling College as Pierre Mark Mathabane.

Founded in 1959, Dowling was a predominantly white private college with nearly three thousand students, about three hundred of whom were graduate students. The college was renowned for its aeronautics program; its escadrille team yearly won top honors at the National Intercollegiate Flying Association (NIFA) tournament. Located in the small Long Island town of Oakdale, approximately fifty miles east of New York City, Dowling had begun as a liberal arts institution. But lately the college had started shifting its emphasis to "job-oriented courses," largely because the Reagan administration's financial aid cutbacks, which led to higher tuition costs, made students view a liberal arts degree as a luxury they couldn't afford. Many opted for business majors in the hope of finding jobs upon graduation to pay back hefty student loans.

The majority of Dowling teachers were liberal-minded and laid-back. Classes were small. The mentality among many of the undergraduates, who had lived all their lives on Long Island, was provincial. The goal of many was to graduate with a business degree, find a well-paying job, preferably with Grummans, the big aerospace company next door, marry a hometown sweetheart, settle down in the suburbs, raise a family, and vote Republican. The Suffolk County part of Long Island was Reagan country.

By this time I was familiar with the history of American students. My temperament and radical ideas made me long for the sixties. Not the sixties of hippies, wild sex, and mind-altering drugs, but the sixties of the civil rights movement, the Great Society, and the New Frontier, a time when whites and blacks of courage, idealism, and principles stood side by side and championed liberal causes that inspired hope in the future and wrought fundamental changes in American society. In 1964, three such visionaries—two Jews, Michael Schwerner and Andrew Goodman, and a black man, James Chaney—sacrificed their lives in Neshoba County, Mississippi, where they had gone to vindicate the American creed of justice, equality, and the rule of law. Despite the untimely deaths of these visionaries, and many others, the sixties seemed to me to have been a great time to be alive.

But by the eighties the progressive movement in America had lost its soul. Issues like busing, affirmative action, and housing desegregation had turned many northern whites into conservatives, as shown by the election of Ronald Reagan in 1980, and his landslide reelection in 1984, as President of the United States. The once formidable alliance between Jews and blacks had begun disintegrating amid charges of black anti-Semitism and Jewish insensitivity to black issues. At colleges and universities across the country, droves of students were rejecting liberalism in favor of conservatism. There was a palpable backlash against the radicalism of the sixties and early seventies.

The popularity of Reagan's conservative ideology, and his rabid denunciations of liberalism as something sordid, almost akin to communism, made it easy for students who misunderstood what "liberalism" meant to stop challenging authority when it abused its power, and championing idealistic causes like social justice and peace. In 1983 Grenada was invaded to resounding student applause. As a replacement for social activism, most students became preoccupied with self, money, and materialism.

Few students at Dowling possessed any in-depth knowledge of the apartheid issue. Many had an appalling sense of geography and American history. The handful of black and Puerto Rican students who attended Dowling came mostly from poor families. Many depended for financial support on the Higher Education Opportunity Program (HEOP). Ironically, to some of these students the civil rights struggle was like a fairy tale. They found it hard to believe that a form of apartheid, with legally segregated schools, lunch counters, and buses, ever existed in America. They saw nothing miraculous in their being able to attend a white institution like Dowling or to vote.

The day I arrived at Dowling, the dorm director, a muscle-bound Italian body builder named Chris Ungarino, who ran the establishment like his own private company, apparently concluded I was a sissy because of my polite manners. Many macho Americans, it seems, associate good breeding in men with femininity. Anyway, what is wrong with men having a little dose of femininity in their character? After all, they're born of man and woman, not of two men.

Chris assigned me as a roommate to a bearded white senior named Bill. I was unaware that Bill was a homosexual, that other students had declined him as a roommate, for except for his strange tight-fitting outfits, he seemed polite and helpful. But, later, rumors began circulating around the dormitory that I was "gay" because I shared a room with Bill (he freely admitted his homosexuality), had no girlfriend, had "feminine manners" and a mellifluous accent, and dressed like a dandy. One time I wore a green Stanley Blacker sport coat, and when people gaped at me, I claimed that I was a black Irishman.

As I harbored no particular prejudice toward homosexuals, I would have ignored the whole situation and continued to treat and respect Bill as an individual, except that Bill began telling some of his friends that I was about to become his lover and would soon be "coming out." From time to time he praised my athletic physique. The situation became intolerable and I asked Chris to transfer me to another apartment, but he dragged his feet. One night I learned that Stan Smith had called me a couple days before and had left a message with Bill to call him. Bill withheld the message, for what reason I don't know. That was the last straw. A fight erupted. All my ghetto instincts took over. I threatened to blow Bill's brains out with a gun I didn't possess. Terrified, he pleaded with the dorm director that I be removed from the apartment. I was at last tranferred to another apartment, where my roommate was a sensible black tennis player.

So determined was I to make the soccer team that I spent most of the summer of 1981 training, while taking a course in Fundamentals of Speech. I ran about ten miles every other day, joined a nearby gym where I lifted weights, and participated in a local summer soccer league. The hard work paid off. I performed well in preseason workouts and was considered one of the better players on the team. But once the fall soccer season began, I noticed that the coach's attitude toward me had changed. Game after game he kept me on the bench. Exasperated, I asked him why he wasn't playing me.

He replied that he preferred using veteran players from last year's team and those newcomers who had performed well at the Summer Empire State Games (only American citizens who were residents of New York State were eligible), but that if the occasion arose he would use me. I continued warming the bench till the season was almost over. What was most nettling was that his team of veterans (all of them white) was plagued by injuries, yet the coach chose to play hobbling players and left me in the cold. Paul, the only other black player on the team, got some playing time because he was the best defenseman on the team. I was one of several good forwards, so apparently I was disposable.

"What do you make of this?" I asked Paul one afternoon following a game in which I had again been benched. Paul, a Jamaican from Hempstead, Long Island, was a steady friend and both of us were avid fans of Bob Marley's revolutionary music. He worked to put himself through college. He couldn't afford to live in the dormitory, so he commuted everyday.

"This smells like prejudice to me, my good man," he said with a Jamaican accent. His long face broke into a grin. Paul always reacted to prejudice with humor; he believed that since "there's so much prejudice in America," for a black man to react with rage is futile and self-destructive. I still had to learn his sound maxim.

"But why are they prejudiced against me?" I demanded.

"I hear rumors that some players consider your attitude the problem. And these white boys have the coach's ear."

"What do they mean by my attitude?"

"For one thing they say you're proud," Paul said. "They say you think you're better than them."

Again, it seemed, my refusal to drink, womanize, attend wild parties, and act like one of the boys, my unwillingness to accept as "cute" and "innocuous" tasteless jokes about women and minorities, led white teammates to conclude that I was stuck-up and belligerent, and looked down on them.

"You know me well, Paul," I said. "You know that that's not true."

"Well, the way I see things is that an independent black man is a threat to most white people," Paul said.

It is interesting that, in America, just as in South Africa, those blacks who act unintelligent and happy-go-lucky, and those willing to flatter the vanity of some whites and make them feel superior, are much loved by white folks. The minute blacks become assertive, independent, and stand up for their rights, they're seen as threats and called "sassy, uppity niggers" or "cheeky Kaffirs."

"But this isn't fair," I said.

"The word 'fairness,' my good man, is not part of the vocabulary of too many white people."

"I'll quit the team."

"That's exactly what they want us to do."

I didn't immediately quit the team. In part because I didn't believe that Coach Jamieson was racist since his overall treatment of other blacks and myself had always seemed fair. I still hoped that he would give me a scholarship to offset the cost of attending Dowling, about $6,000 a year, and lessen my dependency on Stan. But as the season wore on, I continued warming the bench. Whenever Coach Jamieson chose to play me it was only for a few minutes, hardly enough time for me to get warmed up. Despite that I still scored a couple of goals. We played against teams from Long Island University, Adelphi, Hofstra, and other area schools.

But as the season wound down, it became clear that I would get no scholarship. Unwilling to have my spirit broken or to be humiliated, I finally quit the soccer team. As a further act of defiance I also left the tennis team, where I was the number-one player, thus keeping my vow never to allow white people to exploit my athletic ability or run my life, no matter who they were or how much power they wielded. I also vowed that come what may, I would graduate from Dowling College. The stage was set for a confrontation of wills.

My decision to stay at Dowling was also influenced by my recollection of the moral in W. Somerset Maugham's story "Appointment in Samarra." A merchant in Baghdad sends his servant to market, where the servant sees Death. Terrified, the servant borrows his master's horse and flees to Samarra. Later in the day, while strolling in his garden, the merchant meets Death and asks, "Why did you threaten my servant?" Death replies, "I did not threaten him; I only showed surprise at seeing him in Baghdad when I have an appointment with him tonight in Samarra." I did not want to be like the servant; I wanted to confront my fate.

I spent the 1981 Christmas, my fourth in America, with Stan and Margie. I explained to Stan why there was little hope that I would be receiving any scholarship money and that I had quit the soccer team.

"Well," Stan said. "I've stood by you thus far. It won't make any sense abandoning you now, will it?"

"I wish there was a way I could stand on my own two feet," I replied. "I hate being such a burden to you and Margie."

"No, you're not a burden. You're a friend."

"But I've caused you nothing but trouble since I came to this country. I'm always transferring schools and enraging coaches because of what is called my attitude. You don't owe me anything. You've done all you can for me. You gave me the opportunity and I'm squandering it. I don't think any other person would have had so much patience with me."

"You're a good student. That matters a lot to me and Margie. You need that education, and if we can help you get it, we're happy."

I have never had truer friends than Stan and Margie Smith. Before I met them I had considered the expression "A friend in need is a friend indeed" a pious platitude, but they have made it real. Each time I think of them, one of the better truisms of the sententious Polonius in Hamlet comes to mind: "The friends thou hast, and their adoption tried, grapple them to thy soul with hoops of steel."

Stan's and Margie's backgrounds hardly qualified them to befriend a radical black South African. Margie (Marjory), *née* Gengler, the second of seven children—five girls and two boys—was born into a comfortable family in Locust Valley, Long Island. She led a relatively sheltered childhood, going to private and boarding schools. While an honors student at Bishop, a girls' boarding school in La Jolla, California, she blazed through Junior Tennis. In the fall of 1970 she entered Princeton University, where she majored in American history and as the number-one tennis player led the women's team to three undefeated seasons. She was part of the first class of graduating women in 1974. Having been the top-ranked woman in the tough Eastern Tennis Association for four straight years, Margie could have played professional tennis if she wanted to. Instead, she married Stan in 1974 and now describes herself as "a happily married housewife and mother of four lovely children (two boys and two girls)."

Stan grew up in Pasadena and attended the University of Southern California, where he graduated with a B.A. in business finance in 1969. He was a devout nondenominational Christian, believed in traditional family values and a strong national defense, and loved and had served his country honorably as a private in the army. During the Vietnam War he and Arthur Ashe, a graduate of U.C.L.A. who was then a data-processing instructor at West Point, visited hospitals in South Vietnam after they had won the Davis Cup against a formidable Australian team. For their character, sportsmanship, and goodwill, the two were renowned across the world as "the gentlemen" of tennis, and parents everywhere urged their children who picked up the game to emulate "Stan Smith or Arthur Ashe, the true champions."

Above all, Stan was a devoted family man. He possessed the rare ability of relating to people of all colors, creeds, and ideologies as human beings, even when meeting them for the first time. There was nothing artificial about him. His unpretentiousness and honesty often struck people as naïveté, since we live in a world where, as Milton put it, many have banished from their lives their "happiest life, simplicity, and spotless innocence." Others took advantage of him. But for as long as I have known him, he has never ceased to believe in the basic goodness of humanity, to abide by the simple values of love, tolerance, compassion, and generosity to which humankind owes its survival.

MY MOTHER IS CURED OF HER INSANITY; VOODOO IS IMPLICATED; THE FATE WHICH BEFELL THE WIZARD'S SONS; GRAPPLING WITH THE REALITY OR UNREALITY OF WITCHCRAFT; GHETTO AND CONCENTRATION CAMP PSYCHOSES COMPARED

Upon returning to Dowling in the new year, 1982, I found a letter from home waiting for me with the miraculous news: my mother had finally been cured of her insanity. I was overwhelmed with joy. The contents of the letter related how Aunt Queen, the *isangoma*, had spent over a year treating my mother. She was said to have used *muti* (tribal medicine), consisting of special herbs, bark, and roots—and divination, a seeing into the past and future using bones.

Apparently my mother's kindness had done her in. While in South Africa she had, against my protestations and those of the family, taken in as boarders from the Giyani homeland in the Northern Transvaal a tall, raw-boned *nyanga* (medicine man) with bloodshot eyes, named Mathebula, and his family of five. They had nowhere else to go. The shack became home for about fifteen people; some slept under the tables, others curled up in corners and near the stove; there was no privacy. My mother had made it clear that their moving in with us was only a temporary measure, to provide them a roof over their heads while they hunted for their own shack. When months passed without the Mathebulas making any attempts at finding alternative housing, my mother had politely requested them to leave. This angered the wizard, a proud and chauvinistic man. Nonetheless he speedily constructed a shack in one of the rat-infested alleyways. But he never forgave my mother.

From strands of my mother's hair and pieces of her clothing, which he had gathered while he lived in our house, he allegedly concocted his voodoo and drove my mother mad. It took Aunt Queen almost a year to piece together what she deemed a "dastardly plot." Daily, out in the yard, under the hot African sun, with my mother seated cross-legged across from her, my aunt shook bones and tossed them onto the ground. From interpreting their final positions she believed that she was able to name the sorcerer and the method he used to bewitch my mother. To a Western mind this of course sounds incredible and primitive. But witchcraft is a time-honored tradition among many African tribes, where convenient scapegoats are always blamed for events which, through limited knowledge and technology, seem inexplicable. Belief in witchcraft can be compared to a Westerner's belief in astrology holding answers to man's future and fate.

"Now you know the truth," Aunt Queen said to my mother at the end of her confinement, when she was finally cured. The two spoke in Tsonga. "What do you want me to do?"

"Protect my family from further mischief."

"Is that all?"

"That's all."

"Don't you want revenge? Are you simply going to let him go scot-free?"

"I'm not a witch. I'm a child of God. I harbor no malice toward him or his family. I seek no revenge." My mother, despite her belief in witchcraft, still considered the Christian God to be all-powerful. This position of course had its contradictions, and since this episode occurred I have pointed them out to her from time to time. She has modified her beliefs and is now more under the sway of Christianity.

"But your ancestors must be satisfied," Aunt Queen said. "And what about the pain he caused you? Do you know that he intended to kill you?"

"But Christ prevented that. He led me to you and gave you the power to cure me."

"You know, Mudjaji [my mother's maiden name], you're so

loving that it's impossible for me to understand why anyone would want to harm you. The only thing left for me to do to complete your cure and prevent a relapse is to send the mischief back to its perpetrator." It was believed that no cure of witchcraft was complete until the black magic had reverted to the sorcerer.

"Please don't do anything that would harm him or his family," my mother pleaded.

"The gods will decide," Aunt Queen said.

Two weeks after my mother returned to Alexandra, the sorcerer's favorite son was stabbed to death during an argument in a *shebeen*. Hardly had he been buried when another of his sons was stabbed to death by *tsotsis* (gangsters) during a robbery and dumped in a ditch. My mother felt remorse over the deaths and grieved for the sorcerer's family. Aunt Queen told her that there was nothing she could have done to prevent their fate.

Here I was in America, in the heart of Western civilization itself, having to grapple with the reality or unreality of witchcraft. I remember how my mother's incredible story tested my "civilized mentality," my Western education, my dependency on reason, my faith in science and philosophy. But in the end I realized that her insanity, of course, had rational causes, just as did Uncle Piet's gambling, matrimonial problems, my father's alcoholism, and the family's poverty—all of which they tended to blame on witchcraft. Either my mother's diagnosed and shoddily treated diabetes or the oppressive conditions under which she lived, or a combination of the two, had deranged her. Aunt Queen was the tribal equivalent of a shrink. Her "magical" treatments of diseases owed much to the power of suggestion and her keen knowledge of the medicinal effects of certain herbs, bark, leaves, and roots, from which, it has been discovered, a good deal of Western medicine has gained real remedies. As for the deaths of the wizard's sons, this was, of course, pure coincidence, since Alexandra, especially the neighborhood in which my family lived, was an extremely violent place: on one weekend over a dozen murders were committed.

I realized all this from the knowledge I had gained since coming to America and discovering that there was a branch of medicine of which I had been completely ignorant while I lived in South Africa: psychoanalysis and psychiatry. The inhuman suffering experienced by blacks under apartheid had devastating effects on their mental and physical well-being. Given the primitive state of health care in the ghettos, endemic illiteracy, and the sway of tribal beliefs, my mother and most blacks were ignorant of causal relationships. They therefore blamed witchcraft for mental illnesses like schizophrenia and paranoia; diseases like malnutrition and tuberculosis; problems like unemployment, alcoholism, and gambling; and unlucky coincidences, such as being arrested during a pass raid while neighbors escaped, or being fired from a job. Their lack of access to qualified medical doctors, psychotherapists, and social workers forced them to rely on the dubious and often dangerous "cures" of *isangomas,* especially since such "cures" at least offered the victim much-needed psychological relief.

Superstition is present in Western societies as well, astrology being one example. Some people also blame their misfortunes on the Devil. And many govern their lives through card-reading and palmistry, and rely on charlatans to cure them of cancer, AIDS, blindness, varicose veins, and other diseases. Until education dispelled my ignorance and fortified my reason I was to a degree superstitious and believed in witchcraft.

The psychological problems experienced by blacks in South African ghettos are somewhat similar to those experienced by inmates of concentration camps during the Second World War. *From Death-Camp to Existentialism,* by Viktor E. Frankl, explains how psychotic behavior can become a "normal" way of life, a means of survival, for helpless people whose sense of identity and self-worth are under constant attack by an all-powerful oppressor. Jews in concentration camps were at the mercy of their Nazi guards, just as blacks in the ghettos of South Africa are at the mercy of apartheid's Gestapo-like police. Some victims of oppression even come to identify with their oppressors and persecute with relish their own kind. There are cases of Jews, known as Capos, who, in return for special privileges like food and cigarettes doled out by SS guards, treated other Jews sadistically and even herded them into crematoriums and gas chambers. In South Africa black policemen, in return for special privileges such as better housing, residential permits, and passbooks for relatives, shoot and kill unarmed black protesters, torture them in jail, uproot black communities under the homeland policy, and launch brutal raids into the ghettos to enforce Kafkaesque apartheid laws. Such are the evil consequences of unbearable pressures.

15

CAUGHT BETWEEN CULTURES; I BECOME EDITOR
OF COLLEGE PAPER

The witchcraft episode brought to a head a dilemma I had grappled with since leaving South Africa. How could I reconcile the tribal traditions of my ancestors with a Western education? How could I weave these two seemingly incongruous strands into a harmonious whole? The only solution that made sense was for me to preserve what was good and useful in my African heritage, and not blindly embrace Western civilization. As a starting point, I chose to uphold and venerate the African practices of extended family, community spirit, filial piety, traditional music and folklore, and respect for nature as the giver and preserver of all life. I rejected witchcraft, *lobola* (wife-buying), taboos, polygamy, and mountain schools with their cruel and dangerous circumcision methods.

Materialism, selfishness, and the nuclear family concept were among Western practices which I abjured. I admit that the nuclear family serves an important social function in Western societies, but among Africans, the extended family is considered the ideal. Relatives, referred to in Tsonga as *bakweru* (those of our home), are seen as so many fathers and mothers. Grandparents remain throughout life an active, integral part of the family and of the community. Their wisdom and experience are cherished and harnessed. For instance, grandmothers often act as midwives; along with grandfathers they often take care of the little ones while parents are off working; they teach the young morality and share with them traditional music and folklore, thereby preserving the language and the culture. Farming the elderly to nursing homes—the concept is yet uncommon in the

102

ghettos—would be considered abandonment, a disgrace not worthy of a loving and respectful child.

Through trial and error and an open mind I eventually was able to strike a balance between my heritage as an African and my Western education and civilization—a balance by no means perfect, but one which my conscience could live with.

Such a balance made me realize that there was no longer anything to be ashamed of in who I was and where I came from. I was, like Tennyson's Ulysses, "a part of all that I had met." As an individual I had the responsibility of defining who I was, and letting the world take me as I am. I was young, gifted, and black, and could hold my ground against anyone. I should insist upon and fight for my rights as a human being. Now that I was in America, I should not allow apartheid, which I had fought against all my life in South Africa, to triumph over me by dictating how I thought, felt, and acted. I had convictions and responsibilities. I must make my presence felt, known.

It was with these thoughts in mind that, a year and a half after I arrived at Dowling, I volunteered to become the first black editor of the college newspaper, *The Lion's Voice*. I had little knowledge of how a newspaper was run. All I had was a vision. I wanted to turn *The Lion's Voice* into a muckraking publication, an organ for unpopular radical causes, a paper whose main purpose would be to jolt students out of their apathy, complacency, and fear of authority.

Some students laughed at my audacity. One black friend, a sophomore majoring in aeronautics, said he hardly knew of a newspaper run by blacks.

"There are a few," I said, and named the *Amsterdam News* and the *Chicago Defender*.

"Those are exceptions."

"Well, add another exception to the few exceptions."

"I wish you luck. Remember a lot is riding on you, brother. There are many people who expect you to fail."

I knew that and I was determined to prove them wrong.

When one of my English professors, the late Dr. Clinton Trowbridge, who taught a seminar on the poetry of Robert Frost, heard that I was the new editor-in-chief, he said to me, "You know, don't you, that few students wrote for the *Voice* under the previous editor. How do you plan to overcome such apathy?"

"I'll write the entire paper alone if I have to," I said with a little arrogance. "The student paper is just too important an organ of student power to lie useless."

"How can you write an entire paper by yourself?" Dr. Trowbridge asked. "Do you know what that means? Aren't you a junior? Aren't you teaching tennis?"

"Yes, but I can do it."

"Well, you have my support and best wishes."

Putting out the first issue was a monumental task. I almost failed. The entire twelve-page paper consisted of one or two stories, publicity handouts printed verbatim for lack of reporters, ads, and a page-long editorial by me. On the day of publication I took the material to the print shop in Sayville, Long Island, owned and operated by the wife of Peter Cohalan, the Suffolk County supervisor. Mrs. Ronnie Wacker, the paper's faculty adviser, and I spent the entire afternoon arranging the stories, copy-editing, and writing headlines and captions. We had fun. The staff at the print shop gave us valuable assistance and pointers. When Monday came, issues of *The Lion's Voice* were at various locations around campus. People were astounded. I had attended all my classes and kept up with my assignments. I had been seen jogging around Oakdale and teaching tennis. I had even found time to attend a party over the weekend. How had I accomplished all that and still put out a newspaper? Everyone wanted to know. I didn't know the answer either.

Mistakes had been made. The paper contained numerous spelling errors. My editorial sounded unctuous and more like a revival sermon. But we had met the deadline and the paper had been produced. People began looking at me with new eyes. Teachers praised me and marveled at my energy. I felt a sense of power and responsibility I had never before known. I had gained the respect I had long sought as a black person—not the ephemeral athletic respect which I enjoyed as an athlete, but the intellectual respect which so often eludes many black people. I was ambitious. My brain teemed with ideas and innovations for the paper, one of which was to recruit black students as reporters, and in that way have a black slant to the news to counter the pervasive white slant in media across the U.S.

My dream of an intellectual "insurrection" among black students went nowhere because of one of the black community's greatest enemies: apathy. Some black students thought it amusing and rather silly that I devoted so much time to the paper when I could be partying, watching television, visiting malls, or attending a basketball game. Others found the idea of openly expressing their views to the all-powerful white establishment of the college intimidating. And others simply did not think that they, black students, had the intellectual capacity to write things that others, whites at that, would care to read.

"I'd only be making a fool of myself," one intelligent basketball player said when I approached him about the idea of writing a regular sports column for the paper.

"But I'm making a fool of myself and loving it," I said.

"Well, that's your problem."

I probably was making a fool of myself when I wrote, in an article on weight training: "The bodybuilding phobia is especially widespread among women. Nightmarish tales of hippopotamic females with massive deltoids are haunting women the world over. Most women are thus shying away from weight training because of this widely held stigma that associates muscularity with masculinity; a muscular woman with freakish behavior." And in one on tennis, which began, God knows why, with the opening stanza from Keat's poem, "To Autumn," and was followed by: "There's no better time for an athlete to indulge in the quintessent loveliness of nature than in autumn; that glorious season that John Keats so brilliantly celebrated in his poem, 'To Autumn,' written nearly two centuries ago.

"For many people today the advent of autumn affords the opportunity to be outdoors and playing tennis, while at the same time savoring the fresh air, and delighting in the splendor of the rustic and colored leaves so full of a fleeting life."

But my eccentric approach to journalism eventually led several students to join the paper, perhaps eager to display their quirks. Among them were two black students. Both were children of immigrant blacks from the West Indies. They confirmed a phenomenon I had encountered before. I had discovered that most black students from immigrant families were less inclined to allow white racism to prevent them from realizing their dreams. They were hardworking, and came from stable families which adhered to strict values of respect, discipline, pride, and success. They knew that racism existed in America; they everywhere confronted obstacles and setbacks; yet they kept fighting, and eventually succeeded in spite of bigotry.

Edna LaRoche and Antoine Pierre-Pierre were children of Haitian immigrants. The travails of Haitians are familiar to many. Yet despite having suffered under the detestable Duvalier regime and its dreaded Tonton Macoute, despite being kept in poverty and illiteracy by a small and wealthy elite, the destitute Haitian immigrants who managed to escape to the U.S., sometimes on flimsy boats, brought with them a determination to succeed. And succeed they often did. The same can be said of Vietnamese refugees, whose strong family ties, discipline, and Catholic faith are largely responsible for their children graduating near the top of their classes from institutions like West Point, Harvard, and Stanford a few years after arriving in the U.S. barely able to speak a word of English.

Edna, whose mother, Olivina, paid her way through college, wrote articles whenever she was freed from her work-study jobs. Antoine helped with photography, owned a jalopy, and occasionally gave me rides to the print shop. The rest of *The Lion's Voice* staff was white, and included one radical student, Tracy Parlemo, who opposed the Reagan administration's foreign policy and wrote a column attacking it.

Working on the paper, and determined to maintain my 3.5 grade-point average, and to coach tennis privately to earn money to defray some of my bills, I was fearful that I would hardly have time left to do anything else. But resolved to combat student apathy through example, I joined the curriculum committee and became a student representative, along with two white students, on the President's Council, a body responsible for advising President Victor Meskill on the state and direction of the various parts of the college. The two were the student government president, Steve Keogh, a plump, jovial, and pliant senior, and treasurer Mike Ring, a portly, bespectacled junior with a penetrating mind, whose Machiavellian sagacity allowed him to run the student government without seeming to.

In these committees Mike and I often took President Meskill and his assistants, seasoned administrators who were secure in their positions of power, to task about issues we felt they either misunderstood or were skirting. In one meeting I impressed upon Meskill and his associates the concern expressed by both faculty and students about cutbacks in liberal arts courses.

"I think it's a mistake to sacrifice liberal arts courses for business courses," I said. "It's my belief that a liberal arts education is essential even to those students who plan to pursue business careers."

"That's not and never has been our intention," said President Meskill, a shrewd and eloquent administrator.

"Then why are so many liberal arts courses being discontinued?"

I asked. Several English, philosophy, economics, and sociology courses had been scrapped.

"It's because some of those courses don't attract enough students to make them economical," Meskill said. "The school has suffered severe cutbacks in federal financial aid, as you know."

A few months ago the paper had run a front-page article on a meeting of the presidents of Long Island colleges to assess the extent of the financial aid loss from Reagan administration budget cuts. Statistics showed that Dowling's funding of $3,583,500 would be reduced to $1,507,789.

"We've been forced to make some tough choices," Meskill continued. "If we don't reduce expenses, would students welcome a tuition increase?"

"No," I said. "But I still think that a liberal arts education is the most important asset a Dowling graduate can have. Despite the cuts, the college mustn't forget Jefferson's warning that a liberal education for all is the best safeguard for American democracy."

"No one in this room will disagree with that point," Meskill said. "Believe me, we'll do everything possible to retain our tradition as a liberal arts college. But tough and unpopular decisions will have to be made so long as the Reagan administration pursues its misguided educational policies."

My outspokenness won me the respect of President Meskill and his colleagues. They knew that ultimately their interests and those of the college were not served by flattery. Besides, I posed no threat to their power anyway. I wondered what would happen when I began jeopardizing the entrenched and comfortable careers of white men who brooked no opposition to their power, even from fellow white males. What would they do to me? How would they go about "lynching" me?

16 NEED FOR BLACK STUDIES

In my classes I was learning about Nietzsche, Sartre, Camus, Hobbes, Mill, Thoreau, Robert Frost, Plato, Alexis de Tocqueville, Wordsworth, Niebuhr, Whitman, Hegel, Keynes, and Adam Smith, and studying French. Outside of class I voraciously read Richard Wright, Aime Cesaire, James Baldwin, Langston Hughes, Chinua Achebe, Zora Neale Hurston, Wole Soyinka, Frederick Douglass, Léopold Sédar Senghor, and Du Bois. My desultory reading also led me to books and articles about Paul Robeson, Marcus Garvey, Fannie Lou Hamer, Nkwame Nkrumah, Rosa Parks, Sojourner Truth, Toussaint L'Ouverture, Nelson Mandela, and many other champions of black liberation. Mandela's writings were banned in South Africa; I now understood why. The leader of the African National Congress (ANC) was neither a terrorist nor a fiend thirsty for white blood and revenge, as the Pretoria regime claimed. He is a true democrat, a born leader, and an intrepid freedom fighter.

How could a man, despite being imprisoned for over twenty years on Robben Island, the Bastille of South Africa, despite the suffering and death blacks have endured under white domination, still steadfastly maintain that all blacks want is to live together with whites as equals and as brothers and sisters? In his own defense in 1964, before being hauled off to Robben Island, Nelson Mandela, an accomplished lawyer, said: "During my lifetime I have dedicated myself to the struggle of the African people. I have fought against white domination, and I have fought against black domination. I have cherished the ideal of a democratic and free society in which all persons live together in harmony and with equal opportunities. It is an ideal I hope to live for and to achieve. But if need be, it is an ideal for which I am prepared to die."

Why were there no black professors at Dowling to teach American students about such heroes of our time? Why were there no Black Studies courses to enrich the cultural experience of white America? Such a state of affairs was wrong and had to be corrected. But how? How could things be changed when the majority of black students—out of a sense of hopelessness, out of an unwillingness to rock the boat, out of ignorance about important contributions made by black heroes and black culture—were either apathetic or indifferent?

I discussed the problem with Dr. Jacob Sonny, a short, soft-spoken native of India who lived in Syosset, Long Island. He was a professor of economics and my academic adviser. He was particularly fond of me as a student, and of my work as editor-in-chief. He and other professors knew that for as long as students remained phlegmatic and divided, the school would be run according to the narrow dictates of administrators. Student apathy, indifference, and complacency weren't unique to Dowling. The malaise, largely the result of a back-lash against the activist sixties, afflicted students from coast to coast, and manifested itself in their focusing on materialism and looking out for number one.

"Why don't you write about this problem in *The Lion's Voice*?" Dr. Sonny said to me. "I, too, would like to see a black professor and Black Studies taught at this school. It would enrich the whole Dowling experience."

"I considered writing about it," I said. "But I don't think the timing is right. I hardly have the support of students on this issue. And the paper is still struggling with financing. Too much controversy may lead to its shutdown."

"Well," Dr. Sonny said. "I'll bring up the issue of a black professor at one of our faculty meetings. We need another economics instructor and I'll try to convince my colleagues that we actively seek a black person to fill the position."

Exams came and I made the dean's list for the third time in a row, with a 4.0 average. The year was 1982. I was awarded a merit scholarship worth about $1,000. Professors began forecasting a future for me in the newspaper world.

"You did a splendid job with the paper," Ronnie Wacker, the

faculty adviser, said at the end of the year. "Have you thought about working as a journalist after graduation?"

"No," I said. "But it sounds exciting."

"Well, my husband works for *Newsday,* and I write a column for them periodically. Either of us can be your contact with the paper. Just let me know."

"Thank you."

To work for the prestigious and award-winning *Newsday* would be quite an achievement. But it was all still far out in the future, and in the intervening year before I graduated, anything could happen to change my plans.

17   INTERRACIAL DATING; BARBARA AND THE WIELUNSKIS

One of my convictions was that I would never allow white racism to turn me into a black racist. It was not an easy conviction to abide by, especially when I was aware of frequent indignities against blacks which would have justified fighting back in kind. A respectable black family was hounded out of their newly bought house in a white neighborhood of Deer Park, Long Island; one of my professors, Dr. Faith Pereira, a charming, cultured lady from India, was denied an apartment because she was not white; and in yet another incident a group of white boys harassed a black man and called him "nigger" for walking in a white neighborhood of Islip.

Despite such incidents, and countless others I read about in newspapers and saw reported on television, the lessons of my childhood were not lost to me. I remembered well how my mother always insisted that there were good and bad white people, just as there were good and bad black people, and that I had to strive, despite the difficulty and the pain, despite the convenience of stereotypes, to judge people according to the contents of their characters, and not by the color of their skin. She had proven the truth of her creed many times. The most dramatic was when a white nun at the Alexandra

Health Clinic assisted her in obtaining the birth certificate without which I could not have registered at the local tribal school.

When I found myself dating a white woman, my conviction was put to the severest test. I had heard the myths about black men lusting after white women, how relationships with white women were regarded by some as a sign of black men's latent hatred of black womanhood, and in turn of themselves. I had read Franz Fanon's *Black Skin, White Masks*. I knew that two of my heroes, Richard Wright and Frederick Douglass, were calumniated by blacks and whites for marrying white women. Most important, I was aware of white society's irrational and often vicious reaction to interracial relationships and marriages. I knew that the Ku Klux Klan had been formed ostensibly "to protect white womanhood," and that one of the basic excuses for racist systems like apartheid was to prevent "race mixing," to ensure that there was no social contact between blacks and whites because no white man wanted his daughter to marry a black man, even though white men, during slavery, violated black womanhood with impugnity.

Armed with all that knowledge, I began dating Barbara Wotjek, a sensitive, ebullient eighteen-year-old Polish student with bright blue eyes and a ready smile. Barbara was a native of Bloomfield, New Jersey, and had lost both parents to cancer. When we met she was living with her aunt and uncle, Ziggie and Alice Wielunski, in the small working-class town of Bohemia on the outskirts of Oakdale. She had just graduated from the Academy of St. Joseph, a Catholic school in Brentwood, Long Island, and had enrolled at Dowling for a semester in order to qualify for Social Security benefits under Reagan's restrictive financial aid policy. She planned to attend Barnard College in New York.

Barbara and I occasionally discussed what it meant to be a mixed couple in a predominantly white, conservative community.

"I don't particularly care what people think," she said. "As long as you don't."

"But you may be ostracized by your people."

"If that happens, it will hurt," Barbara said, "but I'll survive."

"You don't mind being called a nigger-lover?"

"No."

"Why?"

"Because you're not a nigger. There's no such thing as a nigger."

We're all human beings. I find you the most understanding person I've ever dated. You care about what I feel and what I think. You aren't like one of those macho freaks who treat their girlfriends as ornaments and possessions. We have been dating for several weeks now and you've shared with me a special world full of poetry, nature, African culture, music, and many things which have enriched my life. You value my companionship and that means a lot to me. To be honest with you, whenever we're together the thought never occurs to me that you're black. You're only a sensitive human being."

"I feel the same about you. But how have your friends reacted?"

"With envy."

I was surprised.

"With envy? Why?"

"Because I tell them the truth about our relationship. Some of them can't believe that you haven't already ripped my clothes off and raped me."

The reaction from some black students to my dating Barbara was negative. Even though I had dated black women before, some black students accused me of being a traitor to the black race, of suffering from an inferiority complex which only the possession of a white woman could allay. The false accusations hurt. At times I felt like severing my friendship with Barbara, but I knew that to do so would be to justify the accusations, to deny my conviction that human love can and should be shared with anyone, regardless of color or creed.

"If at anytime you think it's not worth it," Barbara said, "we can mutually end the relationship."

"I have never allowed the attitudes of people, even my own people, to run my life. And I'm not about to. You're a dear friend. I care deeply about you. I'm prepared to pay any price for our friendship."

I underscored my resolve by escorting Barbara to a banquet hosted by Dowling College, honoring Admiral James D. Watkins, Chief of Naval Operations in the Reagan administration, as the recipient of the Distinguished Citizen Award. I also published poems of mine dedicated to her in a poetry section of *The Lion's Voice*. Most students were open-minded enough to accept and respect our relationship.

The big day came for me to meet Barbara's guardians. I was invited for dinner at their home. I had seen *Guess Who's Coming to Dinner?* several times and went prepared for a Spencer Tracy–like interrogation. Much to my surprise, I found Ziggie and Alice not only warm and hospitable, but eager to talk about issues unrelated to race. It struck me that whenever I and other blacks got together, our conversations almost always centered on racial issues; with whites, I have found the opposite to be true. Ziggie and Alice and I talked about Polish and African music and dances; about the upcoming play, *The Mikado*, being staged at the Dowling theatre, in which their son, Eddie, and Barbara had parts; about the vegetable garden in their backyard; about their other grown-up children, Ellen and Thomas, and their families. Throughout the evening Ziggie had me laughing with all sorts of jokes, including Polish ones. As I was getting ready to leave I cornered Aunt Alice in the kitchen.

"Have you any objections to my dating Barbara?"

"Not at all," she said with her captivating smile. "You know, Barbie has never been this happy before. She's always talking about you. In fact, she wishes she had met you last year so you could have taken her to the senior prom."

A deep friendship developed between the Wielunskis and myself. They treated me like one of the family, even after my relationship with Barbara ended when she moved to New York City to attend Barnard College, where she majored in English; Barbara is now working for a prestigious law firm in New York. They also were responsible for one of the biggest breaks in my life.

18   TAKING FREEDOM FOR GRANTED; STAFF EMPLOYEES STRIKE; CAMPUS PAPER BECOMES MORE CONTROVERSIAL

When college let out for the summer holidays I applied for a student work permit, which was granted, and I was able to work as a soccer instructor at the Ivy League Day Camp in Hauppauge, Long Island. I got the job by replying to an ad. My programs were innovative and had an international flavor.

I quickly became popular with the kids and when camp ended I was voted best instructor. My approach was simple. Knowing how American children were often driven against their will to participate in sports by parents who perversely lived their athletic fantasies through their children, knowing how miserable and averse to sports children subsequently became, and knowing the various psychological and physical traumas they suffered during the ordeal, I ensured that, first and foremost, they enjoyed themselves. Once that was accomplished, teaching them discipline and building their characters were easy.

Almost all the campers were white, came mostly from middle-class families, and were spoiled. One morning, before the commencement of the day's program, I gathered several groups of boys and girls under a large tree. There were about thirty youngsters, between the ages of eight and thirteen. Several counselors—high school students—helped keep the group quiet. I began telling the campers stories of my childhood, of my struggles for food, for an education, of my passion for books and sports, and reminded them how very fortunate they were to live free and comfortable in America. I pointed out that most black children in the ghettos of South Africa had never had the luxury of attending a summer camp and couldn't even afford soccer balls and toys. But they always came up with ingenious ways to have fun. They made "cars" out of wires and empty tins of shoe polish, slingshots out of tree branches and discarded tubes, toys out of clay, and soccer balls out of rags.

The campers were astounded. Some confessed that they couldn't imagine life, and would never be happy leading a life, without Reebok shoes, stereos, camps, lots of hamburgers, television, and designer clothes. But there were several campers to whom my words provided food for thought. I noticed as time went on that they tended to be less wasteful of food during lunch, less demanding that their every whim be satisfied, more attentive during lessons, and eager to help others and to clean up the soccer field at the end of the day.

Another time, to about two dozen teenagers, the oldest group of campers, who with their rebellious "I don't care" and "I know everything" attitude I thought needed the advice the most, I said: "Do not take for granted the freedoms you have. And don't waste or abuse the various opportunities you're blessed with. Whenever you throw away food, remember that in much of the world people are starving. In this very country there are people who eat out of garbage dumps, who are homeless, who do not know how to read or write. Nothing is free in life. You have to earn everything you get, just like your parents earned everything they are giving you."

Well, suffice it to say that I was politely listened to.

I sent part of my earnings home to the family, with instructions that my mother use some of the money to meet the school needs of my siblings. My father had entered his fifth year without a job; he had recently been run down by a car and his left arm was crippled. My mother had started working at a strenuous night job scrubbing floors in a commercial building to augment the pittance she made as a washerwoman during the day. Her starvation wages hardly kept pace with the family's ever-growing needs. Florah had given birth to a baby girl named Angeline and there was talk that the father of the child, Collin, had finally agreed to marry her, due largely to my mother's untiring effort to get him to admit responsibility. She did it this way. When she returned from her long confinement in the homeland on account of her insanity, she had issued Collin's parents the following ultimatum: either your son, as the father of Angeline, marries Florah, or I will keep possession of the child and bar you from ever seeing your grandchild.

I returned from the camp prepared to use my senior year at Dowling to leave a permanent mark on the college. I now had ample assistance on the paper as more students joined the staff. Lori Piro, a senior, wrote features; Maria Kokolakis was chief photographer and arts reviewer; Kelly Gunn covered sports; Jim Dowis, a tall, gray-haired elderly man of lively wit and urbane manners—retired but anxious to continue his education—was our Russell Baker; Andy Edelman, Greg Sarra, Adina Desiati, and Ann Marie Cook contributed articles from time to time. There were now five blacks: Edna, Antoine, Michel Mercer, a poet, Theron Corbin, a promising cartoonist, and myself.

For three semesters in a row I had made the dean's list, and my activities as an editor and student representative on various committees had been commendable; now I wanted to do even better. The first week of classes the staff employees' union, Local 153 of the AFL-CIO, called a strike following a breakdown of contract negotiations with Dowling College. In an open letter to students, the staff employees—secretaries, clerical workers, receptionists, and switchboard operators—stated their grievances:

. . . There are forty (40) of us on the staff and many of us have been here (at Dowling College) 18, 16 and 12 years. The following is a breakdown of the full-time employees' salaries:

2 are making—$6,000–$7,000
3 are making—$7,000–$8,000
8 are making—$8,000–$9,000
12 working 8 years or more are making—$9,000–$10,000
5 working 10 years or more are making—$10–11,000
4 working 12 years or more are making—$11–12,000
2 working 18 years or more are making—$12–13,000
1 working 18 years or more is making—$13,000

Based on the figures above and the present increment rate of $3 a year, it takes many years before we reach the maximum of our pay grades.

President Meskill made about $84,000 a year and other administrators were handsomely paid. What the staff employees wanted was economic justice, in the form of a package which included a wage increase, improved medical care, and a "me-too clause"—a contractual statement in which benefits received by any group of employees in the college community would be automatically due other employees within Dowling College. The administration stuck by its unacceptable offer to the union.

The strike entered its eighth week with no resolution in sight. Registration had been disrupted and now other vital college services suffered, too. Each side blamed the other. Teachers, who had struck at the same time the year before, supported the staff employees. The support of students, who all along had been passive spectators to the fray, was courted actively by each side to enhance their bargaining position. President Meskill addressed the student association and so did union representatives. I wrote an editorial urging the students to seek out the facts, reflect upon them, and then make an informed judgment over which side deserved their support.

Students began speaking out. In polls they supported the staff employees by a margin of four to one. Several students even ventured to state openly their opinions in the newspaper. Al Lepenski, a junior, said, "The wages that these people make are not by any means enough. The administration should just give them the increase instead of paying for extra security and $200 per hour for a lawyer." Liz Irwin, a senior, said, "This is the second year I have been at Dowling and this is the third strike I have seen here. I feel that it is a disgrace that the administration (Dr. Meskill in particular) has done nothing to work things out. I feel that my tuition is not going to better education, it is going to pay for Dr. Meskill's $84,000 annual salary. He should be given a letter of resignation to sign, then send him packing." Other students were ambivalent about the strike. Jesse Mendoza, a black senior, said, "I feel that the strikers are out for a good cause, but I feel that if they get their money, the students' tuition will go up, which would be unfair to students." Gary Gorde, a white sophomore, said, "I don't believe in strikes because the only thing that comes out of them is a lot of poor and hungry people."

But there were some who were openly partial to the administration. Tracy, Liz, myself, and several other student activists fought for the right of students to make a decision that would protect their interests. Inevitably, our actions alienated the pro-administration students. Plans were made to neutralize or, if need be, remove me from the editorship. They failed.

The strike was finally settled, with the administration the apparent winner. I knew that I had increased my enemies on campus, some of whom were capable of doing nasty things to me. But I knew that as long as I kept up with my studies, I would always survive, no matter the obstacles.

The Lion's Voice became more controversial. Several members of the student government clamored for it to be censored. Censorship was tried through indirect means by the student government cutting back on our funding, but even with a shoestring budget the paper continued being an agent provocateur. And more and more students read the paper, which now came out once a week and was free. Stories were written about the faculty-burnout syndrome, about proposed reforms in the college curriculum, about the administration sometimes ignoring the needs of students in the pursuit of economics, about the decline in the support for the liberal arts, about the dangers of student apathy and narrow-mindedness, about the message of movies like *Gandhi*, about the perils of idolizing materialism and ignoring the cultivation of one's soul, about the inadequate funding for sports like tennis, about the pressures put on teachers to lower their standards to suit the needs of lazy students, and about the dangers of a total reliance on the market system, untempered by government concern for the disadvantaged and overall community needs. At the end of the fall semester I again ended up on the dean's list.

19

THE BLACK STRUGGLE IN AMERICA AND SOUTH AFRICA COMPARED

I continued exhorting other black students to become activists for causes but I had little success. It was clear to me that many of these students had been demoralized by the ghetto environment.

Many of these students told wrenching stories of growing up in Harlem, the South Bronx, and other New York ghettos. I could not help but conclude that such places—where a child grows up believing that violence, criminality, drunkenness, drug addiction, and hopelessness are normal aspects of living; where evil seems constantly to triumph over good, and villains become heroes; where teenage pregnancy, high school lawlessness, and dropping out are rampant; where many households are headed by a single parent and the extended family was almost nonexistent—bred apathy, antisocial behavior, and dependency on others. Once the ghetto gets into you, I knew you could only live for the moment, you failed to assume responsibility for your own actions and life, you wallowed in the view that you were a victim of circumstances beyond your control and therefore deserved pity, and you became convinced that there was no use trying to better your condition because the whole world had ganged up against you.

My conclusions were based on my intimate knowledge of such a world. I had grown up in ghettos which bred the same self-destruction. I had survived because, like countless black Americans who have made it out of ghettos, I had been determined, from a very early age, never to allow racism and oppression to define the terms of my humanity, to prescribe my place in life, or to define the limits of my aspirations. My refusal to give up, my taking risks, created opportunities where none seemed to exist.

But that was not all. My mother and grandmother—despite the oppression and degradation they experienced every step of the way, when they were forced to flee their own home in the middle of the night and hide on rooftops and under bridges because they lacked permits allowing the family to be together in Alexandra, and when they were confined to menial jobs which paid them a pittance and left them dead with fatigue—never failed to find the time to instill in us children the values of hard work, love, caring, right and wrong. Without these values, I believe, survival in a racist and oppressive environment is impossible. Why? Because racism and oppression breed rage and hatred in the victims. And the two Hydras, if uncontrolled by an unshaken belief in the worth of one's humanity, despite what others say or do to one, invariably lead to the disintegration of one's personality and ultimately to its dissolution.

Even my father, despite the unimaginable pain of his life, when he was daily emasculated by the system and his humanity twisted into something almost bestial, had some positive influence on me. He never abandoned his family. He accepted responsibility for bringing us into this world, though at times he shirked that responsibility. Then there was the community spirit, the extended family of my grandmother, aunts, uncles, and even neighbors. When my parents were off slaving for white people or hunting for food, they could count on adults in the neighborhood to act as surrogate parents. Finally, there was that precious something which apartheid, try as it did, could never take away from us—our family's dignity.

Such shared experiences reinforced my solidarity with black Americans. And the more I read black literature in the year 1982–83 and became familiar with the history of black life in America, the deeper my identification with their suffering and experiences became. I began to see that, in a way, their struggle was harder, more baffling, more frustrating, because they lived in a society where they were told daily that everyone is free and equal, that the American dream is within the grasp of everyone who tries. And yet, try as they did, many got nowhere. They kept banging against invisible walls of social and economic injustice.

The harried victims often ask themselves: What's holding us back as a people? What's trampling most of us in the mire of poverty and hopelessness? Who is really the black man's enemy? Is it the white man? Which white man? Many blacks have white friends and many whites fought alongside the black man in the struggle for justice. Wait a minute, are those white friends I have truly my friends? Am I sometimes my own oppressor, my own worst enemy? Why do other discriminated ethnic groups—the Vietnamese, the Jews, Hispanics, among others—with handicaps succeed and we usually fail? How many of our problems are due to racism and how many to our own failings? What are our failings?

In seeking answers to these momentous questions, many black Americans, I feel, overlook several important realities. First, the white-male power structure, though formidable, is not unassailable. Blacks and other oppressed groups, such as women, give up their power by failing to take their destiny into their own hands. If blacks can't stand up united, and say enough is enough, we demand our fair share of the American pie, who will do that for them? Most important, the white-male power structure will concede nothing without a demand.

Second, racism alone is not responsible for the black man's plight. The black man, too, bears some responsibility. How can the black community survive when the black family structure is disintegrating? When children beget children and thus perpetuate a legacy of poverty and hopelessness? When role models for most black youngsters are athletes, entertainers, gangsters, and drug pushers instead of doctors, teachers, lawyers, politicians? When black drug dealers feed such poison as cocaine and crack to their own people, especially the young? And when so many blacks, once they have attained success, forget where they came from?

Third, in America, unlike South Africa, blacks have the right to vote; their civil rights are protected under the Constitution; and in 1954 the U.S. Supreme Court, in *Brown* vs. *Board of Education*, outlawed segregated and unequal education. For these important rights Medgar Evers, Malcolm X, Dr. King, and others paid the ultimate sacrifice. These martyrs considered these rights powerful weapons which blacks should use, without apology, to fight for their place in the sun, and their fare share as copartners in the building of the American success story. These martyrs knew that it was dangerous folly for any black man or woman to believe that success will only come to black people when white racism has been completely eliminated. Racism, in one form or another, will exist for as long as there are people on this earth of different colors, fighting for survival. Rather, blacks should be looking for ways to succeed despite racism. And by virtue of their success, they will lessen or neutralize the effects of racism on themselves and on their communities.

And fourth, until black communities acquire economic and political power, they will not prosper, nor will they be able to protect their interests effectively. Economic power will only come when blacks stop spending billions supporting banks, movie theatres, stores, fast-food chains, and other businesses belonging to those who give very little or nothing back to black communities. And political power is gained primarily through the ballot box. No party, Democratic or Republican, and no political candidate, black or white, for local, state, or national office, should be allowed to take the black vote for granted. The black vote should go to those who can deliver tangible benefits to black communities.

Unfortunately, to many black Americans these realities are simply too painful to accept, or too difficult to deal with. For some acceptance of these realities will blur the image of the black man as strictly a victim of racism, to be pitied, to be on welfare, to have things done for him by benevolent and paternalistic whites, many of whom vociferously call for integration—but only in someone else's neighborhood, someone else's school district, or until their sons or daughters marry across the color line. For others acceptance of these realities will let racist whites off the hook, and palliate the shortcomings of the Reagan regime and others indifferent to civil rights. Acceptance of these realities also threatens the careers of those blacks who benefit from the status quo, from the miseries and pain of their brethren. And finally, acceptance of these realities calls for hard choices and concrete solutions.

For black South Africans, at least for the moment, the objective is clear: to win our liberation. The enemy is clearly identified: white oppression in the form of apartheid. Justice and injustice in our society are clearly delineated. South Africa is a society which blatantly guarantees power, privilege, and comfort to a minority and misery, degradation, and suffering to the majority, solely on the basis of skin color. South Africa is a society which has created for whites a relative paradise on earth, and for blacks a hell. Almost all the black man's problems, for the time being, can be blamed upon the white man. We can afford to play the role of victims of apartheid with perfect self-complacency.

But what will happen when we reach the stage that black Americans are in; when institutionalized segregation has been abolished and yet more subtle racism, exploitation, and oppression still persist? How different will South African blacks' problems be from those harrowing black America?

PART THREE

BECOMING
A WRITER

POOR WHITES; THE MISSION OF A JOURNALIST

I spent the Christmas of 1982 on Hilton Head. My year and a half on the paper had so radicalized me that I now began to see the island as largely a haven for the rich, which indeed it is. With some exceptions, the island was a place where developers bought out poor, mostly black families so they could build on it their Vanity Fair, with its resorts, condominiums, chic shopping malls, exclusive golf courses, tennis courts, and beaches. And in this materialistic Shangri-la blacks and poor whites were often exploited.

A case in point is the ordeal undergone by a white friend, Cory "Skip" Beard. Skip, thirty-one, was an amiable, heavyset, blond Southerner who grew up in Ehrhardt, South Carolina. His father, Cory Sr., a proud man of integrity and strong will, who in many ways resembled my father, died in April of that year at the age of sixty-seven. He had been a jack-of-many-trades and was known and respected around the community as a generous man who often did maintenance work for free, especially during the Christmas season. Skip's mother, Mary, sixty-nine, was a native of rural Mississippi. For many years she earned one dollar an hour as a laborer in a sewing factory. She was paid "a couple pennies extra the more she sewed." Her wage improved to sixty dollars a week when she joined a sewing factory where the workers were unionized. She earned that amount until diabetes forced her to retire at the age of sixty-two.

Skip's family of eleven—five boys and six girls—was so poor that as a child Skip sometimes wore to school his sisters' panties as underwear. For a table the family used a propped-up door. Yet

125

Skip's character revealed that his parents had taught him to believe in right and wrong, in the value of integrity, compassion, and selfless love.

On Hilton Head Island, Skip met and married Wendy Marlow, twenty-nine, a warm, lovable Britisher from Essex County, England. Wendy helped Margie around the Smiths' house and with the Smiths' children. Skip was enterprising, talented, and hardworking. Yet he had trouble keeping various jobs because of his honesty. It seemed that several of his employers believed that it was a virtue to make a profit at all cost. One time, while in the employ of a small company, Skip was sent to repair a refrigerator for a wealthy client. He was told by his manager that if the job required less than an hour, he should lengthen it to about three by disassembling and assembling some part of the refrigerator to kill time. He refused to do that and was fired. Another time, while working as a security guard, he caught a colleague selling drugs to a minor. He warned the colleague to desist. The colleague persisted. Skip reported the matter to his superiors; he was fired, along with the drug-dealing colleague. It turned out that others on the security force were involved in the drug-selling racket.

The plight of Skip and his family made it increasingly clear to me that the form of "apartheid" which existed in America wasn't always a black-and-white issue. Most of the time it was an economic issue, the separation of the haves from the have-nots. Often, in order to detract attention from this exploitation, and to prevent the have-nots from uniting and demanding their fair share of the American pie, the haves pitted poor blacks and poor whites against each other by feeding the prejudices of the latter with such slogans as "Watch out for blacks, they'll take your jobs away," or "Don't support things like civil rights, they mean more favor and special treatment for blacks." And the poor whites, ever eager for scapegoats to blame for their dismal lot, generally believed this.

One day Stan introduced me to Terry Plumb, editor of the local paper, *The Island Packet*, with a circulation of about 11,000. A graduate of Notre Dame University, Terry was a short, bright man of liberal politics. He saw the job of a journalist as that of "afflicting the comfortable, and comforting the afflicted." His ideals seemed out of place in a place like Hilton Head. Terry has since been promoted to editor of *The Herald*, a larger, more cosmopolitan paper in Rock Hill, South Carolina.

"How do you manage to write all these stories?" Terry asked, perusing one of the copies of *The Lion's Voice* I had brought along.

"I try to make time and I write as I go."

"Well, you seem to have mastered one important journalistic skill: speed. You should have no trouble meeting deadlines."

Terry then proceeded to give me advice on how to improve the quality of the paper. He emphasized the importance of simple, straightforward sentences, rather than the labyrinths I was accustomed to, in which I would lose my meaning. I had once considered them a mark of artistic perfection, but now I saw that I only confused readers.

"Shakespeare's style of writing, wonderful though it is, would never sell newspapers," Terry said. "Your primary task as a journalist is to answer the five W's: Who, What, Where, When, and Why. Once that's done, your story is complete. Everything additional is superfluous, and in the newspaper world space is valuable. And, finally, keep your feelings to yourself. Don't wear your heart on your sleeve as a journalist. Objectivity is important."

"But my feelings are important to me," I said.

"They may and should be," Terry said. "But in journalism you strive for objectivity. You provide readers with facts so they can make up their minds about the issues. Flowery and subjective writing is for poets."

"I find it almost impossible not to inject my opinion into anything I write," I confessed.

"I can see that from reading what you wrote. And it's a problem all beginning journalists have. But if your goal is to become a good journalist, you must learn to subordinate your feelings to facts."

21 ONE CANNOT BE SEXIST AND FIGHT RACISM EFFECTIVELY

My outspokenness led some redneck white boys at Dowling to threaten me with physical violence. One afternoon I returned to my apartment and found a photo of my face, which usually appeared on the editorial page, pasted to the door with the inscription "Dear Faggot. You don't know what a pussy tastes like. Watch out, black mother-fucker." At other times I received anonymous phone calls in which I was told, "We lynch sassy niggers like you," and "Go back to Africa where you belong, you black ape." My white detractors even succeeded in recruiting a few black students in their campaign against me. I was almost assaulted by one of them, a ghetto-toughened dude, who mistook my nonviolent attitude for cowardice.

I did not take such threats lightly, but I refused to be intimidated. I continued to print what I thought was right, to attempt to provoke students out of their apathy and make them think about issues beyond their selfish interests. In one number of the paper, which appeared on March 15, 1983, I wrote an editorial entitled "114 Years Thereafter: Have There Been Any Real Changes?" in which I argued for the equality of the sexes. My arguments were based on the classic essay *The Subjection of Women*, written by John Stuart Mill in 1869. The editorial concluded with the following thoughts:

> The attainment of full equality between men and women, and the observance of that equality as an inviolable universal truth, if realized, has the potential and the capacity to bring great and wondrous changes to all of humankind. If the union between man and woman becomes finally that of equals, sharing equally both in gain and responsibility, the potential of humankind to achieve and to progress is infinite.
>
> Two independent minds, when fully and equally harnessed, and their potentials brought together to form an inseparable unit, can and will produce a synergism to top all synergisms. However, as long as one mind considers itself more capable than the other; and when the other mind becomes reduced to a state of reflexive response, where it does, involuntarily, the bidding of "the superior and capable" mind, the future of humankind looks bleak indeed. For, sooner or later, the enormous and crushing burden of shouldering the responsibilities of the entire world on one person's shoulders, namely, that of the male specie, while, all along, there is an equally capable but largely ignored friend on the side, would become too oppressive as man continues to walk the Primrose Path.
>
> Woman and Man can and should work together toward a common destiny without one having to become the slave of the other. It's been one hundred and fourteen years since John Stuart

Mill told us that: Therefore let us, now as we celebrate National Women's week, remember his impassioned pleas. Let's set women free.

This editorial earned me more "Dear Faggot" letters. Some male students openly questioned and cracked jokes about my manhood. I merely scoffed at them, and exulted in the thought that I had succeeded in drawing attention to the sexual discrimination on campus, and in forcing men to reevaluate their misconceptions and stereotypes about women. I felt particularly proud having written the editorial. It was in a way an opportunity to pay tribute to the two women who first emancipated me from male chauvinism—my mother and Granny— and taught me that a man can feel, cry, love, cook, clean house, change diapers, and still be a man. But I was shocked by the response of some of the female students on campus. They had been so conditioned into their roles of subordination and subservience to men that they were frightened of their own true identities. They equated a liberated woman with a lesbian. These women were similar to those who, when approached to sign a petition for the Equal Rights Amendment, told the petitioner to come back when their husbands were at home.

But many women agreed with my views. They supported and defended me. One of them, Lisa Caputo, an elementary education major who worked part-time in the library, said, "You've upset so many men because what you're saying is true."

Later that year I sat in on a newly founded women's studies course taught by a feminist professor and attended mostly by older women. The course was canceled after only one semester. The professor and her students were ridiculed as lesbians by many male and female students. What this course—and one-to-one discussions with several of the women who took it—revealed about the nature of male-female relationships and marriages in America shocked me. They poignantly described their suppressed rage; the wanton infidelity of the men in their lives; the blatant attempts by husbands and boyfriends to mold or abase the personalities of their wives and girlfriends according to what best served their selfish needs and gratified their brittle machismo; the sadistic comments about fading beauty, damaged merchandise, neuroticism, inadequate sexual performance; the pressures some husbands and boyfriends put on their wives and girlfriends to undergo dangerous operations to change the shapes and sizes of their vaginas, breasts, and other parts of their bodies.

Despite my sympathies, I realized how much I still had to learn about women. The course, one of the most instructive I have ever attended at any college, increased my sensitivity to women's issues. It drove home the point that in South Africa and America black men could not hope to triumph over apartheid and racism as long as they kept black women in bondage: one cannot be sexist and fight racism effectively.

CAREER CHOICE; CONRAD'S INFLUENCE; ENCOURAGEMENT FROM PROFESSORS; THE BIRTH OF *Kaffir Boy*

It was my final semester in college. I began thinking about what I wanted to do with my life following graduation. Many students had already made up their minds to pursue business careers. I conferred with Professor Sonny and told him that I intended to declare my major in economics.

"Do you plan to go on to graduate school?" Dr. Sonny asked. "You can be admitted into about any graduate studies program because of your grades and accomplishments as a student leader."

I replied that for a while I had toyed with the idea of applying to Harvard Business School, but that the more I learned about the sharkish nature of the business world, I had lost my enthusiasm for that sort of life and career.

"What about becoming an economist?" asked Dr. Sonny. "There are Ph.D. programs around the country which offer generous fellowships. Such a degree will be useful should you return to South Africa."

"A Ph.D. in economics wouldn't be bad. A free South Africa will certainly need economists. But to tell you the truth, I want to do something with the written word," I said.

"Become a journalist, you mean?"

"Something like that."

"Why don't you discuss that with John Rather?" John Rather, no relation to Dan Rather of CBS, was the paper's new faculty adviser and a stringer for *The New York Times*. He had just arrived on campus but he and I had already developed a positive rapport. He admired my printing controversial articles and had once given me a rundown of what my rights were as a journalist.

"As long as you print the truth," John said, "no one can touch you. Your right to publish is protected by the First Amendment."

"Can't the college stop me from publishing a damaging article if it wanted to?"

"No. That's censorship. And they can be taken to court. And most likely you'll win."

To me there's never been a greater wonder about American society than its system of laws as the guardians of justice and freedom for all, in total contrast to South Africa. I often wish that more Americans, especially the young, who are the future protectors and interpreters of these laws, would attempt to understand through reason, and not just by rote, the meaning of the Declaration of Independence, the Constitution, and the Bill of Rights. These three unique documents specifically protect individual and civil liberties, justify the right of revolution against unrepentant tyrannical government, and establish the separation of powers, accountability in public officials, fair representation, and an independent judiciary, among many other blessings—all in order to "form a more perfect Union." How lucky Americans are, in a world where many nations groan and bleed under the yoke of despotism, to have such canons as the foundation of their society!

John Rather recommended that I apply to *The New York Times* for a position as a copy boy.

"Copy boy?" I cried. "I want to be a foreign correspondent."

He laughed. "Maybe after twenty or forty years in the business you'll be able to do that."

"What!"

"Forget all that rubbish about the glamour of newspaper reporting," John said. "That world is a bureaucracy just like any other. There are steps to be climbed, gradually, painfully. The best thing for you would probably be to start off at some small local paper somewhere in Nebraska covering courts and writing obituaries, and then work your way up to the big city papers. You have the distinct advantage of having a worldview of life. Most papers value that. Why don't you attend the minority recruiting session next week?" He showed me the announcement he had received from the organizers of the event.

Armed with a portfolio of newspaper clippings, a résumé, and dressed like a young executive, I took the Long Island Railroad to the nearby campus of C. W. Post where the recruiting session was to be held. It was an overcast day with an intermittent drizzle. The taxi got lost and I almost missed the occasion. There were recruiters from various major and small but reputable papers around the country. There was apparently an affirmative-action push in the newspaper business to hire more minorities, especially as reporters, so that the news could be more balanced and less a white male's view of the world.

My credentials impressed recruiters from such powerful papers as *The Washington Post*, the *Memphis Commercial Appeal*, the *St. Petersburg Times*, *The New York Times*, and *Newsday*. The recruiter from *Newsday*, a black man of radical politics who had written extensively on African issues and was at one time stationed in an African country, was so impressed that he scheduled a second interview session with me, out of which came a job offer upon graduation. I went back home elated. I shared the news with John Rather and he was proud.

"You know, John," I said to him several days later. "The job offer from *Newsday* sounds unbelievable, and I should be happy. But I'm not. I don't think I want to be writing for some paper where I would have no artistic control over what I write. I want to write essays, books, like my heroes Richard Wright and James Baldwin. I want to influence the world, to change people's attitudes for the better on issues of importance. I don't want to be covering courts and writing obituaries all my life."

"Why don't you become a writer then?" John said.

"That's what I really want to be. But who's ever heard of a twenty-two-year-old writer getting published? There are white-haired professors at Dowling who have been writing all their lives and never been published."

"You may be the exception. Besides, what harm is there in trying?"

Yes, what harm was there in trying? I resuscitated unfinished short stories which I had serialized the year before in *The Lion's Voice*, in the style of Dickens's *Pickwick Papers*. The themes were exotic, replete with dazzling African characters and plots. With these short stories transformed into novels I wanted to do for Africa what was done for the sea by Joseph Conrad. I considered Conrad the greatest novelist who ever wrote in the English language. His incredible story of not learning English until his twenties, and not writing a word until thirty-five, made him a tremendous role model. I often wept at the sheer beauty of his prose and insight into human nature. I had read every one of his books I could lay my hands on, from *Almayer's Folly* to *A Personal Record*, and had committed to memory his famous preface on art, which begins: "A work that aspires, however humbly, to the condition of art should carry its justification in every line. And art itself may be defined as a single-minded attempt to render the highest kind of justice to the visible universe, by bringing to light the truth, manifold and one, underlying its every aspect."

"To render the highest kind of justice"; I liked that. But I quickly learned I was no Conrad. It was one thing to dream of writing books, of supplanting *Heart of Darkness* as the finest novella ever written, and another to write puerile and orotund stories like "Terrors of the Jungle" and "Born Free." But the exercise was valuable. It taught me respect for the English language and showed me that with enough discipline and hard work, I could someday write something of value.

Three amiable English professors—Dr. Robert De Maria; Dr. Aaron Kramer, a noted poet and Walt Whitman scholar; and Dr. Thomas Tornquist—encouraged me to write, but left me with no illusions about the many pitfalls along the path to literary glory.

"Why do you want to write books?" Dr. Tornquist asked me one afternoon after class. "Why don't you become a journalist instead? You have the raw talent and with the proper guidance you can become a good newspaperman."

"I want to write books. Can you tell me the secret of successful novel writing?"

"There's no secret that's not already known. First, write about what you know. And write honestly. And your subject must have interest."

I went to the library and looked up books on how to get published. There were dozens of them. Reading them made me despair. The odds were heavily stacked against the beginning writer. Shouldn't I reconsider and become a journalist instead? After all, Dickens, Orwell, Zola, Hemingway, Dreiser, and Steinbeck worked as journalists before they became writers. I read Aristotle's *Poetics* seeking to understand how the classic story was composed. At the same time I read Pope's translation of Homer's *Iliad;* I had read somewhere that for sheer dramatic power and invention Homer was unequaled. I got no nearer to my goal of producing that *chef d'oeuvre.*

Since coming to America I had kept up with works by black South African writers such as Ezekiel Mphahlele and Peter Abrahams. I was constantly chagrined by the fact that, aside from occasional books by the two, few black voices were emerging to tell the truth of apartheid as it was, and that most American readers thought black South Africans were mostly like characters in the books of Paton, Gordimer, Fugard, Coetzee, and others. Despite the fact that these fine white writers regularly, courageously, and eloquently wrote about South African society and the apartheid system, I knew that there was a crucial element missing in their benevolent and sometimes romantic depiction of black characters and black life. Some white writers, I hate to say, were downright condescending.

I had been infected by the fiery and anarchistic eloquence of Richard Wright. I shared his feeling after he had read H. L. Mencken's *Prefaces* and been jarred and dazzled by its contents. "Could words be weapons?" Richard Wright had asked himself. I already knew the answer.

One spring morning I woke up, pulled out my electric typewriter from its black case, and took it to the lounge lest I awake my sleeping roommate. I sat down, inserted a blank page, and began writing. Thus began the chronicle that was later to become the best-seller *Kaffir Boy.* I didn't know what I was going to write about, except that there was something lodged deep within my soul that needed to see the light of day. That day I wrote twenty pages. I knew no hunger; I was oblivious to the passage of time. I existed only in the memories that I was digging out of a tormented past. I wrote like a man possessed. I cried and I laughed with the memories, many of which I had thought long gone, dead and buried, memories which over the years I had suppressed or sought to deny as they reminded me of a nightmare that I wished desperately to forget, to believe had never happened.

I was back in South Africa, in the dusty and miserable ghetto of Alexandra. I felt the pain, the hunger, the suffering, the joy, the love, the humiliation, and the rage, as if the events were happening as I wrote. The last scene I wrote that day was a humorous one. I was five or six years old and my friends had dragged me to the local Kings cinema to see my first movie. As we sat in utter darkness, before huge, red curtains covering the silver screen, I was terrified.

"Why is it so dark here?" I said. "I want to go home."

"Don't worry. The movie will begin soon and you'll have the best time of your life."

"Why is that big man slapping all those boys sitting on the benches?" I pointed at the usher.

"He keeps order in the Bioscope. If you don't shut up, he'll give you the hot five."

Music rumbled. I turned my head to see where the door was, in case . . . While my head was turned I heard the sound of a truck traveling at top speed. I whirled and saw a huge gray truck coming right at me! I screamed and leaped off the bench to get out of the way.

"Sit down, you fool!" My friend pulled me back.

"The truck! The truck!" I screamed, pointing at the screen, my head turned back.

"What truck?"

I turned and looked at the screen. The truck had vanished. Instead, a herd of elephants stampeded toward me.

"Mama, help me!"

The usher lammed me on the head with his flashlight. He ordered me to sit down or get out. I sat, shaken. My friends later told me how everything on the silver screen only took place in the white world.

After I wrote this scene I quit the typewriter, exhausted but exhilarated. I instantly knew in my heart that I had written something that frightened me with its power. I had opened a passage to my inner self which would let in much-needed and curative light. I had made a confession about things which had long harrowed my soul. I was relieved. I was thankful to the Muses for their kindness.

In the space of two months, while saddled with the duties of editor-in-chief and studying for end-of-semester exams, I completed about a hundred pages of my secret book. I dreaded showing it to anyone. What would people say? How would I be looked at? People wondered why I was always typing, typing, typing. Word got out that I was writing a book, but what sort of book, nobody knew.

I showed several chapters to Dr. Tornquist and he told me that the story was interesting but overwritten. He suggested that I use James Joyce's *Portrait of the Artist As a Young Man* as a model. I read the book. Though I enjoyed it, I felt that its style was unsuitable for my story. I wanted to write like a fighter, I wanted my books to throb with the blood of reality, to be naturalistic, not impressionistic.

To fictionalize the brutal reality of black life in South Africa, the reality that I had incredibly survived, the reality which many found too nightmarish to be believable, would be to reduce its impact and immediacy. I wanted people to know the truth, to be shocked by it, to be enraged, and never be able to hide behind the excuse that "after all, this is fiction." "Art for art's sake" was all right, provided the inhumanity of apartheid was not taking place and people were not suffering and dying in South Africa. One cannot conduct a symphony in the middle of a war. The writer must be in the front line, a fighter with the mighty sword of a pen.

Students were barred from using the college word processors, but I succeeded in obtaining permission to do so at night from the director of the center, Maryanna McCarthy, a kind, motherly white woman whose son I had encouraged to write poetry. After long, hard days I would go down to the center and wait for a vacant terminal, where I would work until the center closed, at about nine. Sometimes there would be so much administrative work that I had only fifteen minutes on the word processor before the center closed. Gradually I won Mrs. McCarthy's confidence and she let me continue for an hour after the center was closed. She almost got in trouble for her kindness. Those who knew I was writing a book dismissed my attempt as futile.

I felt alone, terribly alone. I was constantly plagued by doubts: What if they were right? What if I was merely wasting my time? I could have been pursuing those job offers as a reporter. I was comforted by the remembrance that there had been times when one person had been right and the multitude wrong.

23   IRREGULARITIES DURING STUDENT ELECTIONS; CONTESTING THE RESULTS; GRADUATION

During the final exams in May 1983 elections were held for next year's student council. Several radical students stood as candidates. They promised to reform the student council and rid it of nepotism, incompetence, and tacit alignment with the administration. They also promised to fight for integrity in teaching, especially since one teacher, Dr. A. Arturburn, had already been unjustly dismissed.

He was a newly hired instructor, with a Ph.D. in economics and a law degree. At the recommendation of Dr. Sonny I took his course. I found Dr. Arturburn highly competent. He constantly challenged students to think rather than memorize. He also gave us a fair amount of homework. Two other students and myself enjoyed this refreshing approach, but our preference was not shared by the eight other students in class. They began complaining to the dean of students that Dr. Arturburn wasn't a good teacher and should be replaced. Sometimes they ridiculed Dr. Arturburn for dressing in three-quarter-size clothes, like the character Squeers in *Nicholas Nickleby*. Whenever he tried explaining simple economics concepts such as supply and demand and GNP using graphs, some students grunted their disapproval. Dr. Arturburn tried asserting his authority by demanding that the disrespectful students shut up or walk out. During one class two or three walked out. Unbeknownst to Dr. Arturburn, those who walked out were organizing a boycott of his class if he continued using graphs. He did, partly because there was no way of teaching economic concepts like supply and demand effectively without using graphs, and partly because of his pride as a competent teacher.

The graph haters—about two-thirds of the class—absented themselves from several important classes. The final exam came and several questions required the use of graphs in answering them. In the middle of the exam the graph haters marched en masse to the dean's office and complained that the exam required them to know material "they had never been taught." I don't know if other charges were trumped up against the innocent teacher. For several days Dr. Arturburn's job hung in the balance as the case brought against him by essentially lazy students was being debated by the administration. Faculty internal politics—apparently there was a power struggle within the social sciences division—prevented the new and untenured Dr. Arturburn from getting faculty support. Dr. Sonny was his lone supporter. I and a female colleague, Janice Jacobs, a senior who majored in economics and math, pleaded that Dr. Arturburn not be fired for doing his job. Our impassioned pleas could not save him. He was let go by the administration and the students' grades were adjusted to reflect their dislike for graphs. For days I spoke out against such unfair treatment of a qualified and competent teacher, and in doing so acquired more enemies.

I knew that if the Student Government Association elections were fair, the radical candidates could defeat those candidates—many of them incumbents—who were favored by the administration. I organized a group of poll watchers. We discussed tactics on how to ensure a clean election for positions of president, vice president, treasurer, and secretary on the Student Government Association. Election watchers were posted at every polling station to guard against irregularities. The voter turnout was surprisingly heavy. Throughout the day Tracy Parlemo, myself, and several colleagues visited each polling station and were met by the same remarks from the poll watchers:

"The administration's darlings are running scared. They know that if this election is fair, they might lose."

"Long live student power!"

"Next year there will be genuine student government."

"Student power will change the direction of this college."

Polls closed. Expectation mounted that the ballots would be read in public by student vote counters. This had been explicitly agreed upon by all candidates. Now several of the incumbents insisted that the ballots be counted in secret, in the office of the dean of students. Students were in an uproar. They insisted on an open vote count. The incumbents pointed to an obscure section of the election bylaws to support their self-serving claim.

"What about the agreement?" I asked.

"The law is the law," responded one incumbent.

"What's to prevent your stuffing the ballots when you and your buddies have to do the counting, and in secret for that matter?" I retorted.

"We will allow an independent observer of your choice during the counting," the incumbent replied.

Tracy Parlemo was chosen as the independent observer. Later that evening she burst into my apartment in a rage.

"This election was a sham!" she cried.

"What happened? Who won?" I asked.

"Who won? Of course they won."

"Who are they?"

"The administration's puppets."

"What! They won? Did you witness the vote count?"

"I was never allowed into the damn office."

"What?"

"I was kept outside in the hall and only told the results. I reminded them of their promise but I was ignored."

"Hell, no!"

"Hell, yes!"

"But they promised—"

"They knew they had lost—so they made a promise they knew they would break. All they wanted was to lay their paws on the ballot boxes. I tell you this election was a downright sham!"

Something had to be done, that was certain. But what? The obvious course of action was to have the elections declared null and void. We could easily galvanize students into calling for another election provided we had hard evidence of any fraud. That night Tracy, Liz Irwin, another radical student, and myself plotted strategies on how to proceed.

"Is pursuing this thing worth it?" Liz asked. "Won't we simply be stirring up a hornet's nest? After all, the majority of students couldn't care less who won and who lost."

"We must make them care," Tracy said.

The first thing our ad-hoc committee did was to demand a recount. When stalling tactics were used to prevent an immediate recount, we set up tables in the student center and asked students to sign a petition demanding a new election on the grounds that the last one was improperly conducted. We gathered enough signatures, which we presented to the election committee. In the meantime I conferred with John Rather about running the story in *The Lion's Voice*.

"You know this is a big story," Rather said. "It must be handled carefully. You must have all your facts straight."

"Presently much of our evidence is circumstantial," I said.

"But you're sure they refused to allow Tracy to be present, after first agreeing to it?" John asked.

"Yes."

He grilled me on the facts of the story and in the end he was satisfied that we should print it.

I sat down to write the story but was unable to complete it for several days because of exams. Since the paper was a bimonthly, and only one issue remained to be published before the end of the school year, there was enough time to be devoted to the story. Despite the excitement of the moment, my education remained top priority—especially so now, since I knew that if I scored highly there was no way I could fail to graduate. I had made the dean's list for three semesters in a row, and my performance during this semester had been above average. For my final semester I had taken the following courses: Introduction to Eastern Thought, History of Philosophy II, Sociology, Advanced News Preparation, and Arts and Life in Africa, an anthropology course. As added insurance I had already acquired more credits than were necessary to earn a bachelor of arts degree. My exams completed, I set about putting together stories for the last issue of the year. One afternoon while I was at the office, Maria Kokolakis, the paper's photographer and my successor as editor-in-chief, came in.

"Have you heard the news?" she asked.

"What news?"

"There won't be any final issue of *The Lion's Voice*."

"What?"

"I've been told that there won't be a final issue of *The Lion's Voice*," she repeated.

"Who told you?"

"I can't say. But trust me that I'm speaking the truth."

"But we have money to print the last issue."

"There's no money."

"But according to our budget figures there should still be money left for one more issue."

"The Student Association says there's no money."

I went to see Steve Keogh, the outgoing SGA president, about the matter, and he reiterated that there wasn't enough money for another issue of the paper.

"But the final issue was budgeted for," I said.

"Yes. But the SGA is way over budget for the year and we can't afford additional expenses."

When I pressed Steve on the issue, he revealed that the money which had been allocated for the paper was needed for the more important end-of-the-year party. There was nothing I could do.

Although I had no hard evidence, this chain of events led me to conclude that the Student Government Association wanted to kill the story.

I called John Rather and explained the matter to him.

"Is it legal for the Student Government Association to withhold funding for the paper?" John asked.

"Yes. The student paper is under their control."

There was a pause of a few minutes.

"Why would the SGA want to kill the story?" John asked.

"Simple. To prevent a new election," I replied.

"What do you say about the idea of taking this story to *Newsday* or *The New York Times*?" John suggested.

"Is it a big-enough story for them?"

"We'll see."

The story wasn't big enough for the big city papers. There was no final issue of *The Lion's Voice*.

My colleagues and I may have lost the battle but we were determined to win the war. The college was now rife with news of the scandal. Out of nowhere stories began circulating among students that during the year I had embezzled funds for the paper, that I had used the paper to inflate my ego, that I was challenging the election results from an ineradicable streak of mischief, that I was a rebel without a cause, that I had nothing to lose since I was graduating, and other such attacks to assassinate my character. I received anonymous telephone calls in which I was called "nigger," and warned about what white people did to "smart-assed niggers."

Then through the grapevine I heard that my transcripts had been investigated by the dean's office and the discovery made that I had not fulfilled all my requirements for graduation. I never found out if the rumors had any basis in fact. In a panic I consulted Dr. Sonny, my academic adviser, and he assured me that to the best of his knowledge I had met all requirements.

"I'll personally look into the matter," he said.

In the meantime I went to the dean's office to find out for certain what was happening but was told he was out of town. Days of anxiety followed. Tracy and the others who had fought alongside me had received similar threats. One afternoon Tracy and I met.

"Do you think it's worth it?" she said, "Continuing our challenge of the elections?"

"What do you think?"

"Well, Liz and I are concerned about not graduating. I've applied to law school and I need that diploma."

"You know, Tracy," I said, "we've already proved our point. I can assure you that next year's election will be clean."

Somewhat disappointed that justice had not been done, but feeling vindicated that we had fought an honorable battle and had succeeded in raising the consciousness of the college community, we agreed to abandon the fight. The threats vanished. When the dean returned I was told that I had fulfilled all requirements and would be graduating with honors. I never found out whether, in fact, my transcripts had ever been investigated. I would also be awarded a plaque in recognition of "outstanding service to the Student Association through exceptional participation in furthering the aims and goals of student government."

Stan Smith came to my graduation on June 5, 1983. It was a sunny spring day with blue skies and a gentle breeze. The campus teemed with parents, relatives, and friends of the graduates. I felt proud marching in file with other graduates, dressed in a shiny black gown and tasseled cap. The graduating procession was led by administrators in ornate silk gowns. The dean of students, William Condon, awed by Stan's arrival in a limousine, momentarily left the procession to shake hands with him. Ellen Burstyn, the actress and star of the movie *The Ambassador*, gave the commencement address.

The Wielunskis also attended and took photos, several of which I sent home to my family. It was a very special day for me, the achievement of an impossible dream. I wished my mother and Granny had been present, for it was a dream both had nurtured and created opportunities for with their heroic sacrifices. I even wished my father present, so he could see that an education wasn't "a waste of time," as he believed.

"I'm very proud of you," Stan said as I showed him my diploma and the student government award. "And you should be proud of yourself, too."

 DOUBTS ABOUT THE FUTURE; STAN'S SUPPORT; I DEVOTE MYSELF TO WRITING; KATIE, A SOULMATE

What would I do with my future? Caught in the caldron of events during my final semester, I hadn't really focused on this important question. But now I was out of school, armed with a bachelor's degree. Yet I was fearful of returning to South Africa because of renewed violence and repression, and because I was not sure how I would adjust to living under the stifling and inhuman laws of apartheid after having tasted freedom in America. But how would I survive in America? What were my prospects? And what about my immigration status? Now that I was no longer a student I was liable to be deported if found to be out of status.

I saw in *Newsday* ads about free consultations with immigration lawyers. I went to one, was told that my case was almost hopeless, but that if I came up with $2,000 something might be tried. I had no such money. In despair at the thought of being deported, I ransacked my files and discovered to my dismay that my passport was missing (I never found out how it got lost or if it was stolen). I went to the college's foreign student adviser, a genial woman who occupied the post part-time. She was a firm supporter during my tenure as editor-in-chief. Her first impression, too, was that my prospects of staying in America were bleak, but she promised to leave no stone unturned in search of legal ways to prevent my deportation.

A day later I was issued an eviction notice by the dorm director since I was no longer a student. I pleaded for an extension of my stay until at least I had resolved my immigration status as I feared leaving the sanctuary of the campus.

"Dean Condon has to approve such a request," the dorm director said.

I went to see Dean Condon.

"There's no problem with your staying in the dorm a few weeks," he said. "As long as you pay for it."

"Thank you very much, sir. I'll talk to Stan and I foresee no problem in his paying the bill." I rose to leave.

"Not so fast," Dean Condon said. "I have something else to tell you."

What now?

"I hear you're having immigration problems," he said.

"Yes, sir."

"I've looked into the matter. I think something can be done to prevent your being deported," he said with an even voice.

"Something can be done?" I stammered.

"Yes. And it won't be anything illegal. As a graduated senior you're entitled to one year of practical training. It's granted automatically. All you have to do is request it from the INS. Here are the forms. Complete them and bring them back to me. By the way, how's the book coming?"

"Very well, sir," I said with a smile, accepting the forms. "And thank you very much."

It dawned upon me that though we had had our disagreements on several issues, Dean Condon was going out of his way to help me because he truly appreciated by contributions to the college, and my efforts in behalf of students. His fairness gained him my respect.

"Write a good one," he said. "And don't forget to mention Dowling College. It will be good for recruitment, you know."

I did receive a year's practical training permit from the INS; I was allowed to remain at the dorm for the summer; and, most important, I was allowed to continue using the word-processing center.

But how to support myself while I wrote? I doubted that Stan, who had already spent over $40,000 for my tumultuous education, would consent to so preposterous an idea as supporting me for a year while I wrote a book which almost everyone I had talked to dismissed as unpublishable. Was I being realistic in expecting that people would want to read the autobiography of a twenty-two-year-old African student?

Stan returned from a tennis trip to Europe and I called him at home to discuss my future.

"I want to write this book," I said. "But I don't know if it's any good, let alone if it will be published. But I want to write it."

"So what do you want me to do?"

"I would greatly appreciate it if you could support me while I write it."

"You know, it's time you starting supporting yourself, Mark."

"Yes, I know."

"And what about home? Do you intend ever to go back? Don't you miss your family?"

"I miss them dearly. But I also fear for my life if I return home under present conditions. The regime is detaining innocent people right and left. I left with a cloud of suspicion hanging over my head. It would certainly make the security apparatus jubilant to have me safely in prison, especially since I've been denouncing apartheid since I came to America. Besides, I believe I lost my passport."

"If writing is what you want to do," Stan said after a pause, "I'll support you till you finish the book. But be realistic. Think of the odds."

Dr. Ron Killion with three representatives of Limestone College's freshman class (from left to right): Ricky Nelson Hall, Dr. Killion, Patrice Paula Abrams, and David Mark Bomar. *(credit: Limestone College Yearbook Staff)*

ggie and Alice elunski at my gradua- n from Dowling Col- e in 1983. *(credit: Stan ith)*

Ned Bennett and Scott Hardman (far right) along with Tom Getman (not pictured) took my family a copy of *Kaffir Boy* in 1987. To the left of Ned are my mother and sister Florah. *(credit: Tom Getman)*

Granny with a grandchild on her back and my mother admiring themselves in *Kaffir Boy*. *(credit: Tom Getman)*

Uncle Cheeks, who, after his release from jail, became a church choir conductor and assistant minister at the Twelve Apostles Church of God in Alexandra, which my mother attends. *(credit: Mavhunga)*

sister Merriam, 18, who returned to high
ool in 1988 after giving birth to a baby son,
usiso (Gift). *(credit: Tom Getman)*

Gail and my mother meet for the first time at
JFK. *(credit: Debra DiMaio)*

American businessman Bob Brown with my parents in Alexandra in 1988.
(credit: Stedman Graham)

Oprah Winfrey, me, and her boyfriend, Stedman Graham, at JFK Airport awaiting the arrival of my family from South Africa in June 1987. (*credit: Debra DiMaio*)

The family on "The Oprah Winfrey Show." Left to right: Granny, my mother, myself, Oprah, Florah, George. Seated: Linah and Dianah. (*credit: Oprah Winfrey Show staff*)

Gail and I at our wedding on Long Island, August 1, 1987, flanked by Maid of Honor Joanne Matzen and Best Man Stan Smith. *(credit: Marty Van Lith)*

Gail's family and mine at the wedding. *(credit: Marty Van Lith)*

(*Above*) Linah, George, and (*below*) Dianah after a year in America.

(Left to right) Jeanne and Arthur Ashe, myself and Gail, and Stan and Margie Smith in New York. *(credit: Brian C. McLernon)*

Receiving a 1987 Christopher Award from Father John Catoir. The award's motto is: "It is better to light one candle than to curse the darkness." *(credit: 1987 Christopher Awards photographer)*

Schoolchildren in Alexandra with books donated by American schools. *(credit: Linda Twala)*

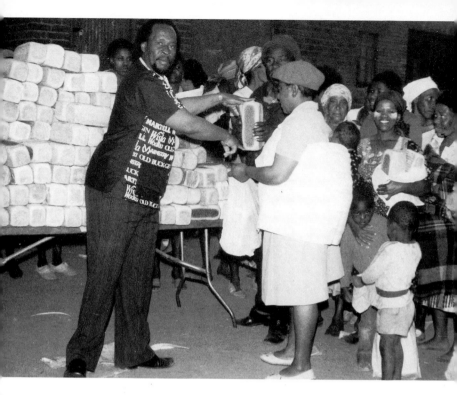

Mr. Linda Twala distruting free bread under
auspices of the Intertional Concern Foundati
(credit: Friends of Alexan

Granny (far right) with thof Alexandra's centenaria
In 1988 Oprah Winfrey
nated $7,000 to provide flunches for Alexandra's
derly for an entire ye
(credit: Linda Twala)

"Thank you very much, Stan," I said.

I thought of the odds, and at times my spirits drooped, but I persevered. Two weeks before college reopened for the 1983–84 academic year, I vacated the apartment and became a lodger at the Sherards, who lived about a mile from Dowling. Uncle Ziggie and Aunt Alice, whom I still kept in touch with, had contacted the Sherards, a middle-aged white couple, about my situation and they had offered me a room. Jim Sherard was a flight engineer with TWA and his wife Barbara a social worker. She is now president of the local chapter of Planned Parenthood and Jim is retired. Both were liberal Democrats and treated me like a son. For a modest monthly rent I had the use of their entire house and pool.

I spent the mornings at the local Connequot library rewriting whatever I had printed the previous evening. In the afternoon I either played tennis with members of the Dowling team, or went for a run in the woods or by the beach with Jim. At about six I would ride the bike to Dowling and there wait for a vacant terminal. I would write until the center closed. Sometimes there would be no vacant terminal, and I would return home having written nothing.

From time to time I encountered familiar faces and I would be asked, "What are you still doing here? I thought you had long graduated."

"I'm writing a book," I would say.

"Whose the publisher?"

"I don't have a publisher yet."

Often there would be looks of pity. Some people thought me demented. I could imagine them thinking, "We have professors in this college who have earned Ph.D.s in English from the most prestigious universities, they have taught for years and know everything about plot, character, action, and the structure of sentences, they have written dissertations on Middle English and literary criticism, they have amassed innumerable ideas and are weighed down with experience and knowledge of human nature, they have piled up in their offices and homes manuscripts on literary theory and psychoanalyses of Shakespeare. Yet these venerable sages of the English language have never written books, only academic treaties. Who do you think you are to succeed where experienced and scholarly professors have failed?"

But I wasn't attempting to write like a professor. I was merely expressing my innermost thoughts and feelings.

Conrad best sums up why I wrote, and in his words I found inspiration:

> The sincere endeavor to accomplish the creative task, to go as far on that road as his strength will carry him, to go undeterred by faltering, weariness, or reproach, is the only valid justification for the worker in prose.
>
> And if his conscience is clear, his answer to those who in the fullness of a wisdom which look for immediate profit, demand specifically to be edified, consoled, amused; who demand to be promptly improved, or encouraged, or frightened, or shocked, or charmed, must run thus: My task which I am trying to achieve is, by the power of the written word to make you hear, to make you feel—it is, before all, to make you *see*.

I wanted to make people hear, to make them see, to make them feel what I experienced as a black boy growing up under the apartheid system. I wanted to "snatch, in a moment of courage, from the remorseless rush of time, a passing phase of life" and to "reveal the substance of its truth" to a world that strikes me as increasingly cynical, myopic, and self-centered. I was determined to let that world know—despite the pain, the anguish, the humiliation, the despair, and the invisible bleeding that such revelation might cost me—the truth about man's inhumanity to man. I was intent on warning others, especially Americans, about the dangers of allowing selfishness, greed, the worship of materialism, exploitation, and intolerance to take root in the human heart and mind, to fester within a free society and to erode those final checks of true liberty—fidelity to simple values and the Golden Rule.

Months went by. I kept writing. Those were exhilarating days. I had no social life worth mentioning, except a dear friendship with a misunderstood but wonderful spirit, a German woman in her fifties who lived next door to the Sherards. Her name was Katie. Many people, including members of her own family, considered her weird, if not moonstruck. But I discovered in the course of our tender friendship that she was a most intelligent and sensitive soul. She was a nuts-'n'-berries health-food enthusiast. She cooked delicious meals and would often set aside supper for me, and, when I returned from the word-processing center, I would visit her. We spent hours talking about poetry, books, philosophy, nature, and about the "True" and the "Beautiful" in life. I often read her my favorite poems (among them "Tintern Abbey" and the "Lucy Gray" poems, by Wordsworth; "On First Looking into Chapman's Homer" and "Ode to a Nightingale," by John Keats; "Dover Beach," by Matthew Arnold; and the sonnets of Shakespeare and Milton), which it often turned out she knew from her desultory reading. We were perfect soulmates.

Over the years Katie had amassed an impressive library of the best works in literature and had used it well. She was a penetrating critic of good writing and of life. Though reticent about her past, she occasionally offered glimpses of her difficult years in Germany. She was orphaned during the Second World War, and forced to wander from foster home to foster home. She met her husband, a man "almost damned in a fair wife," during the war, and he subsequently brought her to America. He was a middle-aged, overweight Spaniard who worked as a milkman.

Before they were married, she would tell me, with glassy eyes, he was romantic and understanding. But after two children were born, the years of matrimonial bliss faded into oblivion, familiarity bred contempt, and finally an unbridgeable rift came between them. He became insensitive to her needs and macho in his behavior. At every turn he and his unemployed brother, who lived with them, sublimated her individuality, disparaged her love of Nature and book learning, and generally treated her as if she were crazy.

The psychological abuse was so constant that Katie sometimes doubted her sanity. My brief entrance into her life, she confessed, was godsent. I was to hear Katie's story of marital psychological torture over and over again. My willingness to listen, my sensitivity and vulnerability, which often led men to call me effeminate and a fag, won me the trust of many women—divorced, single, young, old, black, white—who confided,in me their innermost secrets because I cared. Katie eventually divorced her uncaring husband.

By the time I visited Hilton Head Island for the Christmas holidays I had written nearly half the book. Stan and Margie were surprised when I often locked myself in the condominium for hours, became absentminded, and sometimes forgot to have dinner at their place.

"Anything wrong?" Stan asked one day.

"Nothing. I'm just absorbed in the book I'm writing."

"Can I read it?"

I gave Stan a copy of the manuscript. He was shocked by the depictions of my childhood experiences; it was information I had never before divulged to anyone. He assured me of his continued support until I had completed the book, which I told him would be in a couple months. He promised to show the manuscript to his friends, among them Arthur Ashe, who had contacts in the publishing world.

"You should take a few chapters to Terry Plumb. Remember him? He might have a few suggestions."

I took the manuscript to Terry, editor of *The Island Packet*. He was astounded by the story but was critical of the writing style.

"It's too verbose. Too many words. They get in the way of the story."

"But it's good?"

"Yeah, it's an interesting story. An important story. But you've only written several chapters. If the rest is as powerful as this, you're headed somewhere. But remember, you must work at writing crisp, direct, simple prose, like good journalists do. Wordiness is a sign of vagueness and can be the death of a story, no matter how interesting. Since you've graduated, I would strongly recommend you find a job as a journalist. That will give you the opportunity to hone your skills as a writer. We're a small paper, we don't have many openings and don't pay much, but if you can find a place to stay, I can create a position for you. Talk to Stan about it."

Stan said that though the condominium was where his guests stayed, he was willing to let me use it for a few months while I looked for a place of my own. The cost of living on Hilton Head Island could not be met on an apprentice reporter's pay, so I abandoned that idea.

"Thanks for the offer, Terry," I said. "But I don't think things will work out. I'm going back to Long Island and try to finish the book."

Terry then told me about a journalism writing program conducted by a noted writing teacher, Roy Peter Clark, at the Poynter Media Institute in St. Petersburg, Florida.

"It will be excellent training for you," he said. "The summer fellowships are among the most coveted by aspiring journalists. And I think you have the qualifications to win one of them. If you want me to I'll write Roy and he'll send you the application forms."

"Please do," I said gratefully, seeing no harm in having alternatives to fall back on.

25

SIBLINGS' TROUBLES; MY FATHER'S WORSENING
ALCOHOLISM; CHOICE OF EXILE; APPLYING TO
JOURNALISM GRADUATE SCHOOL

Letters reached me from home that the family's poverty had worsened. My mother had become frail from her untreated diabetes, but she continued to work the night shift, operating a heavy cleaning machine which left her exhausted and wracked by body aches. But as always she never complained. My brother George, from whom I received at least two letters imploring me to bring him to the U.S. to study, had become a follower of a religious cult. His letters were fire-and-brimstone sermons. Thus far he had escaped the fate of many of his peers, who were either murdered in the continuing and escalating violence in the ghettos or had simply disappeared. Yet throughout this ordeal he continued to believe in the value of an education, to hold out the hope that some day things would get better.

Florah had left her job at Kirschoff's flower shop following a quarrel with Collin. Maria, because of disrupted black schooling which left teenage boys and girls with nothing to do all day but mostly fool around—often, alas, without access to contraceptives—had become a teenage mother. She remained unemployed. My mother prayed every day that my three remaining sisters—Linah, Dianah, and Merriam—would not fall victims to teenage motherhood. But she knew that she was fighting a losing battle because apartheid, it seemed, by disrupting black schooling, was bent on creating the conditions that made it easy for children to bear children. Schools, with their rigorous discipline and strict morality, were often the only places where black children were safe from some of the deadly aspects of ghetto life: gangs, criminality, and early experimentation with sex.

149

My father had apparently given up all hope of ever becoming gainfully employed. He now drank heavily and every day. His reign of terror in the house had become a permanent and ugly fixture. He constantly demanded for liquor whatever little food money was brought in by my mother. I also learned that an educated neighbor had helped my father sue the driver who lamed him and had received an out-of-court settlement of about five hundred rands (about $250). Instead of bringing the money home and supporting his family, he had given it to a *shebeen* keeper for safekeeping, and within weeks drank all of it.

"Child," my mother said. "I'm deeply hurt by what your father did. Not only that he drank all that money, but that he trusted a *shebeen* keeper over me, his wife. But I still love him. I'll continue to pray for him. He will someday come to see the light."

I was again asked when I was coming home to take over as head of the family since I had graduated. Pictures of my graduation were the pride of the family and my mother constantly showed them to her white employers, who, she said, were green with envy. I also learned that Granny was getting old and was plagued by numerous health problems. She wished to see me before she died.

"She's determined not to die," my mother said. "She's willing to endure the worst pain the Devil can afflict her with so long as she can live to hold you, her beloved grandchild, in her arms. But, child, your grandma is truly suffering. Her heart is withering every day because of the suffering of her chidren. Especially Uncle Piet, who now has a large and growing family and no job."

Why wasn't I home? Why was I being selfish? If I returned to South Africa with an American degree, and caused the authorities no trouble by openly professing what I had learned in America about freedom, I could write my ticket to prosperity and all my family's miseries would be ended. But as days passed, as news of escalating repression and violence and death made headlines in the American media, as I continued speaking out against the injustices of apartheid, I knew that I might never see my native land again, and the faces that I loved and missed.

The die was cast. Life in America had taught me that to submit to injustice of any kind, to make peace with apartheid servitude under any terms, however favorable, was to contradict the laws of God, of Nature, and of Reason. Even animals never willingly consent to their captivity. Such captivity denatures them. Thomas Jefferson in the

Declaration of Independence; Thomas Paine in *Common Sense* and *The Rights of Man;* John Locke in *Second Treatise on Government;* Alexander Hamilton, John Jay, and James Madison in *The Federalist Papers;* Mary Wollstonecraft in *A Vindication of the Rights of Woman;* Algernon Sidney in *Discourses on Government;* John Stuart Mill in *On Liberty* and *Representative Government;* Karl Marx in *The Communist Manifesto* and *Das Kapital;* John Milton in *First and Second Defense of the English People;* Jean-Jacques Rousseau in *The Social Contract;* Percy Bysshe Shelley in *Mask of Anarchy;* Thoreau in *Civil Disobedience;* Étienne de la Boetie's *Discourse on Voluntary Servitude;* and Frederick Douglass in his essays and speeches such as "The Negro and the Fourth of July": all these radical writers had led me to conclude that apartheid was nothing but a form of twentieth-century slavery, an evil which could not be reformed but had to be completely abolished, and that it was my duty, and the sacred duty of all lovers of liberty and justice, to fight such tyrannies wherever they reared their damned head.

But to fight meant exile, and the thought of exile frightened me. South Africa was a part of me and of my soul. I could not unlearn the radical ideas about freedom and democracy America had instilled in me. At the same time I knew that the Pretoria regime would never allow me to spread those radical ideas among my compatriots. What would I do?

I chose exile so I could continue to fight. For weeks I felt lonely and depressed at having taken such a momentous step. Where would it lead me? Was it the right thing to do? Many nights, as I lay curled up in bed, I thought of escaping from the conundrums of reality into the world of drugs, sex, fantasy, and alcohol. Many in America with problems they cannot solve seem to be escaping from them; why shouldn't I? Just a little marijuana or cocaine, a little promiscuous sex, a little alcohol, wouldn't do me any harm. I could quit any time I wanted to. I would only be lost in sweet forgetfulness.

But I was mortally afraid of taking that first sip, that first sniff. I thought of what alcohol had done to my father, and how drugs were bedeviling America, and the havoc wrought by the deadly disease AIDS. No, in such self-destruction I could never lose my pain. I would only make it worse. Yes, my soul was in agony, but my suffering paled in comparison to the suffering of my family and of millions of other people in places like Afghanistan, India, Ethiopia, Haiti, and the Middle East, who were not as fortunate as myself to live in America, to have a roof over my head and a full meal each day. I owed it to myself to live. Life was too precious a gift to let a little trouble take it away.

More days filled with the anguish of exile and loneliness followed. I continued to write, finding solace in the emotions which poured out of me with the fury of harpies. Books became my opium: I read and read and read, mostly philosophy, history, religion, ethics, poetry. My guides to good books were often the authors themselves, who praised or cited other books which had influenced them.

From time to time I visited the Wielunskis and occasionally accompanied them to folk dances, community theatre, and films. I had become something of a spectacle at Dowling, akin to one of Shakespeare's fools, full of sound and fury but signifying nothing.

One day I had lunch with Professor Tornquist. He told me of his days at Columbia University, how he worked as an elevator operator to pay his way through school. By degrees our discussion turned to me and my future.

"Have you thought of applying to the Columbia Graduate School of Journalism?" he asked. "They have one of the finest programs in the country. And there you can hone your skills as a journalist. You can always write books. But you must earn a living in order to write. Your determination and drive will someday get you published. But that someday may be a long time coming."

I heeded his advice and wrote to the journalism school at Columbia. Marianne Kellogg, the admissions coordinator, sent me a cordial letter, forms, and intimidating information about New York City, the curriculum at the J-school, the renowned professors, and the stringent admission policy where hundreds applied but only a selected few were admitted. Columbia's alumni list read like a *Who's Who* in the media. Last year's applicants for the one-year degree program had attended some of the best undergraduate schools in the world, and I learned that the school seldom accepted people who hadn't at least a few years practical experience in the news business. What then was I doing applying to such an elite school with my undergraduate degree from obscure Dowling?

But I was desperate. I wrote an intensely personal essay and hoped that, just as at Limestone, it would not be my grades or titles but my convictions, ambition, burning desire, and courage to believe in myself that would win me passage, that would separate me from the pack.

"Anyway," I thought, "even if I am not accepted, at least I will have tried." About the same time I received a package from Roy Clark containing brochures and application forms for the summer newswriting program in Florida. The fellowship was worth about $2,500. I applied.

My practical training permission expired in a few months. I couldn't dwell on what I would do if I wasn't accepted at Columbia or awarded the fellowship at the Poynter Institute; I would have gone crazy to do so. I continued to write.

One day the Wielunskis invited me to address a Unitarian fellowship in Bellport of which they were members. I was reluctant to go at first. I remembered how a year ago, eager to please some white acquaintances—a husband, his wife, and their three children—who lived in Oakdale, I had accompanied them to a charismatic church in Sayville, where the congregation supposedly spoke in tongues. During the service, the wife of my acquaintance, with whom I sat, started talking what I thought was gibberish. The minister, a tall, angular fellow with a military haircut, saw the bewilderment on my face. He took it to mean that I, too, was about to be struck by the prophetic spirit. He came over to me and urged me to let go.

"Don't be shy," he said with a paternal look on his face. "I can tell that the Lord wants to speak through you. Don't stop Him. Let go of yourself. Just open your mouth."

"But if I let go I may talk nonsense," I said.

"There's no nonsense in the eyes of the Lord," he said.

I didn't let go. Since that day, I swore that never would I attend any church where reason was abjured, blind faith edified, and scandalous deeds committed in the sacred name of God.

VISIT TO UNITARIAN CHURCH; I ACQUIRE A LITERARY AGENT; PUBLISHING HOUSES BID FOR *Kaffir Boy*; SUMMER AT POYNTER INSTITUTE; MY FIRST ARTICLE IS PUBLISHED IN THE *St. Petersburg Times*

The visit to the Unitarian church changed my life. Most members of the group were liberal intellectuals and their faith was firmly embedded in reality. I gave an impassioned speech in which I related how I had grown up black in the ghetto, and how I survived the nightmares of my childhood and gained passage to America on a tennis scholarship. The audience was spellbound. I received a standing ovation and people came forward and congratulated me. Unbeknownst to me, in the audience were two published authors: Charles Hession, a retired professor of economics at City College in New York, whose controversial biography of British economist John Maynard Keynes was about to be published by Macmillan, under the editorship of Edward T. Chase; and Phyllis Whitney, the world-famous mystery writer whose books, among them *Vermillion* and *Rainbow in the Mist*, have sold over forty million copies. I shook hands and engaged in an animated discussion with both.

"That was a very moving presentation," Phyllis Whitney said. At eighty years old she was remarkably vivacious and healthy. "And you told your painful story so well. It was uplifting in its sorrow. Have you written it down somewhere?"

"Yes," I said eagerly. "As a matter of fact I'm currently working on a book about my life in South Africa."

"Are you? Do you have a publisher?"

"No, ma'am. But I would like to have publishers look at it."

"Do you write as well as you speak?"

"I think so."

Charles Hession told me of his book and added that he would be happy to recommend my manuscript to his editor at Macmillan.

"But I don't have a completed manuscript yet," I said. "I have only written about half the book."

"How many pages?"

"Two hundred or so."

"I think that's enough to give publishers a pretty good idea of whether a book is publishable. Don't you think so, Phyllis?"

"Yes."

"Really?" I was under the impression that only completed manuscripts were acceptable to publishers.

"I would suggest you send what you've written so far to Ned Chase, my editor. I'll call him first thing tomorrow morning and tell him to expect your manuscript." He then told me that Ned Chase was a noted editor of dozens of best-sellers and the father of Chevy Chase, the movie actor. I was impressed.

Phyllis countered by suggesting that I should also send the two hundred pages to her agent in New York, Julie Fallowfield, at McIntosh & Otis, who, if she was interested, would then submit it to publishers.

"In this business you need a good agent," and Phyllis.

I returned home giddy with joy. I could not believe my good fortune. Finally, I thought, I had gained a foothold into the publishing world. Over the next few days I meticulously edited the two hundred pages, made several copies, wrote cover letters, gave a brief biography of myself, and sent the material to Julie Fallowfield and Ned Chase. I prayed every day. I kept the news of my lucky break to myself for fear of being disappointed. But I wrote with renewed courage and confidence.

At the fellowship I also met Stewart and Claudia Malloy, a mixed couple of liberal politics. The two actively championed the cause of blacks in South Africa and Namibia, and were also dedicated peace activists in their conservative community. Stew was a stockbroker with Merrill Lynch and Claudia a schoolteacher. Their odyssey as a mixed couple was painful but heart warming. Claudia became estranged from her parents when she defied their wishes and married a black man. Only years later had they been reconciled. Stew and Claudia welcomed me into their home, and with their three lovely children, Leta, Sudi, and Shani, I shared many a warm and memorable family moment.

I was forced to look for other lodgings when one of the Sherards' children returned home. I found a small but neat and sunny room near the library. My landlord was Mr. Maltby, a soft-spoken elderly man who once worked for *The New Yorker* magazine. The walls of his study were lined with first-edition classics and framed, autographed photos of old movie stars such as Marlene Dietrich and Humphrey Bogart. Mr. Maltby also owned a tribe of cats. He was seldom home so I was able to work undisturbed.

A few days after I had mailed the copies of my unfinished manuscript to New York, the phone rang. It was Ned Chase. He thought my manuscript was incredible and wanted to right away offer me a contract for Macmillan to publish "the amazing book" I had written. How much longer did I have to go on the book? he asked. Could I send him what I had thus far written? Would I like to come to Manhattan and have lunch with him? He was anxious to meet me. How old was I? Did I know so-and-so? Had I read such-and-such a book? He was an ardent admirer of Stan Smith and an avid tennis player, and personally knew such tennis greats as Jack Kramer and Gardnar Mulloy. I was overwhelmed. He said he would give me time to think things over, and asked me to please call him back, collect.

Shortly thereafter another call came. It was from Julie Fallowfield. She, too, found my manuscript incredible. She had wept reading it. It was the most important book on South Africa she had ever read. Could I come to New York to meet with her? McIntosh & Otis, if I didn't know, was one of the biggest agencies in the business, and so exclusive their name wasn't even listed in *The Writer's Market*. They represented such celebrated writers as Walker Percy, John Steinbeck, and, of course, Phyllis Whitney. Wow! She would give me time to digest everything, and I should call her back, collect.

I walked from the phone to my room in a daze. Could it be true? Or was I dreaming? Did these people have the right manuscript? How could my words have moved them so deeply? I pulled out a copy of the manuscript and read a page: "My tenth birthday came and went away, like all the other nine, uncelebrated. Having never had a normal childhood, I didn't miss birthdays; to me they were simply like other days: to be survived. Strangely, however, on each birthday I somehow got the feeling that I had aged more than a year. Suffering seemed to age me more than birthdays. Though I was only ten, black life seemed to have, all along, been teaching me the same lessons of survival, and making the same demands upon me for that survival, as it was doing to grown-ups. Thus, emotionally, I had aged far beyond my years."

I saw nothing magical in these words, or the thousands of others I had written. I had written simply and candidly. I had made my appeal to the human heart by which we all feel. Words are indeed weapons. Conrad was right: the right word and the right accent could move the world. I didn't know how to proceed in dealing with the two offers. I needed advice before committing myself to anything. I called Stan Smith and explained what happened.

"Amazing," he said.

"I don't believe it either."

"You know, a few days ago I told Arthur Ashe about your manuscript and he promised to do something. He knows and has dealt with literary agents and publishers." Arthur Ashe had written a poignant autobiography called *Portrait in Motion*. His latest work, *A Hard Road to Glory: A History of the African-American Athlete,* was described by *The New York Times Book Review* as a monumental accomplishment. "I would suggest that you go ahead and meet with

Julie Fallowfield and Ned Chase. But don't be pressured into signing anything."

I had never been to Manhattan. I only knew the city from books, newspapers, and the nightly news. So when I emerged from the tunnel at Penn Station, and took my first tentative steps, like a newborn babe, along Thirty-forth Street on my way to 475 Fifth Avenue, I was overawed, intimidated, and a little terrified. I constantly threw my eyes at the gigantic buildings that almost touched the sky, puzzled over the stern, cold, impassive faces in the hurrying and jostling crowds and scores of honking yellow cabs. My ears were blasted by the Miltonian cacophony. Feeling dizzy, I leaned against a wall. So this was the world-famous Manhattan, a jungle of concrete and steel where fortunes are made and squandered, where the lights always shine on Broadway, where celebrities and power brokers have their chic apartments on the East Side and blacks and other minorities languish in grinding poverty in places like Harlem and the South Bronx. This is the city that had filled James Baldwin with such eloquent rage, and inspired Claude Brown to write the masterpiece *Manchild in the Promised Land.* This is the city where daring robberies and grisly murders were committed, where drugs ruled and ruined lives, where pornography was flaunted in Midtown, where the Darwinian law of survival of the fittest applied. Yet the city had an irresistible fascination, almost like "the fascination of the abominable." It seemed the only place in the world to be.

Julie Fallowfield explained the duties of the agent. Should I enlist her as my agent she intended to make a multiple submission of the manuscript to the best publishing houses in the business–Random House, Simon & Schuster, Knopf, Macmillan, and others. She had no doubt they would trip over each other to publish my "extraordinary book."

"When can you have it completed?"

"In a couple of months."

I then told her that I needed a few days to consider her offer of representation. I telephoned Ned and told him that I was flattered by his praise of my manuscript and his willingness to offer me a contract, but that I preferred to first acquire an agent who would get me the best deal.

We discussed the pros and cons of various agents under the circumstances, and Ned spoke encouragingly of the prospects of an offer from Macmillan.

"I think I will be better off with an agent," I insisted. "I'm new to this business and I need professional guidance."

"All right," he agreed. "If that's what you want, go ahead. Who's your agent?"

"I'm talking to Julie Fallowfield."

"Oh, I know Julie. I'll be in touch with her. Call me anytime. I want your book and I'm determined to get it."

As if my good fortune was not enough, a few days later a letter came from the Poynter Institute. I had won the fellowship. Then another miracle followed a few days later. Marianne Kellogg called from the Columbia Journalism School. I had been accepted on a full-tuition scholarship. Stan called the following morning and I told him the good news.

"Well, I don't know what to say," he said. "It seems you're off and running."

"Do I really deserve all this?"

"Well, you've worked hard."

"Thanks for believing in me, Stan," I said.

Stan informed me that Arthur had recommended that I see his literary agent, Fifi Oscard, in order to have a choice between agents. I again went into Manhattan and met Fifi, a kindhearted, convivial but astute veteran agent. She was well known in literary and entertainment circles, having represented performers like Orson Welles, Jack Palance, Warren Beatty, and Bernadette Peters, and writers like Piri Thomas, the author of the classic *Down These Mean Streets*. I also conferred with Kevin McShane, her tall, sharp-minded Irish associate, who negotiated many of the book deals.

"This is a fantastic book," Kevin said. "I have never read anything like it. Once I began it I couldn't put it down. Did all these things you write about really happen?"

"Yes."

"Americans, even those who are experts on South Africa and apartheid, have never spoken so vividly and dramatically about the horrors of the terrible system," Kevin said. "It's like slavery."

"That's one reason I wrote the book," I replied. "I knew that much had been written about the politics and economics of apartheid. But few books have told the human story. Especially from the black man's point of view."

"I have a feeling that this book will do for blacks in South Africa what *Manchild in the Promised Land* did for blacks in America," Kevin said prophetically. "But it must be well packaged. And there are some scenes which may have to be rewritten."

"I don't want the style changed," I said. "Its imperfections, whatever they are, are part of its message. I wrote this book as I felt it, not as I thought it."

"No, no, no," Kevin said. "You don't get my point. I won't change your style for all the world. After all, it is your style, your tone, which makes this book powerful. All I mean is that some things would have to be more clearly explained to the average American reader who, you must admit, hardly knows anything about the true nature of the apartheid tragedy."

A few days later I agreed to be represented by Fifi Oscard Associates. I conveyed my decision to Julie Fallowfield, and she wished me well. I gave Kevin and Fifi my address and telephone number in St. Petersburg, Florida, where I was headed the following week to begin my internship at the Poynter Media Institute.

Several of the fellows in the writing program were graduates of Princeton University, Bennington College, and Carleton College. They displayed command of the liberal arts. They spoke with ease about existentialism, St. Thomas Aquinas, Plato, and semiotics. The newswriting program was under the direction of Roy Peter Clark, a well-known journalist, media critic, and writing teacher whose antics, gregariousness, and penchant for sports won him the friendship of all the fellows.

The focus of the program was on writing. Day after day we wrote and rewrote. Roy led us in severe but constructive criticism of each other's stories. We learned how to write under deadline, how to edit, how to arrange a news story in the pyramid style, and how to identify the most important parts of a story. Roy was fastidious about the English language, a fact which delighted me. He encouraged us to adopt as models the best writers, something I had tried to do all along. One day we read and analyzed an essay which had a profound effect on my temperament as a writer. It was George Orwell's "Politics and the English Language." I agreed with Orwell's contention that "the decline of language must ultimately have political and economic causes," and that a good deal of modern English prose is full of bad habits spread by imitation which can be avoided if the writer is willing to take the trouble to think clearly. Even at college I was scornful of many modern novels because of what I considered their abuse of the English language masquerading as innovations and improvements. My reading fare consisted mainly of classics, which is why I considered a collection of Shakespeare's works, or Gibbon's *Decline and Fall of the Roman Empire*, the perfect light reading for a bus or plane ride.

Bad English prose, Orwell went on, arises whenever "the concrete melts into the abstract and no one seems to be able to think of turns of speech that are not hackneyed; prose consists less and less of words chosen for their meaning, and more and more of words tacked together like sections of a prefabricated henhouse." That short essay became my literary Bible. I no longer felt odd or defensive about my preference for good literature and for good English.

The *St. Petersburg Times*, the South's largest independent and locally owned newspaper, became our laboratory. I was fascinated at how a major daily was put together; the electric energy in the newsroom, the teamwork, the competition, the idealistic resolve among journalists to "afflict the comfortable and comfort the afflicted." Midway through the program Roy offered to submit any interesting and timely story we wrote to the *St. Petersburg Times* for publication. There was competition among us each time we fanned out into the community hunting for newsworthy stories. Aware that any story from the community would most likely already have been covered by a staff reporter at the *St. Petersburg Times*, it occurred to me that I might be able to come up with story ideas of which I would be the sole or immediately available authority. I came from South Africa, I had lived in a ghetto, I was a student of race relations, I was writing a book of many themes, so I decided to use my experience to generate ideas.

My first article in the *St. Petersburg Times*, for which I was paid $170, was about the 1984 Summer Olympics in Los Angeles. Since 1960 South Africa had been banned from Olympic competition; I wrote a piece explaining the reasons why. This early success confirmed my belief that instead of seeking to become a journalist as an impersonal reporter, I should write about things I knew without graduate degrees or years of apprenticeship. All that remained for me to do was hone my skills. And I could do so by wide and discriminating reading and writing. I made several friends on the paper, among them Clay Bennett, the cartoonist; Andrew Barnes, editor and president; and Malcolm Jones, the book editor, for whom I later reviewed several books by white South African writers.

One day a phone call came from New York. Kevin and Fifi had sent out several copies of my manuscript and top publishers were eager to bid on it. An auction date had been set. Simon & Schuster, Knopf, Random House, and Macmillan were among the bidders. I was stunned. Wasn't this, after all, the same book which frustration almost made me consign to the flames? Over the next few days I received calls from editors at the various publishing houses eager to entice me into selling the book to them.

"I have edited books by South African writers," one said. "It will be an honor to edit your book, which is the finest I have ever read on the subject of apartheid."

"I grew up in the South," another said. "I was involved in the civil rights movement and I have the sensitivity to edit your book well. Don't let money be the only issue that decides who gets your book."

The bidding began. I was told by Kevin that normally a writer's first book, especially one on a topic that seemed so far removed from American society, would fetch a modest advance. The next call I received from Kevin informed me that Knopf and Macmillan were the two bidders remaining. "Ned really wants the book," Kevin said.

Ned Chase, a child of the Depression, was a Phi Beta Kappa graduate of Princeton University and had taught English at Stanford University. He had a long and distinguished record as a liberal editor. While vice president and editor-in-chief of New American Library he had purchased the paperback rights to *Manchild in the Promised Land* for some $100,000, and helped make the book a major best-seller. He had recently published James North's book on South Africa entitled *Freedom Rising*.

A few days later Macmillan's counteroffer came. They were prepared to pay $35,000 for the hardcover rights to the manuscript. Thirty-five thousand dollars! That was more money than I had ever dreamed of having. With that kind of money I could build my family a decent home, set up a trust fund for the education of my siblings, and still have a small fortune left to live independently and write in America.

27

MOVE TO NEW YORK CITY; DISENCHANTMENT WITH JOURNALISM SCHOOL; STAY AT INTERNATIONAL HOUSE

Shortly after I signed the contract with Macmillan, I moved to New York City to begin my term at the Columbia Graduate School of Journalism. I was part of the class of 1985. After the first few weeks of classes, I realized that I had made a mistake in going to journalism school. Having rebelled against apartheid laws which sought to prescribe my place in life, having throughout college resisted pressures to have me conform to the role of a dutiful black student who should be grateful and deferential to his white benefactors, having defied attempts by black Americans to define what sort of a black person I should be, I could not see myself accepting, this late in life, when I had already found my calling, the general attitude that prevailed at the J-school that I and my colleagues were essentially blank slates upon which sage professors were entrusted with the solemn duty of inscribing inviolable precepts on how we should write. I knew I was already a writer, imperfect though my skills were. I could not see myself ignoring or discarding my writing style, let alone suppressing my feelings about life, which invariably colored everything I wrote, in pursuit of the sacrosanct "objective" journalism—a thing I doubt exists.

There were exceptions. In a once-a-week course, Journalism, the Law and Society, taught jointly by *New York Times* columnist Anthony Lewis, author of *Gideon's Trumpet*, and Benno Schmidt, then dean of the Columbia Law School and now president of Yale University, fellow graduate students and I vigorously discussed celebrated First Amendment cases. One case was *CBS* vs. *Westmoreland*, in which General William C. Westmoreland, America's Vietnam commander and army chief of staff, sued "CBS Reports" for allegedly libeling him in its 1982 documentary "The Uncounted Enemy: A Vietnam Deception." The class listened to a well-reasoned presentation by the lawyers for CBS, asked questions, and discussed various thorny elements of the case. The course taught me that journalists, by virtue of the power they had under the First Amendment, had to be responsible in its use.

Another course I enjoyed was Writing with Style, taught by Peter Prescott, a senior writer and book reviewer at *Newsweek*. The suggested reading list included works by Edmund Wilson, H. L. Mencken, Strunk and White, George Bernard Shaw, James Agee, Ernest Hemingway, and George Orwell. The class was a departure from straightforward, objective journalism: it was designed to help us acquire a "highly distinctive style and a developed personality—a persona."

Despite my enjoyment of the two classes, I still opposed the overall emphasis at the journalism school. I had half a mind to withdraw from the program. But such a move might result in serious complications. Aside from disappointing all those well-intentioned people—Marianne Kellogg and others—who were partly responsible for my being accepted and awarded the $10,000 tuition scholarship, by dropping out I stood to lose my student visa. Then there was the undeniable fact that I wanted to experience New York City. I wanted to see Harlem and to enjoy the intellectual stimulation the city's many incongruous aspects never failed to provide.

Also, if I quit the J-school I could be thrown out of International House—I-House, as it was popularly called—where I rented a room on the condition that I remain a full-time graduate student. The environment I found at I-House was unique and refreshing. Founded sixty-three years ago by the Rockefellers and the Cleveland H. Dodge family, I-House, a gray ten-story building located next to Riverside Church on the Upper West Side, was dedicated to fostering peace, brotherhood, and sisterhood among the nations of the world. It sought to accomplish this partly by offering affordable housing to about 530 graduate students, interns, and trainees, 30 percent of whom were Americans; the remainder represented about eighty foreign nations. In turn, residents of I-House interacted with each other and with the New York City community.

I-House regularly sponsored lectures by such notables as Jesse

Jackson; Justice Sandra Day O'Connor; Mayor Ed Koch; Malcolm Fraser, the former prime minister of Australia; Beverly Sills; and Bishop Tutu, the Nobel Peace Prize winner. There were also weekly movies, parties, athletic events, and free or discounted theatre tickets. I-House also had its resident orchestra and dance troupe. The residents came in all stripes—from revolutionaries and flaming liberals to apolitical musicians and neoconservative business students. During meals I found myself engaged in heated and far-ranging discussions with students from Latin America, Scandinavia, Europe, the Middle East, the Far East, North America, Australia, and Africa.

The regular intellectual diet of my coterie, which included Americans who planned to work for UN development and relief agencies and the Peace Corps, was literature, culture, and politics— more specifically, criticizing the Reagan administration's bad policies. We blamed the administration for giving comfort to the apartheid regime through its policy of "constructive engagement"; for the perpetuation of the contra war in Nicaragua; and for propping up the dictatorships of Duvalier, Pinochet, Noriega, and Marcos. On the home front, the Reagan administration was charged with failing to protect the hard-won gains of the civil rights movement; with worsening poverty and homelessness through its "reverse Robin Hood economic policies" of giving tax breaks to the rich and slashing social programs for the poor; and with fostering, in the name of "America is back and standing tall," a false patriotism which distorted U.S. foreign policy and made Americans disliked around the world.

The thought didn't escape my mind that America was one of the few countries in the world where, because of the right to freedom of speech, even foreigners could openly criticize the government, without fear of persecution or imprisonment. By contrast, in South Africa, in the Soviet Union, in Eastern Europe, in various countries throughout Latin America, Asia, the Middle East, and Africa, governments routinely harass, jail, torture, and even murder their critics.

But our criticisms were not limited to the Reagan administration. The Kremlin also came under fire for its blind faith in communism, its military intervention in countries like Afghanistan, its support for totalitarian regimes on the left, and its suppression of free speech and violation of human rights in the Soviet Union. The corruption, brutality, and despotism of many African governments were also condemned. The point was made that black totalitarian rule only impoverished Africa, encouraged stereotypes of Africans in the West, and undermined the struggle against apartheid by justifying the fears many white South Africans have, that should blacks take over, it would be "one man, one vote" only one time.

It is unconscionable that millions of Africans were asked to make great sacrifices during the bloody struggles against colonialism, only to end up, when independence had been achieved, being oppressed, exploited, starved, and butchered by despots of their own color. How does one justify the lavish palaces and personal wealth of dictators like President Mobutu of Zaire, and their families and cronies? Zaire is one of the poorest countries on earth; its social needs are dire and manifold; its per capita income of $180 is the eighth lowest in the world—yet the personal fortune of President Mobutu is estimated at $5 billion. Incidentally, Mobutu, whom many believe was responsible for the murder of nationalist Patrice Lumumba, "the hero of Africa," came to power in 1965 with assistance from the U.S. government and the CIA.

How does one explain the cruel withholding of relief supplies such as medicine and food, to starving innocent men, women, and children, by the warring factions in the civil wars in Ethiopia and the Sudan? And how does one explain the massacre in 1987 of nearly five thousand subjugated Hutus by the Tutsi tribe in Burundi, a black-ruled country in central Africa? The Hutus make up 85 percent of Burundi's population; the Tutsis, led by strongman Jean Baptiste Bagaza, are a minority much like the Afrikaners and control the economy and government, including a brutal army. The tragic thing is that such corruption and genocide often meet with little outrage and punishment from other African countries and the world community. Why? I often ask myself. Is exploiting, starving, and slaughtering black people only reprehensible when whites do it? Or are there certain crimes against humanity about which the world simply doesn't care?

28 I CONTEMPLATE QUITTING JOURNALISM SCHOOL; MORE VIOLENCE IN SOUTH AFRICA

The intellectual stimulation at I-House was unending. Daily in the dining hall and in the lobby I listened in fascination as Palestinians, Nicaraguans, Afghans, Filipinos, Chileans, Sikhs, and black Americans talked about their various struggles for justice and freedom. Some advocated peaceful solutions; others insisted that violence should be met with violence and bullets with bullets. FBI agents were rumored to be in our midst but that did not deter most students from professing openly their radical ideas. How I wished I had had such stimulation during my years as an undergraduate. But I consoled myself with the thought that those years had not exactly been wasted. I had used them to stockpile ideas and to sharpen my reasoning and convictions through introspection. Most people mistook me for a graduate of one of the Ivy League schools and were surprised to learn I had attended a small college they had never heard of.

"It doesn't matter what school one attends," I would say. "If one has access to books, can think critically, is open-minded, and dares to be a Daniel, one will mature intellectually."

There was probably an egotistical element in all this. But in the main it was my love for the free exchange of ideas, the unfettered pursuit of knowledge, the idealism that the world could be changed for the better if only people had causes and worked together, which spurred me, and made me a rebel against any form of intellectual tyranny and student apathy wherever I found them.

I began making my dissatisfaction about the J-school known. Classmates warned me about the consequences of my actions.

"You're throwing your future away, Mark," said Michele Nayman, an Australian journalist and fiction writer. "Do you know how coveted a J-school degree is?"

"I do."

"Don't you want it? Imagine the sort of job a person of your talent and background can get."

"I don't want it at the expense of being unable to write what I really want to say."

"What do you mean?"

"Straight journalism is not for me. I just can't keep my feelings out of anything I write."

"Then pretend."

"I can't pretend."

"For God's sake, Mark, don't be stubborn."

I wasn't being stubborn. Deep down I believed that a person learned how to write not by going to journalism school but by writing. I continued attending classes, doing the assignments, and participating in the lectures, but my heart was not in it. My disenchantment was compounded by the depressing news from home. The Pretoria regime had once more cracked down on black dissent. A group of mourners had recently been massacred, churches fire-bombed, activists detained without trial and held incommunicado, and freedom fighters hanged as terrorists. I had recently written a couple of letters home but received no reply. For some reason whenever there was an outbreak of black unrest, letters sent through the post office in Alexandra failed to reach my family. Presumably the white authorities intercepted my letters to intimidate me into not writing or speaking out on the apartheid issue at this time. I tried calling my mother's workplace but was told by a frightened white woman that my mother no longer worked there. I asked the white woman to please contact her in Alexandra as I was concerned about the safety of the family. The white woman, for whom my mother had worked for over four years, did not know where Alexandra was; neither did she know my mother's full name. To her, my mother had simply been "Magdaline, the girl," a piece of labor, discarded when no longer needed. I began to show my anxiety in class. My mind was plagued by the question "What if my family has been killed along with the dozens who have died in Alexandra since the new violence erupted?"

I approached Osborne Elliot, dean of the J-school, and asked him for help in contacting my family. He had contacts in the Johannesburg

English-speaking community. A few days later the reply came back that my family was still alive but financially strapped. I was due to receive the first installment of my advance, so I made plans to send some money home.

RELATING TO OTHER SOUTH AFRICANS AT I-HOUSE; MY FRIEND PHISTOS; REACHING OUT TO THE CHILDREN OF HARLEM

There was a small community of black South African students at I-House, many of whom kept such a low profile that one would have had great difficulty identifying them as being from a country seething with injustice, violence, and death. Because of my antiapartheid activity many of these students were wary of associating with me, perhaps for fear of reprisals from the regime. I knew that the regime was monitoring my actions. I had been indirectly warned to desist, reminded that I still had family in South Africa whose safety I was jeopardizing with my activism. But I had crossed the Rubicon; there was no turning back. I could not pretend that I had not tasted of freedom, that I had not learned what it meant to be a human being, that I had not discovered that black South Africans, too, had unalienable rights and that apartheid had to be abolished for my compatriots to enjoy those rights. I couldn't renege on the promise I had made to myself when I left South Africa, that I would use every ounce of my strength to fight for what was right, no matter the personal price to be paid.

I was therefore impatient with those black South African students who seemingly had allowed themselves to be cowed and silenced by the apartheid regime. I sought to reason with them about the duty we all owed to our brothers and sisters back home to speak out, to tell the world about the realities of apartheid from the black man's, the victim's, point of view, but some dismissed my exhortations with versions of "prescribe not us our duty." A few, who came from middle-class families and were accustomed to looking down on those like me from peasant stock, resented my outspokenness. They accused me of currying favor with Americans without the credentials, of having no right to speak in behalf of black South Africans.

"I represent nobody but my own conscience and convictions," I replied. "For as long as I'm a human being, I'll speak out against the suffering of other human beings without a prompter."

I further made it known that I would not isolate myself from other students out of some false sense of black pride or solidarity. Like David Bomar back at Limestone, in the cafeteria I sat at tables where the conversation was serious. Two black South African students came up to me one day and said, "Mark, what you're saying is right. We are all part of the struggle, whether we like it or not. We too want to do something. There's a lot of lies being believed by the American people about what is truly happening in South Africa. We want to do something to change that. But we still have families back home and we're worried about what the regime may do to them."

"I have family, too, and I worry about them," I replied. "But the truth about apartheid must be revealed. If we don't speak for ourselves, others will. And they won't tell the whole truth, however sympathetic they may be to our cause, because they don't know the black man's life as we know it. That is one of the problems with blacks in this country, too. They have all this freedom but they let others champion their cause. You must remember that few white people will put the interests of black folks before those of their own people."

"But we're not politicians."

"Neither am I. But I'm a human being, and I know right from wrong. I know that in South Africa people, our own brothers and sisters, are suffering and dying. You don't have to spout party lines or wave banners. You should make a contribution as best you can. You know that the Pretoria regime has saturated America with propaganda about what is the cause of the violence and who's to blame. That has to be countered, neutralized, overcome."

"Yes. But it's easy for you to fight because you're a writer. You're good with words. We're not writers."

"You don't have to be a writer to speak the truth. Just tell people about your experiences in South Africa. Tell them about what you saw, what you felt, what you suffered, what you endured, what you and your comrades believe in. Tell them about life in Soweto, Guguletu, Crossroads, and the other ghettos where you've lived. Tell them about life in the impoverished and corrupt homelands. That sort of personal testimony is worth a thousand political speeches," I said.

"The regime has informants all over the place, you know that. How do we know that you're not one of them? How do we know that you're not telling us to jump out of the frying pan and into the fire?" one asked.

I marveled at the reach of apartheid: it could influence the way people thousands of miles away thought, felt, and acted; it could silence them at will; it could defeat them without a shot being fired. It now became clear why some of these students isolated themselves from the rest of the I-House community, why they consciously or unconsciously expected others to fight their own battle, and why, living on the edge of Harlem, daily witnessing and reading about the effects of racism on black America, they failed to make known the similarities between the destruction of black life in the ghettos of America and the destruction of black life in the ghettos where they came from, by some of the same forces: drugs, teen pregnancy, gangs, black-on-black violence, white racism, crime, alcoholism, negative role models, and police brutality, as in the cases of Eleanor Bumpurs and Michael Stewart.

Michael Stewart, a twenty-five-year-old black artist's model, was beaten to death in September 1983 by eleven white transit police officers for allegedly scrawling graffiti on a subway wall. On October 29, 1984, Eleanor Bumpurs, a sixty-six-year-old black grandmother, was shot to death in her Bronx apartment by a policeman's shotgun at close range. Arthritic, overweight, with heart problems and high blood pressure, Eleanor Bumpurs was accused of resisting arrest and threatening six burly, armed white police officers, wearing bullet-proof vests, who came to force this highly disturbed invalid to leave her home for unpaid back rent.

The few black South African students who felt the truth spoke out, despite the dangers involved. Among them were Phistos Stone, a native of Soweto, and Joseph Diescho, a Namibian. Joseph, a Fulbright scholar at Columbia University, later wrote *Born of the Sun,* a fascinating and revealing novel about the history and plight of the Namibian people under South African occupation. Phistos was a short, soft-spoken graduate student in labor relations at the New York Institute of Technology. His ambition was to acquire the know-how to help strengthen the fledgling labor movement in South Africa, which has become a formidable vehicle for change. When his friends began seeing him in my company, they ostracized him.

"Don't worry, Phistos," I said to him. "You'll always have a friend in me. In life always do what you think is right, not what will make you popular."

Phistos and I became steadfast friends. He came to me with his problems and I went to him with mine. We pledged to ourselves that we would do everything to raise the consciousness of students by sharing with them our own experiences of the injustices of apartheid.

At I-House there were also a few white South Africans who had just arrived in the U.S. Along with the flood of white professionals—several thousands a month—who were emigrating from South Africa because they saw no peaceful resolution of apartheid in sight, there was now a steady stream of young white men leaving the country to avoid being drafted into the apartheid army. Two of these whites—André and Andrew—were staying at I-House for a few months. In their early twenties, both were active members of the United Democratic Front (UDF), the largest antiapartheid group, whose patrons included Bishop Tutu, Walter Sisulu, Nelson Mandela, and Reverend Alan Boesak.

The UDF, which has over one million followers, is a nonracial grass-roots movement and includes churches, labor unions, community groups, and high school and university students. The UDF is relentlessly persecuted by the government because its existence proves that blacks and whites can find common ground in the struggle for justice. At the writing of this book, the UDF, along with over a dozen other antiapartheid groups, had been banned. In other words, non-violent protest against the injustices of apartheid has been effectively outlawed in South Africa.

One evening in the cafeteria I approached André and Andrew and we became acquainted. They told me about the shock of finding themselves reviled by Americans as racist simply because they were white South Africans. This unfortunate situation is mainly the result of the simplistic understanding many Americans have of apartheid, which views all blacks as saints and all whites as devils. The irony was that back home, André and Andrew, as members of the UDF, were at the forefront of the black liberation struggle. But what was even more shocking to André was being shunned by most black South Africans at I-House.

"There's a great deal of fear among black South Africans in the U.S.," I explained to André and Andrew. "Your being shunned may be because your whiteness makes you suspect."

"But back home we are part of the struggle," André said. "We've campaigned against the draft, we've participated in countless anti-apartheid rallies, we've denounced the regime and called for the release of Nelson Mandela and all other political prisoners and for the legalization of the ANC. You know, Mark, in the UDF our black comrades consider us brothers."

"I believe you," I said. "And I consider you brothers, too. But remember that to people in whom apartheid has bred paranoia, your very connection with the UDF is reason to be wary of you since all opposition groups in South Africa, particularly the UDF, are full of government informants. And some of these informants are among the most prominent and vociferous critics of apartheid."

André and Andrew shook their heads in amazement and frustration at the realization of how far the tentacles of apartheid reached. Both have since returned home, to continue the internal struggle against apartheid. They smuggled copies of the banned *Kaffir Boy* to give to relatives and friends.

I was at this time writing more commentary articles for the *St. Petersburg Times* on events in South Africa than learning the basics of objective journalism. I poured my time into completing *Kaffir Boy*; wandered about Harlem comparing the black experience there with that in South Africa's ghettos; read the speeches of Malcolm X, the essays of James Baldwin, and the poetry of Langston Hughes; and taught tennis to black youngsters who were part of the I-House tutorial program. I shared with them my experiences growing up in Alexandra, and the important role education had played in my life. I encouraged them never to give up the fight to escape from the ghetto; it could be done, I said, provided they believed in themselves, kept away from drugs and gangs, and never allowed villains to become their role models and peer pressure to force them to do bad things.

I was able to reach many of these youngsters because they trusted me, and considered me a celebrity because I was friends with Stan Smith and Arthur Ashe. It wrung my heart to realize that most of these kids were as impressionable and talented as kids anywhere, but that in their case the lack of positive role models and support systems, the deadly influence and lure of street life, the disintegration of black family life and the attendant loss of positive values, and the inhumanity of life in New York City for the powerless and the have-nots would eventually derail them into the dead-end life of crime and drugs and teenage motherhood.

The only way I could fight their struggle, I clearly saw, was to become a role model to them, in much the same way as Arthur Ashe had been one to me. But I was quick to warn them that they could not all hope to become professional athletes; that they could not all be Diana Ross or Michael Jackson; but that they could all become proud and productive human beings by becoming educated. Many wondered why I made such a big deal about an education, and challenged me to show them blacks who, because of an education, were as famous or as rich as the athletes and entertainers or the drug dealers with the fancy cars, expensive jewelry, flashy clothes, and Rolex watches.

I brought up the names of famous black achievers, including Jesse Jackson, A. Philip Randolph, Harriet Tubman, Paul Robeson, Ralph Bunche, Marian Anderson, Maya Angelou, and George Washington Carver. Except for Jackson, they hardly recognized any of the names.

"These men and women have more power than most of your athletes and entertainers and all of the drug dealers you know."

"What you mean? Do they have a lot of money?" asked a thirteen-year-old boy.

"Many don't. But they have something more valuable than money."

"What could be more valuable than money?" asked a twelve-year-old boy.

"An educated mind."

"What's that?" a fifteen-year-old girl asked facetiously.

"You see, money, fancy clothes, Rolexes, chains, all that can be lost, can be taken away from you. But the treasures in your mind, those no one can ever take away from you. And by the treasures of the mind I mean knowledge. Knowledge of what freedom means. Knowledge of what you can do despite what others may say. Knowledge of what your rights and responsibilities are as an American citizen. Knowledge of how computers work. Knowledge of how to read and write. Knowledge of your true heritage as a black person. And through knowledge one can overcome the greatest oppression of all: mental slavery. Any of you heard of Bob Marley?"

A few had heard the legend's music.

"Well, Bob Marley once wrote a song called 'Redemption Song,' in which he said that to be truly free black people must liberate themselves from mental slavery, and that none but ourselves can free our minds. So instead of getting high on drugs why don't we get high on knowledge? You know, a free mind is a most powerful weapon.

Armed with it you'll be able to fight for what is yours, to define who you are, rather than have others do things for you, set limits to your aspirations, and end up running your life."

Some of the youngsters seemed unable to grasp the full meaning of my words; but there was no doubt that I had made some impression on all of them. I hoped that in time, whatever seeds I had planted in their young minds would blossom into a determination to be educated, to realize their potential as human beings, no matter what the obstacles.

"How many of you visit the library every day?" I asked.

"Every day?"

"Yes, every day," I said.

No one.

"Once a week?"

Out of about a dozen only two girls raised their hands.

"Once a month?"

Still the same two hands.

"Do you love reading and doing your homework?"

A resounding "No" mingled with some laughter.

"How many watch television every day?"

Everyone raised their hands.

"Do you love to watch television?"

A deafening "Yes!"

I knew from experience that most television left black children with a bad self-image, inferiority complexes, and unrealistic expectations. Except for programs like "The Bill Cosby Show," many television programs featured blacks mainly in stereotypical roles. I remember how insignificant I often felt growing up in a white-dominated world in which "black" often stood for bad, buffoonery, filth, and servility, and white stood for good, cleanliness, intelligence, and success. In fact, for a long time, under the label of a "Christian" education, white schoolchildren were taught that blacks had smaller brains and were devoid of normal human feelings. In America no such lessons are now taught (though they were during the heyday of segregation in the South), but many a black child still associates intelligence, beauty, and success with being white.

All this made me want to write and convinced me that I was wasting my time at the journalism school because I already had a cause. Pursuing degrees for their own sake was as pointless as eating, not because one is hungry, but because food is available. I had learned enough. It was time I put my knowledge to practical use.

Having signed the contract with Macmillan under which I promised to deliver the completed manuscript of *Kaffir Boy* by the spring of 1985, and aware that the journalism program required total immersion, I knew that I could not long continue serving two masters. Midway through the first semester I made up my mind to quit. I conferred with Stan. He advised me to stay in school and obtain that "important master's degree."

"You know that a master's degree is a very important credential in America," Stan said. "People will listen to you not because you know anything, but because you have this or that degree, from this or that school."

"I'm aware of that."

"Then how can you throw away a free ride from one of the best journalism schools in America?" Stan asked. "What if your book is a bomb? What would you fall back on?"

I had considered all those reasons and remained determined to leave. Journalism school would not make me a writer if I was not already one, and the surest way to test if I was a writer was by writing. But since leaving journalism school meant losing my visa as a student, I began making plans to apply for a green card. Friends warned me that I was deluding myself into believing I could obtain one, given the friendly attitude of the Reagan administration toward the Botha regime. They reminded me of the case of Dennis Brutus, who was almost deported to Zimbabwe after his request for asylum had been turned down, despite irrefutable evidence that the Pretoria regime was trying to murder him for his activism against apartheid. There were some who believed that Pretoria had secretly requested that he be kicked out of the country.

"What if my application is refused and I'm deported back to South Africa?" I wondered anxiously.

30　I quit J-school; Ellie and Hans Spiegel; immigration trouble

During Christmas of 1984, which I spent on Hilton Head Island, I told Stan that my decision to quit the J-school was final. I was going to devote myself full-time to the writing of *Kaffir Boy*. I received my first check of the advance from Macmillan, a kingly sum of $17,500. I immediately paid Stan $6,000, which he had loaned me to cover my living expenses while I awaited the Macmillan check. I sent $2,000 home through an American friend on a visit to South Africa. Given the problems I was having with the Pretoria regime, I couldn't risk sending the money by mail. I instructed my mother to pay off all her debts, and with the balance open a savings account, and use only the interest to meet the family's daily expenses. Two thousand dollars, substantial money even in America, was a fortune in South Africa: earning fifty dollars a month, my mother would have toiled almost four years to earn $2,000.

Like any person who finds himself with a small fortune, I went on a spending spree. Since childhood I had dreamed of owning a library of my favorite books, believing that a book worth reading was worth owning. So over several weeks I bought about $3,000 worth of classics, including sets of the *Encyclopaedia Britannica*, Harvard Classics, and *Great Books of the Western World*, from my favorite bookstores: the Strand downtown and NRS Books on the corner of Amsterdam Avenue and 118th Street.

Despite ample forewarning, people were hit like a bombshell by the news that I had quit the J-school. Friends questioned my sanity. I was accused of having thrown my future away. Dean Elliot, Marianne

Kellogg, and other administrators attempted to persuade me to remain but I clung to my decision. I was prepared to live with its consequences.

A week after school reopened for the spring term, I received a note in my mailbox informing me that if I was no longer a student, I would have to leave I-House. I went to see Eleanor Spiegel, a white friend and the program director at I-House. Ellie, as she was popularly known, and her husband, Hans, a professor of urban affairs and planning at Hunter College, lived in the suburb of Leonia, New Jersey. Both were liberal Democrats and staunch advocates of civil rights and affirmative action. Hans, a classmate of Coretta Scott King at Antioch College in the 1940s, was a renowned expert on urban affairs. He had served on the President's Task Force in the War Against Poverty and had taught public administration at universities in Kenya, India, Korea, and the Philippines. Before coming to I-House, Ellie, a graduate of Northwestern University in anthropology and sociology, worked for the Fair Housing Administration in New Jersey.

"I've quit journalism school," I told Ellie as we sat in her office. "But I would like to continue living at I-House while I finish my book. Who should I see about this notice?" I showed her the note.

"Someone in admissions should be able to help you," she said.

I went to the admissions office and discussed my situation with John Naughton and Marian Sylla, the admissions coordinators. They told me that the matter might have to be referred to the president of I-House, Gordon Evans. Gordon, a friendly and much-traveled Republican, hobnobbed with the Kissingers and Rockefellers and ran a tight ship at I-House.

"Is there any hope an exception can be made?" I asked.

"We'll see," John said. "But we can't make any promises."

I went back to Ellie and requested that she put in a good word for me should my situation be brought up at a meeting.

"I honestly don't think you'll be kicked out," Ellie reassured me. "If you have to leave, you can always stay at our place. I don't think Hans will mind."

The exception was made and I was allowed to stay at I-House till the end of the school year.

A few days later I received a letter from the foreign student office at Columbia University informing me that if I did not return to the J-school for the spring term, I would be out of status, and the

Immigration and Naturalization Service would have to be notified. Having expected such a move, I promptly went to see my editor, Ned Chase. He spoke to his son, Edward, Jr., a New York lawyer. His son recommended that I see a colleague of his on Madison Avenue who specialized in immigration cases.

"Your situation doesn't look good," the lawyer said, after I described my case. "Your best choice at this moment is to return to school and complete the program."

"But I don't want to. Is there no other visa I can apply for? What about a green card?"

He shook his head solemnly and said, "It's almost impossible for people in your situation to be issued green cards. The INS has tightened the rules for eligibility."

"What can I do?"

"As I said, your best bet is to return to the journalism school and complete the program. With that degree you can possibly find an employer who'd make the green-card application in your behalf."

"But I don't want to return to school," I insisted. I had already lost the remaining half of the $10,000 tuition scholarship, which, upon my withdrawal, had been given to other needy students.

After a brief pause the lawyer said, "There's one category of work permits for which you may be eligible. But I'll be frank with you: that, too, is risky."

"Nothing is too risky for me," I said in desperation.

I paid the lawyer a deposit of $1,500 and he immediately went to work. He instructed me to gather information that would present an effective case to the INS that I was "a person of distinguished merit and ability" and therefore should be granted an H-1 work permit. The basis for the application would be that at the age of twenty-four, despite having suffered numerous deprivations under apartheid, I had graduated with honors from an American college, edited a campus newspaper, regularly wrote articles for influential newspapers, and was about to have an important book published by a prestigious house. I submitted along with the application letters of recommendation from the following: Ned Chase at Macmillan Publishing Co., Roy Peter Clark at the Poynter Institute, and Andrew Barnes, editor and president of the *St. Petersburg Times*. All sent the lawyer panegyrics on my modest abilities. Weeks of anxiety followed, during which I explored alternatives should my application be rejected. There were few.

31

I MEET GAIL; THREATS AGAINST MY LIFE; AP-
PLYING FOR A NEW PASSPORT; EDITING *Kaffir Boy*

One winter's evening after I had returned from Christmas break at Stan and Margie's on Hilton Head, I was in the laundry room of I-House taking my shrunken and deformed clothes out of the overheated dryer when I recognized two fellow journalism students, Katie King and Gail Ernsberger. Katie, a slim, tall American, had studied in Spain and now works for Reuters.

Gail, twenty-three, tall and athletic looking with short blond hair, was describing to Katie her visit to a shelter for battered women in Harlem. I joined their conversation and soon the three of us were discussing various women's issues. During our talk Gail remarked that she was amazed by my understanding of and compassion for women, and we parted with a feeling of mutual respect for one another.

A few days later I was preparing for my regular evening exercise when I ran into Gail again. I found her doing sit-ups and stretching out in the I-House gym after a solo run through Riverside Park. Unaccustomed to finding anyone there, I hesitated for a moment at the door, then entered carrying my tennis rackets and jump rope. I commented on the cold weather, and we fell into small talk. She told me she loved snow, since she came from Minnesota, and that her favorite sport was cross-country skiing. I made her laugh with my stories of how amazed I was at seeing my first snowfall in America. I thought snowflakes would hurt, like hail, when they landed on me.

I started practicing my ground strokes by hitting the tennis ball smoothly and rhythmically against the wall. As usual I had brought more than one racket with me, in case a string broke, and a basketful of tennis balls. Gail asked if she could join me. She said she had not played tennis much since she was eleven, so I gave her a few pointers.

We played for nearly an hour. As she prepared to leave, in an unexpected burst of courage that surprised even myself, I asked her if she wanted to accompany me to the Volvo Masters Tennis Championships at Madison Square Garden on Sunday afternoon.

"I'd love to," Gail replied.

With Stan's help, I was able to get two good seats for the tournament. Sunday morning I called Gail's room.

"Could I take a rain check?" she asked.

"Of course," I replied, stifling my surprise and disappointment. Though I found someone else to accompany me, I remained puzzled by Gail's sudden change of mind. When I returned from Madison Square Garden, I found in my mailbox a kind note from Gail. In it she regretted that too much schoolwork had forced her to miss the tennis match. I wrote her back and proposed another date.

In the days that followed, we spent as much time together as possible. When she was not working on her master's project on foreign artists in the East Village or attending a Russian class at Barnard or developing photographs in the darkroom, and when I was not busy writing the second half of *Kaffir Boy*, we would go to museums or for walks. I recall our walking along the rugged cliffs near the Cloisters, arm in arm, discussing the tapestries and unicorns we had just seen in the monastery. We spent hours at the Museum of Natural History, in the Africa section, where I pointed out the traditional toys, music instruments, masks, and dresses, and explained to her the religion and customs of my ancestors. We exchanged classical music and reggae tapes and books; she was fond of Russian writers like Tolstoy and Dostoevsky. I would read her my favorite poems and she would read me passages from books she found thought-provoking and would serenade me on her guitar. I knew I was falling in love with this sensitive woman.

As I got to know Gail better, I learned she had graduated near the top of her class from Blake School in Minneapolis, which she attended on a merit scholarship and where she starred in track and cross-country skiing. She had previously attended public schools in Ohio, Texas, and Minneapolis. Her family moved so much because her father, David, a former pastor who had attended Yale Divinity School and Union Theological Seminary, kept being promoted to churches with larger and larger congregations. In 1972 the family moved to

Austin, where her father received his Ph.D. in clinical psychology at the University of Texas. He is now a practicing consulting psychologist in Minneapolis and has written three books on Christian education and reviving the church. Gail's mother, Deborah Scott, the daughter of a Congregational minister who was Richard Nixon's pastor in Washington, graduated from Mount Holyoke in Massachusetts and is a schoolteacher for children with learning disabilities.

Gail's parents had raised her to believe that racism was an evil. Her father's sermons regularly dealt with civil rights issues, and some congregations found him too "radical." In 1961, as a minister at the Countryside Presbyterian Church in Saginaw, Michigan, he preached on "Housing Segregation and Christian Justice." Another time he delivered a sermon on gay liberation to a conservative congregation in Westchester, New York, and was never invited back. One time in Texas, Gail's mother, while driving Gail and her two schoolmates home, overheard one of the girls use the word "nigger." She slammed on the brakes and ordered the girl to walk home. The girl and her friend got out, and later told Gail that they thought her mother was "weird" for being upset over a term their parents regularly used. It may have been this type of background that made Gail see me first as a person, not a black.

From Blake, Gail had gone to Brown University, where she graduated magna cum laude in East European Studies and was influenced by writer Susan Sontag and other feminist professors there. She was fluent in Hungarian and German and conversant in Russian, had traveled extensively throughout Eastern and Western Europe, and studied for five months at the University of Budapest. Her ambition was to become a foreign correspondent.

As the trust between us deepened, we occasionally discussed my precarious status. She was concerned for my safety and was surprised that I seemed resigned to the fact that I might be deported.

"Maybe going back home may not be a bad idea," I said. "I've been away nearly seven years. And my family is suffering without me."

"But you may be imprisoned or killed once Pretoria gets hold of you."

"I wouldn't be the first one."

On one rare occasion when I was able to reach my family by phone at a neighbor's home in Alexandra, I told my mother about Gail. Though Gail was sitting right beside me, she could not understand a word of the conversation, which was in Tsonga. My mother insisted on speaking to her, so Gail got on the phone and said a few words, which I'm certain my mother did not understand but was very happy to hear anyhow. I tried to tell my mother about the book I was writing, but she only wanted to hear more about Gail.

"When are you getting married?" she demanded. "Where are my grandchildren?" Apparently my mother could somehow tell from Gail's voice that she was white, for she said, "Did you know there's no apartheid in marriage anymore?" She was referring to the recent repeal of the Mixed Marriages Act. Gail and I simply laughed with embarrassment at my mother's eagerness, not realizing that any of my mother's dreams for us as a couple would ever come true.

I wrote furiously from morning to afternoon, determined to have the book completed before the INS handed down its judgment. Gail was also growing disillusioned with the journalism school. One time she was sent to do a story about paramedics in Harlem. She interviewed several blacks in the four hours she was there, and wrote a fine piece on a black paramedic's rage against discrimination in his profession. Upon evaluating the story, Gail's professor told her that she had been too "caught up with the emotions" of her subject. Like myself, Gail was finding it too hard to keep her feelings out of her stories, and one after the other, her assignments were returned with the following remarks: "Keep your opinions to yourself. Stick to the facts. Don't show emotion. Don't wear your heart on your sleeve. This is editorial, not news." But Gail persevered in the program and eventually earned her degree.

Despite my hectic schedule—I wrote ten to fifteen pages a day—I still found time to write commentary for newspapers on the deteriorating situation in South Africa. In April 1985, following the massacre of black protesters in one of the ghettos, I wrote a piece, published in *Newsday*, entitled "Can Apartheid End Peacefully?" In it I attempted to show why blacks were turning into radicals and revolutionaries and why they believed that only a violent revolution could bring about the complete abolition of the apartheid system. I concluded the article with the following statement:

> Just as it took the American Revolution to end Britain's tyranny over these United States, just as it took the U.S. Civil War to eradicate slavery, just as it took World War II to vanquish the

Nazis, it is clear that apartheid will last only as long as there is no *telling* cost for it.

Moral outrage and condemnatory speeches are "costs" Pretoria can live with. As for the new constitution for whites, Coloureds, and Asians only, and the vague promises of as yet undefined political rights for urban blacks, these are only attempts to make the chains of apartheid comfortable. Apartheid, a form of twentieth-century slavery, is inherently evil and cannot be reformed.

Such rhetoric brought threats against my life. I received about half a dozen calls, all male voices. "Be careful, Kaffir boy," said one caller with a South African accent. "You're playing with fire. Stop attacking whites or else you'll be very sorry." Another caller, with an American accent, after calling me a communist, asked when I would start condemning black-on-black violence and black totalitarian rule throughout Africa. I knew that my dossier at the South African consulate in New York was growing with each article I wrote and each speech I delivered, and that my life and my family's were increasingly endangered. But the fact that my mother approved of my actions and urged me to keep on fighting lessened the guilt I sometimes felt at jeopardizing their lives by my activism. I warned Gail that BOSS—the Bureau of State Security—might already know about her connection with me. I did not want to scare her, but I felt I had to let her know that by spending time with me, she had unwittingly become involved in South African politics.

One day I received a call from the immigration lawyer.

"Do you have a valid passport?" he asked.

"No."

"What!"

"I lost it sometime back and have been meaning to apply for a new one."

"Oh, hell," he said. "How do you hope to travel without a passport? How quickly can you get a new one?"

"I don't know," I replied. "I'm not even sure the South African government will give me one because of my attacks against apartheid."

"You need a passport," he said. "I'm expecting a verdict soon on your application from the INS. Should you be granted the work permit, you will have to get it stamped on your passport. That means going to a U.S. consulate abroad and reentering the States."

Oh, boy, what would I do now? Dare I face officials of the Pretoria regime, whose consulate on Park Avenue had lately been besieged by antiapartheid protesters and was now being moved to an obscure location? I had attended a couple of the protests, which had been videotaped by South African agents. What would be their reaction when I appeared and requested a passport? Was it worth my while even to try?

I showed up at the heavily guarded consulate one morning and went to the window and identified myself. I was given such looks I feared that I might never leave the building alive. The officials were brusque with me. The chief of the consulate even came out and got a glimpse of me.

"Can I see your reference book [passbook], please?" the woman behind the thick glass asked.

I was enraged. How dare she request my passbook.

"I don't have it. I lost it." In fact, I had ripped to pieces the hated document shortly after arriving in the U.S. in 1978. Its sight evoked painful memories of midnight pass raids, humiliating interrogations, and police brutality.

"That will delay the processing of your application," she said matter-of-factly.

Did she think this was South Africa where I was expected to carry the damn thing with me all the time and produce it upon demand?

She handed me several forms and told me to obtain a set of fingerprints. As I prepared to leave I had the audacity to request that they expedite my application as I needed to travel soon.

"It should be ready in a few weeks," the woman said with a smile.

I had a feeling she was lying. I nevertheless thanked her and wished her good-day.

I brought the completed forms back, along with the fingerprints, which I had made at a Harlem police precinct. A few weeks later I called the consulate and was told that Pretoria was having difficulties processing my application without my passbook, that a thorough background check had to be made, and that I would be notified as soon as the passport was ready.

It took me only two months to write the final three hundred pages of the manuscript. My editors at Macmillan were surprised and happy.

"Authors are notorious for requesting extensions," Ned said.

"Well, I figured I'd better have the book completed before I'm deported," I said, smiling.

"They won't deport you," Ned said. "The United States government will never allow those bastards to lay their racist hands on you."

"You don't know the Reagan administration," I said. "It has been trying to deport opponents of its tyrant friends left and right."

"Then we'd better get this book out soon," Ned said. He and Dominick, his assistant, promised to edit the manuscript carefully, line by line. That way they could reduce it to reasonable length while improving the quality of the story. When the edited manuscript came back I was outraged by some of the changes I was requested to make. I stormed into Ned and Dominick's office demanding an explanation for what I saw as the mutilation of my book.

"First of all," I fumed, "this is a book about South Africa, not America. Its language and tone should not be changed to suit American tastes."

"You don't understand how this business works, Mark," Ned said. "Dom and I aren't seeking to change your book. Your style is the most effective in telling your story. But you must remember that many Americans aren't familiar with many of the things you describe in the book."

"Then they will learn by reading the book," I said.

"You must help readers along by explaining some of the terms you use," Dominick said. "For instance, what does *sjambok* mean?"

"It's a rawhide whip with a metal tip," I said. "It's used to enforce apartheid."

"But most readers don't know that," Dominick said.

"But *Kaffir Boy* isn't supposed to be a guide to apartheid," I said. "If a reader doesn't understand certain words, he or she should look them up in a good dictionary or gather their meaning from the context. I deliberately used South African words because I wanted the American public to be familiar with another culture. Why does everything have to be Americanized?"

"That's not the issue here, Mark," Ned said. "The real issue is clarity and effectiveness. You must give concrete and specific details."

Despite my protests I adopted several of their recommendations after Ned and Dominick had convinced me of their usefulness. We now addressed the touchy issue of the book's length. It was over six hundred pages long and had to be cut almost in half.

"But to truncate my book in this arbitrary fashion," I cried, "would certainly destroy its power."

"It will make the book better, Mark, believe me," Ned said.

"How better?"

"Because parts of it are overwritten," Ned said.

"But many of the sections you've recommended I should cut out are among the most important in the story."

"You've made the same points elsewhere in the book," Ned said.

The more carefully I thought the changes over, the more convinced I became that shortening the length of the book would make it effective without the story's message being lost or watered down. Over the next month I painstakingly rewrote *Kaffir Boy*. Much of the advice on effective writing I had received from Roy Clark and Peter Prescott came in handy, particularly the following recommendations in George Orwell's essay "Politics and the English Language":

1. Never use a metaphor, simile or other figure of speech which you are used to seeing in print.
2. Never use a long word where a short one will do.
3. If it is possible to cut a word out, always cut it out.
4. Never use the passive where you can use the active.
5. Never use a foreign phrase, a scientific word or a jargon word if you can think of an everyday English equivalent.
6. Break any of these rules sooner than say anything outright barbarous.

SPEECHES AT PREP SCHOOLS; ENCOUNTERS WITH RACISM IN HOUSING; MORE THREATS AGAINST MY LIFE; DENIED PASSPORT; THE RULE OF LAW

On May 7, 1985, I was invited to speak before children of the wealthy and powerful at the prestigious Spence School for girls in Manhattan. Before the speech, in answer to a student's question about the nature of the struggle in South Africa, I had this to say:

The struggle in South Africa is not between blacks and whites, as it's often portrayed in the Western media. Such a portrayal is simplistic and dangerous. Rather, the struggle in South Africa is between those who believe in justice against those who are determined to perpetuate, by law and by violence, the status quo. There are black people who have a stake in the system and have allowed themselves to be used as tools of oppression. They run the homelands, they have joined the police force, they exercise a reign of terror in the ghettos as vigilantes, and some are members of the city councils. On the other hand there are whites who have embraced the liberation struggle and paid the price. Some of these whites are young men who refuse to serve in the military. Some are antiapartheid leaders like Beyers Naude and Molly Blackburn. Some are writers like Alan Paton, Nadine Gordimer, and Breyten Breytenbach. Some are defiant Afrikaner ministers like the Reverend Nico Smith. Nico and his family chose to live with his black parishioners in Mamelodi (place of music), a ghetto of Pretoria, rather than in a white suburb. Some are individuals like Dr. Ivan Toms, who operates a clinic in the poverty-stricken squatters camp of Crossroads. [At the writing of this book, Dr. Ivan Toms, a conscientious objector, was serving a twenty-one-month prison sentence for refusing to serve in the South African Army.]

The speech was an emotional description of growing up black in a South African ghetto. The lecture received a standing ovation from the students, several of whom cried. Shortly following my visit a teacher from the Spence School, Jackie Percheck, wrote me a letter. "Thank you once again for speaking in assembly last week," she said. "You cannot imagine the impact you had on our students! As a result of your talk, there have been many discussions both in classes and outside in the halls, at home with parents. . . ."

Other schools for the wealthy, Brunswick Academy in Greenwich, Connecticut, and Trinity School in Manhattan, heard about the Spence lecture and invited me to address their students. During the time when I appeared at the two schools, the American media was saturated with stories of black-on-black violence. Many reactionaries in Congress, led by Senators Jesse Helms and Orrin Hatch, cited this as justification for the Draconian measures taken by Botha to quell black protests. I addressed this issue of "black-on-black violence" during a question-and-answer session.

Isn't it strange that now, when the Pretoria regime is under intense international pressure to abolish apartheid, we have a proliferation of stories on black-on-black violence? First, what is the source of this violence? And is it new? No, it's not new. And it's not an indication that the various black tribes have irreconcilable differences. Rather, it is the result of deliberate apartheid policies. How should black tribes react when they are pitted against each other? When land is taken from one tribe and given to another? And in the ghettos, what should happen when desperate people are quarantined without hope; and when a few, like the black policemen, allow themselves to be used as tools of oppression? You see the results of black desperation and hopelessness even in the ghettos of America, in the form of black-on-black violence.

Of course the various tribes in South Africa have their differences. My own mother and father belong to two different tribes. My mother is Tsonga and my father is Venda. But that hasn't prevented them from living together. There aren't matrimonial tribal wars in the shack. When I lived in Alexandra our neighbors were Zulus, Sothos, Xhosas, Pedis, and members of other tribes, but that didn't prevent us from getting along, from speaking each other's dialect, fron intermarrying, until, that is, black children went to the segregated government-sponsored tribal schools, where they learned to regard each other as enemies by reading history books written by whites to justify apartheid. Blacks of every tribe have common cause in the fight against apartheid. In fact the various tribes have more in common than white South Africans, who are a hodgepodge of Greeks, Afrikaners, Italians, Jews, Britons, Spaniards, Portuguese, and so on. Yet whites regard themselves as a single group, because unity serves their interests, just as by dividing blacks it is easy to conquer them.

I was particularly pleased at this opportunity to address these children, most of whom were hardly aware of the reality of human suffering beyond their sheltered worlds. I reminded them that an education wasn't intended as a tool for making more money. Rather, it was meant to create better human beings, and it was better human beings who made better lawyers, politicians, bankers, doctors, chief executive officers, entrepreneurs, and so forth, and not the other way around. The way these students' attention was riveted I had the feeling, perhaps naïve, that when the time came for them to inherit wealth or assume positions of leadership in the world of business and politics, they would know a reality and feel a moral responsibility that would help them make their priority decisions based on right and wrong.

At the end of June 1985 my stay at I-House expired. Finding alternative accommodations proved a nightmare and gave me a bitter foretaste of racism in housing.

A friend at I-House told me about affordable apartments on Staten Island. I scanned the papers and came upon an enticing ad for a beachfront apartment in Tottenville. I called the owner and he eagerly agreed to show me the apartment. "It's one of the best," he said. "And it looks out on the ocean." It took me almost two hours to reach the place by subway, ferry, and bus. I was neatly dressed in a brown suit, pressed white shirt, checkered bow tie, and shined black shoes. I carried a black Samsonite attaché case and with my gold-rimmed glasses looked in every way a respectable Buppie (black upwardly mobile professional). When I knocked at the front gate of the landlord's, a young white boy of about twelve, in short pants and a beach shirt, came and told me no one was home.

"But I just called this morning and was told to come at two o'clock," I said.

The white boy laughed and ran to the back of the yard. I saw the window curtains in one of the rooms move: I was being watched; there were people home. I waited a few minutes but left at the vicious barking of a dog. That evening I called the owner and he told me that he didn't rent his property to blacks.

"You know you're discriminating," I said. "And it's against the law."

"It's my property," he said and hung up.

Another time I lost my self-control and unleashed a tirade of accusations of bigotry at one landlord in Howard Beach. He threatened to call the police. I dared him to but when I remembered my precarious immigration status and the stories I had heard about the racist nature of some of New York City's police precincts, I left. Some landlords—in Queens, Yonkers, Long Island, and Brooklyn—were obviously embarrassed by their bigotry and would say, at seeing that I was black, "I'm sorry, this apartment is already rented. But I can show you other apartments, if you want me to." Knowing that these were usually run-down garrets in the worst neighborhoods, I would decline.

To confirm my suspicions of racism, I would have Gail or a friend call the same landlord; almost always the apartment was still available. It seemed that my accent often fooled bigots into thinking I was British and white. Now I finally understood what the black American felt at having to battle such attitudes daily, and why James Baldwin could have written, "To be black in America is to be in rage all the time." It didn't matter to the landlords that I could pay, that I was well mannered and educated, that I had no criminal record and did not drink or smoke. The fact that I was black was enough. The apartment was being held for a white renter, no matter his or her character.

At other times Gail and I tried, to no avail, a tactic we had learned from Stew and Claudia Malloy, the mixed couple on Long Island. As new arrivals to Long Island, Stew and Claudia had innocently gone about hunting for their first home. They had enough money for a down payment; both were college graduates and held well-paying jobs. Stew and Claudia were puzzled as to why the real estate agents steered them to houses in poor black neighborhoods. At first the two didn't suspect racism; after all, the real estate agents seemed the most charming and helpful people, and Stew and Claudia knew of the psychological danger of ascribing racism to every white person's action. But finally it dawned upon Stew and Claudia that race was a factor. So the two decided to have Claudia show up alone at real esate offices. She was shown lovely homes in the best neighborhoods. But when Stew showed up for the negotiating and signing of the contract, the real estate agent would suddenly tell them the owner was no longer selling the house. Their frustration and anger started to show, especially in Claudia, a feisty, no-nonsense Irishwoman, who began embarrassing real estate agents by exposing their racism.

Stew and Claudia finally managed to buy a lovely two-story house in the white section of Bellport (blacks live on the other side of the railroad tracks) mainly because the white couple, in the middle of a bitter divorce, were desperate to sell.

I was continually angered and dismayed by the unwritten "laws," the steering by white real estate agents, the intimidations and the threats of violence by white mobs, which excluded blacks in America from so-called "white neighborhoods." They bore an ugly resemblance to the Group Areas Act in South Africa, which accomplished the same thing by mandating segregated neighborhoods. Of course there were major differences: in South Africa segregation was the law of the land and in America the equal rights of all races were guaranteed by the Bill of Rights. But that is why America's *defacto* segregation was often the more painful, for it went counter to the American creed and the law of the land, and hence was doubly demoralizing to blacks.

I finally found a place in St. George on Staten Island. It was a two-room, dim, dank basement apartment which, despite its gloomy aspect, its rats, its fire-code violations, and its creaky, rotting floors, offered some privacy. It was, of course, in one of the worst sections of town. The rent was $525 a month. To get to Manhattan I had to take the ferry, which was a soothing and scenic ride compared to the subway, and it cost only twenty-five cents.

Away from the distractions of Manhattan, I followed an even more disciplined regimen. I worked on *Kaffir Boy* from early morning until one or two in the afternoon, sometimes missing breakfast and lunch because I was so engrossed. In the afternoon I would go for a run or lift weights or skip rope, handy substitutes for tennis, which I had temporarily abandoned because the expense of playing it in New York was prohibitive. I went into Manhattan about twice a week to visit Gail, who had just returned from three months in Germany and had moved in with her brother Paul and sister-in-law Debbie. We would browse through bookstores, visit museums, and see friends around the city. Most evenings I stayed home writing letters, book reviews, or op-ed page articles for newspapers.

Watching the 1985 Wimbledon championships, I saw Kevin Curren blast his way with cannonball serves and impeccable volleys to his first Wimbledon final, and listened to praises of the progress made by South African tennis. I also heard some American commentators urge that South Africa be readmitted into the Olympics and other international sporting events, as apartheid no longer existed in sports. I thus felt compelled to remind Americans of the reality faced by black athletes, particularly tennis players, in the ghettos of South Africa, and of the impossibility of having normal sports in an abnormal society.

I wrote an article entitled "Apartheid Faults at Center Court." In it I described the youngsters to whom I had taught the game in Alexandra and other ghettos. I spoke of the dilapidated sand courts with broken fences and torn nets and potholes they played on, the warped rackets with broken strings they took turns in using, the dozen or so worn tennis balls, with no bounces, and the lack of qualified black coaches for scores of ragged, mostly barefoot youngsters who, inspired by the exploits of Arthur Ashe in 1976, were raring to learn tennis.

I ended the article with the following observation:

> As long as apartheid remains the way of life in South Africa, it is unlikely that any of those youngsters I taught—if the lot have not given up the game out of frustration and anger at getting nowhere—will ever grace the grass courts of the game's oldest and most prestigious tennis tournament, and stun the world the way Arthur Ashe and Althea Gibson did.
>
> I have no doubt, however, that were courage, determination, eagerness, and resiliency all it took to produce tennis champions, there would certainly have been at least one or two blacks among the many white South Africans at this year's Wimbledon. Who knows, one of them might even have ended up facing Boris Becker or Martina Navratilova, and again painted Wimbledon black, instead of facing police bullets and painting the dusty streets of Alexandra red.

This article brought me more threats. Strangers called in the middle of the night and warned me that I was playing with fire, that if I did not desist in my attacks of white South Africans, something tragic would happen to me and those I loved. I took the threats seriously and contacted the local police, but they merely told me that if anything happened to me, they would investigate.

"But my life may be in danger. I may be killed."

"By whom?"

"By agents of the South African regime."

"Why would they want to kill you?"

"Because of my opposition to apartheid."

"I'm opposed to apartheid. Why haven't I been killed?"

"Because you're not a black South African."

"Listen here, man. There are Russians in this country who criticize the communist regime in Moscow. But they aren't calling us about threats by the KGB to kill them."

"But you don't know the Pretoria racists," I said. "They're meaner than communists."

I could hear the policeman laughing on the other side of the phone. He hung up. He probably thought I was some lunatic, especially when I dared suggest that the Pretoria regime, which the Reagan administration and conservatives across the country regarded as an ally and friend of the U.S., was worse than "the evil empire." I got an unlisted phone number but the calls continued. I became paranoid. I seldom went out at night, and I always barred the door before going to sleep. Staten Island was isolated, and had a reputation as the home of mob figures. To my worked-up imagination it presented the perfect cover for an elimination.

Despite the pledge I had made myself never to touch liquor as long as I lived, since I had witnessed my father's life ruined by alcohol, I began drinking wine each night. It numbed my fears, gave me a false sense of security, and enabled me to sleep without nightmares. I had developed migraines and stomach problems but I ignored the pain.

One morning in July 1985 I received a call from the immigration lawyer informing me that my application for a work permit had been approved. Overwhelmed with relief and joy, I stammered my gratefulness.

"To be honest with you I, too, am amazed they granted it," the lawyer said. "Others whose cases were more solid than yours had their applications rejected. You should consider yourself very lucky." I suspect that the high caliber of the letters of recommendation accompanying my application played a major role in getting me the work permit.

"Is that the end of the ordeal?" I asked.

"By no means," the lawyer said. "You still have to go to Canada or some other country to get the permit. Have you obtained the passport yet?"

"No. I'm told it's still being processed."

"You'd better get one soon. There isn't time to waste."

"What if Pretoria refuses to give me the passport?"

"Then this permit is useless," he said.

He went on to explain that should my passport application be rejected by Pretoria, and complications arise, I would need a different lawyer to defend me against possible deportation.

His invaluable services had cost me about $2,500. I had almost exhausted the advance from Macmillan. There was no way I could afford the exorbitant cost of another lawyer. I had no alternative but to await anxiously the verdict from Pretoria. I kept calling the consulate and was told repeatedly that my passport application was still being processed. It had been almost two months since I applied. I wondered if my desperation was being used against me.

One afternoon I received a call from the consulate informing me that my passport was ready for pickup. Elated, I went to Manhattan but got caught in traffic jams and found the place closed. I returned home and completed an article *Newsday* had commissioned, in which I assessed the impact of Botha's much-awaited but disappointing "Rubicon speech" delivered on August 15, 1985. I exposed Botha's euphemistic propaganda designed to delude a gullible West into believing that apartheid was being abolished.

> The speech had been eagerly anticipated in the United States and around the world as a momentous one, in which Botha would finally rise to the statesmanship of, say, a Charles de Gaulle during the turmoil and bloodshed in preindependence Algeria, to lead his beleaguered nation in a new direction of justice and equality.
>
> Botha did nothing of the kind. Instead, the South African leader retreated behind a figurative *laager* [Afrikaans for a circle of wagons] and from there, with characteristic histrionics and arrogance, he hurled at an incredulous world the traditional excuses of his racist regime.

The article was also published in the *St. Petersburg Times* under the heading "Botha Offers an Old Song and Dance."

A day after the article appeared, on the twenty-sixth of August, I went to the South African consulate to pick up my passport. I was ready for anything. I could tell from the looks of the officials that they knew of the article. Behind a thick glass window, the white woman listened coldly to my request.

"I came to pick up my passport," I said.

"Who are you?"

I gave her my name.

"Wait a minute," she said, and slipped behind a door. She came back minutes later.

"Your passport is not ready," she said.

"That's strange. I was told it was ready."

"Let me go check something." She again vanished behind a door. She returned.

"Take a seat over there," she said. "You'll be attended to shortly." I wondered what she meant. Several tall and tough-looking

Afrikaner men, presumably agents of BOSS, emerged from the side door, stared at me, and then left the building. There were several Americans at the windows who had come to apply for visas, and their presence reassured me. I had heard of the Pretoria regime's tactic of abducting its foes. Half an hour passed. Finally a woman called me to a side door.

"Here's your document, Mr. Mathabane," she said, and then vanished behind the door without another word.

I was stunned. They had given me the passport, I thought. As I walked out of the building I perused the document to ascertain its validity. To my horror I saw that it was not a passport. It was a freshly made travel document, the type given to enemies of the regime who are denied real passports. I remembered Bishop Tutu, during a visit to International House in 1984, two weeks before he was awarded the Nobel Peace Prize, showing an audience his, which listed his nationality as "undetermined." My nationality was listed as Venda. I had been stripped of South African citizenship and made a citizen of the Venda tribal reserve, a bogus nation which was run by a ruthless dictator named Mphephu, chosen and kept in power by Pretoria. Despite the loss of several elections, Mphephu continued to cling to power through untempered brutality and repression. His goons had detained and tortured Reverend Farisane, whose case Amnesty International widely publicized.

How could I have been told that my passport was ready, only to be issued a travel document? I had no doubt that my passport was ready and somewhere in the building. I speculated that it probably would have been issued but for the appearance of my article in *Newsday* attacking Botha's speech, which had been heavily promoted by Pretoria's propaganda machinery as signaling major changes in South Africa. I did not regret having published the article.

But did I dare travel to Canada on such a dubious document? No other government except the Pretoria regime recognized these fake, so-called independent states, which were nothing but islands of poverty, misery, corruption, and black-led oppression. I went to the Canadian consulate and applied for a visitor's visa. To my surprise I was issued one without much hassle. Canada had a long-standing policy of treating black refugees from South Africa with sympathy. It was Canada that in the 1960s led Commonwealth countries in imposing sanctions which helped turn Ian Smith's apartheid Rhodesia into free Zimbabwe.

On the morning of September 23, 1985, I flew to Montreal. When the plane landed at Mirabeau International Airport, I pondered the possiblity that, because of my criticism of American foreign policy, I might not be allowed back into the States. Because I arrived late in the day and could find no inexpensive accommodations, I was forced to spend nearly all my money on a room in one of the most expensive hotels in downtown Montreal. Throughout the long night I pondered what I would do if I was denied a visa to reenter the United States.

I woke up early the next morning and headed for the American consulate. The place teemed with people of various nationalities. Some were applying for visitor's visas, others were being interviewed as part of their application to enter the U.S. as immigrants or to obtain work permits. The desperation and fear visible on many people's faces, and their resignation when their applications were rejected for this or that reason, turned me into a nervous wreck while I stood in line. What if I blundered during the interrogation? My turn came.

"How long had you been living in the U.S.?"

"Seven years."

"In what capacity?"

"As a student."

"Have you ever been back to South Africa?"

"No."

A pause.

"What type of work do you do?"

"I'm a writer."

"What do you write?"

"Books and articles for newspapers."

"Be more specific."

"I write about the black experience in South Africa and America," I said.

Another pause.

"How long do you intend to remain in the U.S.?"

"Two years."

"Let's see your passport."

I handed over my travel document and the official scrutinized it.

"Is this your passport?"

"Yes."

She left her seat and disappeared behind a door. She came back a few minutes later.

"Don't you have a proper passport?"

"No."

"Why?"

"The South African government seldom grants blacks passports," I replied.

She again disappeared behind the door. By now I felt hot; my body was soaked in perspiration and my heart was racing. What if? What if?

She came back and told me to take a seat. Half an hour passed. I was finally called to the window and handed my travel document. A multiple-entry work-permit visa, valid for two years, had been stamped on page thirteen. I left the consulate, went to a telephone booth, called Gail in New York, and told her that I was coming back after all. She was greatly relieved.

"Thank God you called," she said. "I've been so worried about you. I haven't slept for two days."

"Me neither," I said. "This whole experience has shaken me up."

"You know, I even thought of flying to Montreal to be with you."

"Really?"

"Yes. Did you think I'd let them send you back to those racists?"

"*Je t'aime*," I said.

"I love you, too," Gail said. "Hurry back."

As I sauntered about Montreal in a jovial mood, before heading for the airport, I wondered at my charmed life. I was grateful to have, in Gail, someone with whom I could share my innermost feelings. I marveled at the fact that I, a harsh critic of American foreign policy, was granted a work permit by the same government I criticized. My respect for the American system of democratic government deepened. I saw clearly that in America the rule of law and the rights of individuals were paramount. It is the rule of law, and only that, which distinguishes man as a species and separates democratic nations from tyrannies. This is why groups like the American Civil Liberties Union, which unflinchingly protect the rights of everyone, from Oliver North to the Ku Klux Klan, are so indispensable as watchdogs and deserve the support of all Americans.

33 THE ASSASSINATION OF BROTHERS-IN-LAW; DIFFICULTY GETTING THROUGH TO MY FAMILY

A few weeks after returning to the United States I received an Express Mail letter from my family informing me that my two brothers-in-law had been murdered by the police. The dead were Collin, the father of Florah's four-year-old daughter, Angeline; and the father, also named Collin, of Maria's four-year-old son, Given. The two Collins were close friends. The murders, it turned out, had occurred a few days after my article exposing the duplicity of Botha's speech was published in *Newsday*. The coincidence jolted me. Were they killed because of me? There seemed no other motive behind their untimely deaths.

This is how they died. Both Collins, hardworking young men who had already assumed responsibility for the raising of their children, and who talked of marrying my two sisters as soon as they had saved enough money, were sitting on the front porch of a house that morning, having obeyed a stay-at-home order from militants in the ghetto. Out of nowhere came an armed black policeman. Without a word, he opened fire with a handgun at point-blank range. Maria's Collin was killed instantly. Florah's Collin died a week later in the hospital, from a bullet lodged in his neck; doctors said they couldn't remove it without jeopardizing his life. To the end he kept asking why he had been targeted. The assassin went unprosecuted.

"It's just a coincidence," Gail said, trying to comfort me. "Your article had nothing to do with their tragic and cowardly murder."

"I've been warned," I said, "and I refused to listen."

"Don't blame yourself. There must be some other reason they were killed. The details are still sketchy."

"There's nothing sketchy about the threats I've been receiving."

"What do you intend to do?"

"I don't know. I'm so confused."

"Whatever you do," Gail said, "don't blame yourself. You didn't kill them."

I wasn't convinced. For weeks I was consumed with guilt that I was responsible for the assassinations. I was unable to think or write. Night and day I brooded over the brutal and senseless murders and wondered if my family would be next. My problems were worsened by the fact that I could not reach them. The neighbor's phone in Alexandra, through which I usually contacted them, was inexplicably off the hook each time I called. I began having second thoughts about publishing *Kaffir Boy*. Would publication of the book be my family's death knell? Were they already dead?

I talked the matter over with Ned, Dominick, Kevin, and Fifi. The four were sympathetic and promised to do whatever was necessary to help me find out what had happened to my family.

"If you want me to," Ned said, "I can get in touch with some people in the State Department and have them put pressure on those bastards."

My distrust of the Reagan administration made me doubt the wisdom of such a move. It could make matters worse, I told Ned.

He thought hard for a moment and then said, "I just remembered that some acquaintances of mine will soon be leaving for South Africa on a fact-finding mission. I don't know if they will be going anywhere near Alexandra. I think we should give them a copy of your manuscript and have them try to find out what's happened to your family."

I agreed, even though I feared that the manuscript might fall into the wrong hands.

"In the meantime my advice to you, Mark, is to go ahead with publication of the book," Ned said. "Its notoriety can provide some protection for your family."

"What if it doesn't?"

"If anything happens to your family because of the book," he swore, "I'll personally see to it that the American media creates hell for that racist regime."

"If only I could reach my family," I said, "and know that they're safe, I would sleep easier."

"Let's keep trying, kiddo."

Days passed without success. I was beside myself with worry. I finally reached my mother through the help of white South African friends who had been away on vacation. She was relieved to hear my voice as she had been concerned when I hadn't answered the urgent letter sent to me about two months ago. Not wanting to alarm her, I didn't mention that the letters I had written her had been intercepted by the authorities, and that my calls to her in Alexandra were prevented from getting through by the same. She informed me that Florah and Maria had borne their grief well but had lost their jobs for having taken several days off for mourning. Prospects of their getting other jobs were bleak since they were high school dropouts and the South African economy was depressed. The burden now rested on my mother to provide for their two fatherless children. The motives behind the murder of the two Collins still remained a mystery. When I told her of my suspicions that the deaths might be related to my activism in the United States, and that I was willing to stop speaking out if the family wanted me to, she replied that whether related or not, it was my duty to tell the truth.

"But the truth may get you killed, Mama," I said. "The whole family may be wiped out because of what I write. I'm prepared to stop. Just give the word." I reminded her of instances where families of exiles critical of apartheid had been harassed, detained, and sometimes killed.

"Child," she said in a calm voice. "Do what God has chosen you to do. Stop worrying too much about us, or too much about death. We all have to die someday, you know. We're in this world only a little while. Our permanent home is in heaven, and if God decides to call us home, we should happily go. But if it's not our time, nothing man can do will change God's will."

She went on to relate how one evening a week ago, returning home from visiting an ailing church member, she had escaped being robbed and murdered by outrunning a band of *tsotsis*.

"I'm not a runner, you know, child," she said with captivating laughter. "But that night nothing could have caught me. God had given me angel wings. You should have seen me fly over fences and scream for help."

Comparing herself to Job, she confessed that her faith was being tested every day as she fought to contain her rage at the senseless killings of black children by the soldiers.

"I know God doesn't want me to get angry. He doesn't want me to hate. He teaches and commands us to love even our enemies. But sometimes I can't help it. Just last weekend we buried three more children who were shot dead by the soldiers while playing in the streets.

"What is our world coming to? I repeatedly ask myself. Sometimes I feel like cursing God, child. I feel He has forsaken us, His black children. Every night, in my prayers, I ask Him why He allows His children to suffer and to die needlessly. How long will He allow this darkness to last? I pray every day but things only get worse. I pray for the soldiers, too, you know, so that they can see the light, because they're God's children, too. I'm so glad that you're away from it all. If you had never left, you, too, could have been killed like so many of your friends. We mothers no longer know what to do to protect our children. We weep but tears no longer come out."

I could hear her weeping. I wept, too. Before we parted she uttered a prayer and besought God to bless and protect me. Her courage and equanimity inspired me. If she who every day ran the risk of being killed came up with the courage to keep on believing in the future, to keep on loving and feeling and caring deeply, what did I, who lived in relative security and comfort in America, who had my civil rights protected under American law, who had access to a myriad of opportunities, have to complain about?

SPEAKING OUT AGAINST APARTHEID; *Kaffir Boy* IS PUBLISHED; NADINE GORDIMER; NATIONWIDE BOOK TOUR

I returned with renewed strength to fighting the struggle against apartheid in the only way I knew how. I wrote articles which appeared in the *St. Louis Post-Dispatch*, *Newsday*, and the *St. Petersburg Times*. In these articles I warned Americans to beware of sweet-sounding words and good intentions from Pretoria designed to dupe the Western world into believing that apartheid is being eradicated, when in fact the system is being refined and entrenched. "The South African regime," I said, "is the master of the art of doublespeak."

About the much-heralded new South African constitution I had this to say: "A constitution allowing representation only to Coloureds and Indians and ignoring the aspirations of the black majority is a blatant fraud. There can never be true democracy in South Africa without universal suffrage and the abolishing of apartheid."

I said this about the pass laws: "The abolishing of the pass laws means very little to blacks because the regime has and every day employs other means of achieving the same dastardly results. Color is still being used to define one's place under the sun. Segregated housing is still enforced by the Groups Areas Act. Across the country there are still black and white beaches, schools, hospitals, parks, buses, churches, and ambulances. And thousands of blacks are still being stripped of their South African citizenship and deported to the tribal reserves ruled by corrupt, Pretoria-anointed black dictators."

Such arguments won me the support of Americans of conscience but infuriated apologists of the apartheid regime. The number of threatening phone calls surged. Strange noises began emanating from my phone each time I made a call, leading me to conclude that my phone was probably tapped. I had a feeling of being followed each time I went to Manhattan. But through it all I refused to be intimidated. I knew that the dangers I faced were nothing compared to those faced by blacks in the ghettos of South Africa. Having handed in the revised manuscript, I looked forward to the publication of the book so it could provide me with an even larger audience and platform.

One day I read in the paper that Nadine Gordimer, the noted South African author, was in town for a P.E.N. conference. I told Ned that I had met Gordimer about a year ago while I lived at I-House. She was at the Union Theological Seminary opposite Riverside Church showing several films on South Africa. At the end of the program I had introduced myself and given her a copy of a review I wrote for the *St. Petersburg Times* on her latest collection of short stories, *Something Out There*. She thanked me for it and when she learned that I was studying journalism and writing an autobiography, she urged me to return to South Africa, saying I would be more useful there.

I was somewhat puzzled by this advice because I knew that the Pretoria regime was cracking down on black writers and journalists, and that if I returned to South Africa I risked imprisonment and possibly death. Besides, blacks were forbidden to write as freely as whites under apartheid rules. I wanted to explain this to Nadine Gordimer, but she had become the cynosure of another group of admirers.

"I think it'd be an excellent idea to send Gordimer a copy of your manuscript," Ned suggested.

"But she's too important and busy a person to find the time to read the work of someone as unimportant as myself," I replied.

"But she knows you, Mark," Ned said. "You wrote a favorable review of her book. She's bound to say something encouraging to a new South African writer, especially a black one."

"I don't know if I want to bother her, Ned," I said. "Why don't we let the book succeed or fail on its own merits?"

"Mark, you don't know this business," Ned insisted. "A recommendation from Gordimer would help your book. She's a well-known and admired author in this country."

"If you insist."

Gordimer was staying at the St. Moritz. Ned gave me a copy of the manuscript and I took a cab to the posh hotel. The receptionist rang her room but she was out, so I left the manuscript in her mailbox, with a note explaining who I was and the purpose of my visit.

That evening I called her room and she answered. I introduced myself and she remembered me. She acknowledged receiving the manuscript I had left her.

"But I haven't had a chance to read it," she said. "I intend to take it back with me to South Africa."

"I'll welcome any criticism or comments," I said.

"Do you know Lewis Nkosi?" she asked.

I replied that I had heard of but not met the noted black South African writer living in exile in Zambia.

"You should send him a copy of the manuscript, too," she said. "He's part of the conference."

"I'll try to get one to him," I said. "Thank you very much for your time."

For some reason or other I could not obtain a copy on time to send to Lewis Nkosi. I never heard anything from Nadine Gordimer, and long after the book was published I was bothered that she had never said a word about it. Ned bumped into her one day at an affair in New York where she was being honored, and told her how the book had been doing. Her reply was that the book hardly revealed anything that she didn't already know about black life in South Africa.

Kaffir Boy went into the world with only its contents to recommend it. Early reviews were favorable. *Kirkus Reviews* and *Publishers Weekly* called the book "inspiring, chilling, gruesome; a brave memoir of life under apartheid." People praised as powerful the jacket cover showing a photo of a quietly defiant face of a black youth, taken by Jeanne Moutoussamy-Ashe during a visit to South Africa. The book also carried an insert of photos of my family, scenes from Alexandra, Stan at my graduation, and our shack. Hajima Ota, a Japanese friend from my days at International House, had taken them during a visit to South Africa about a year earlier. My brother George had acted as his guide, thus enabling him to capture much of the truth about black life in the ghettos. Most visitors to South Africa are given government-sponsored tours which are sanitized for Western consumption. The highly publicized Jerry Falwell visit, in which he idiotically called Bishop Tutu "a phony" for leading the opposition to apartheid, is an instance of the effectiveness of these guided tours.

A few days after *Kaffir Boy* was published, Macmillan sent me on a nationwide publicity tour, which began in New York and over the next ten days took me to Washington, Boston, Chicago, and San Francisco, places I had never been. My first television appearance was on CNN during the International Hour. Having never before appeared on television, I was nervous. But the interview went well, despite my disappointment at having been given only a few minutes to explain a complicated book 354 pages long which had taken years to write.

"That's television for you," Ned said.

"But the interviewer didn't even read the book," I complained.

"Consider yourself lucky that you got on the damn thing."

In Washington I stayed at the Jefferson Hotel and had an escort who chauffered me to the various interviews. People who had seen me on television greeted me in the streets, asked for autographs, and wished me well. The celebrity treatment was alien to me, but I took everything in stride: I never wearied of answering questions, many of them very personal, or signing autographs. My task was to increase the audience of *Kaffir Boy*, to spread the word about the black struggle against apartheid, and to thank the American people for caring. If it took playing the role of celebrity to do it, that was a small price to pay. Yet I have never been comfortable in the limelight.

While waiting to appear on "Panorama," a popular Washington, D.C., daytime talk show, I was shocked to learn that the South African ambassador to the United States, Herbert Beukes, had been invited to appear on the same program with me. The host had wanted us to debate one another but the ambassador had insisted that we appear separately, with him coming after me. My mind was thrown into confusion. Should I talk as I am used to or should I be careful about what I said? Until the last minute I was uncertain what to do, but once on the set, I realized the magnitude of the occasion. I was in the nation's capital and I knew the power of television. Thousands of people would be watching the show and what the ambassador and I said about South Africa and apartheid was bound to shape their understanding of the issue. I knew that the ambassador would be armed with formidable propaganda and would pour it into credulous ears without a scruple. I therefore held nothing back. I related in vivid and poignant terms my own experiences growing up under apartheid, aware that such personal evidence would be difficult to refute, even by an artful politician and propagandist like the ambassador. On the other hand, if I argued against apartheid on political grounds, I reasoned, I was bound to be outwitted. As I left the set I met the ambassador in the corridor, surrounded by two burly bodyguards. Apparently they had been watching me on the monitor in the lobby. The ambassador and I shook hands, politely but coldly.

As expected, the ambassador had no defense against my personal testimony except to say that *Kaffir Boy* was on his desk but he hadn't read it, and that my experiences were exaggerated and represented the minority view. He then proceeded to defend his government's indefensible policies. He declared that apartheid was dead and only its reeking corpse remained to be buried. He exaggerated the significance of the cosmetic changes which had taken place in South Africa under President Botha, and warned Americans about "the communistic African National Congress," which, he said, was only interested in turning South Africa into a Marxist-Leninist satellite of the Soviet Union. He did a professional job of masking the evil of institutionalized racism and the duplicity of the Pretoria regime, and of shamelessly exploiting America's paranoia about communism. As he spoke, I had the urge to storm onto the set and shout, "Liar! Liar!" When the show was over we again encountered each other as he left the building. I wondered what was coursing through his mind as he realized that I had thwarted his propaganda, and what possible repercussions our meeting would have on my family back home.

In Boston I appeared on several radio stations and was interviewed for a feature article by Wil Haywood, a black reporter on *The Boston Globe*. From Boston I flew to Chicago, where I gave a well-received address before the Council on Foreign Relations. From Chicago I flew to San Francisco, my first trip to the West Coast. There I appeared on "People Are Talking," the most popular talk show in the Bay area. In all these places I found the audience overwhelmingly sympathetic. Many Americans, even veterans of South African issues, were shocked by the story I had to tell. I in turn was amazed at the amount of propaganda the Pretoria regime was circulating that apartheid no longer existed, that the various black tribes had irreconcilable differences which necessitated the presence of a white master to maintain the peace, that the main issue in South Africa was not white racism and oppression but the need for black economic development and civilization, and that legitimate black leaders like Nelson and Winnie Mandela, Alan Boesak, Bishop Tutu, and others were communists for advocating social justice and an end to apartheid. Unfortunately, there was sympathy for such a message in certain conservative circles. But in the main, Americans turned out to be men and women of goodwill and feeling hearts, and sympathized with people who were fighting for the rights and freedoms Americans couldn't imagine life without.

During my appearance on "People Are Talking," something incredible happened. Many in the audience of mostly conservative whites wept when they heard me describe how my mother had fought against formidable odds to keep us alive; to keep the family together despite repeated attempts by the police to break us apart; to secure her seven children an education which, though illiterate, she firmly believed offered the best hope of our eventually escaping from the pit of poverty and suffering.

The generosity and helpfulness of Americans astounded me. No other country has so many cheerful givers to causes which are explained to them in human terms. People wanted to know what they could do to help improve the lot of blacks and eradicate apartheid. I referred them to antiapartheid groups such as the African National Congress and the American Committee on Africa, both in New York,

TransAfrica in Washington, D.C., and Intercessor, a group in Philadelphia committed to social action and to praying for justice, peace, freedom, and reconciliation in South Africa. I exhorted them to write protest letters to their representatives in Congress, to hold them accountable, to demand that they base their decisions and actions on the South African issue, not on political expediency, but on principle and right; to insist that the American creed and morality not be prostituted for economic interests or narrow and misguided ideological reasons.

"The strength of America," I said during a radio appearance in San Francisco, "its glory and security, lies not in the number of your guns and bombs, nor in your abundant wealth. It lies in the fact that as a nation you have a heart."

Many people thanked me for uttering such words and for writing the book. Aside from educating them about South African society, they said that it had helped them realize how fortunate they were to have been born in America. It had taught them not to take their rights and privileges for granted or abuse them, and to realize that freedom carried with it a heavy responsibility. Above all, *Kaffir Boy* had taught them to have faith in themselves, not to give up easily in the face of obstacles, and to believe in the value of an education and in the redeeming power of love.

I was particularly heartened by the reaction of most black Americans. Many of them, poor inhabitants of ghettos, came up to me and confessed that they had almost given up in their various struggles, that they had begun believing that white racism was unconquerable, that they were often consumed and blinded by anger, self-pity, and hatred, but that *Kaffir Boy*, especially my mother's story, had revived their failing strength and convinced them that the battle could be won. They were now more determined to fight against bigotry and for their fair share in America by using the few opportunities available to them, most important of which were an education and the vote.

At the end of the weeklong publicity tour I was drained. It had been a deeply emotional experience for me. I scarcely believed that a book about the simple daily lives of my people thousands of miles away, a book many had dismissed as unpublishable, as too hard-hitting for American sensibilities, could have touched Americans so deeply. Liberals and conservatives, blacks and whites, religious and irreligious, found its testimony compelling. They saw the people of South Africa, human beings like themselves, laughing and crying, suffering and dying for liberty. They saw why the continued existence of evils like apartheid was an indictment of our collective guilt. They saw that to do nothing to eradicate such evils was to become accomplices in an unpardonable crime: the destruction of ourselves, since everyone is part of the human family, and the suffering of God's children anywhere diminishes our collective humanity. How many innocent lives would have been saved if Hitler's madness had been nipped in the bud? How many innocent lives will be lost if the madness of apartheid is not nipped in the bud?

35 DISAPPOINTING SALES OF *Kaffir Boy*; REVIEWS

Despite the success of the publicity tour, sales of *Kaffir Boy* were disappointing. From the reception I had met with across the country I knew that the book deserved more readers.

"Give it time, Mark," Ned said. "The sales figures will improve."

"But there's such interest out there for the story of *Kaffir Boy*," I argued. "People are clamoring for copies of the book. I assure you that had I carried thousands of copies with me during the publicity tour, I would have sold every one of them."

"I don't doubt it. But that's not how books are sold. Bookstores have to order your book. They will. We're supporting you strongly."

I was constantly on the phone with my publicist, inquiring why such-and-such a city had no copies of *Kaffir Boy*.

"Mark, you're not unusual in your complaints," the publicist said. "All writers accuse the publisher of not doing enough to promote their books. But the reality is that it is in the publisher's interest to sell as many copies as possible. So why wouldn't we want to sell books?"

The much-awaited review in *The New York Times Book Review*, which, if favorable, was expected to boost sales, finally appeared on April 27, 1986. Its brief contents struck me as unfair and inaccurate.

The review appeared in the "In Short" section and the critic, a certain Lilian Thomas, seemed to me to have hardly read the book, for she attacked me for not writing the book in a way I never conceived it. She appeared to take me to task about why I left South Africa, as if she had wanted me to remain there, though she asked, rhetorically, How could one remain there? She seemed to suggest that I had not sufficiently dealt with the issue of apartheid in a personal way. Yet I had written an autobiography.

Despite my anger at the *Times* review, I found consolation in the fact that there were thousands of other papers in the country which, if they assigned *Kaffir Boy* to impartial reviewers, would give the book the recognition it deserved. I was not looking for encomiums. I simply wanted fairness. And though parts of me had been made callous by repeated blows of criticism and scorn, my heart was still composed of penetrable stuff. When cut, it bled. I was not prepared for the sort of reviews which came in over the next months. *The Washington Post*'s *Sunday Book World* devoted an entire page to the review by Charles R. Larson, a professor of literature at American University and author of *The Emergence of African Fiction*. He wrote:

> One irony of the increased American perception of apartheid is that most of the South African writers currently being published in the United States are white. As concerned Americans, we profess our abhorrence of government policies in South Africa, including rampant censorship, though our reading is limited to the country's white literary spokesmen.
>
> Nadine Gordimer, André Brink, Breyten Breytenbach, J. M. Coetzee, Athol Fugard—all of them fine writers—provide us with their liberal views of what's wrong with South Africa, yet, still, for all their concern, the picture is one-dimensional.
>
> Perhaps the publication of *Kaffir Boy* will help change this, though I doubt that Mark Mathabane's autobiography will assuage all liberal guilt. It's too violent and hard-hitting for that. Rather, I'd like to think that *Kaffir Boy* might acquire the same status that Richard Wright's *Black Boy* or Claude Brown's *Manchild in the Promised Land* had for earlier generations of American readers. It is in every way as important and as exciting a book—with the additional factor of showing us the horrors of apartheid through the victim's eyes.

Diane Manuel, in the *Chicago Tribune*, wrote in a similar vein: "What television newscasts did to expose the horrors of the Vietnam

War in the 1960s, books like *Kaffir Boy* may well do for the horrors of apartheid in the 1980s. This is a rare look at life inside the festering adobe shanties of Alexandra. . . . Rare because it comes not from the pen of a liberal white novelist, but from the heart of a passionate young African who grew up there."

MY FAMILY'S STRUGGLES IN SOUTH AFRICA;
LIVING ON A SHOESTRING BUDGET IN NEW YORK;
MEDICAL INSURANCE IN AMERICA

Several months after *Kaffir Boy* was published, I received the remainder of my advance—$17,500—from Macmillan. I immediately sent $2,000 to my family. I mailed the check and letter to my mother's workplace in a white suburb; overseas mail sent to black post offices in the ghettos was often intercepted. My mother was ill with diabetes which had been shoddily treated, my father remained unemployed, and Maria and Florah held jobs one minute and lost them the next, so I essentially supported the family. George at one time had proposed to my mother that, like Uncle Piet before him, he leave school and find some menial job to also help the family, but she wouldn't hear of it. She essentially asked him the same question she had asked me years ago when, at the age of eight, I contemplated quitting school.

"If you leave school, what will you do? What job will you get?"

In the accompanying letter I urged Florah and Maria to finish high school, either by taking correspondence courses or by becoming full-time students. I promised to pay for all their expenses. But whether from shame at how they would be regarded as unwed mothers in high school, or from lack of confidence in how they would perform after years of absence from the classroom, they did not take me up on the offer. Their dilemma resembled that faced by thousands of teenage mothers in the ghettos of America.

On the other hand, the rest of my siblings—Linah, Dianah, and Merriam—promised me that they would stay in school and work hard, despite the continuous disruption of black schooling by violence and unrest. In turn I promised to pay for all their expenses and, upon their graduation from high school, to attempt to bring those who wanted to go to college to America. Liberation, I kept telling my siblings, cannot come to those without the education to understand what it means.

What was left of my advance I added to my savings account at Pro Serve, Stan Smith's representatives in Washington, D. C. Aside from an incurable addiction to books, my needs were modest and I kept on a strict budget. I still lived in that basement apartment on Staten Island. Every other night I had leftovers for dinner. I seldom ate out, preferring to cook my own inexpensive meals of vegetables, fish, and poultry. I figured that since I was in reasonably good health, and had not been to a doctor in years, if I kept up my regimen of good nutrition, regular exercise, and adequate sleep, I could avoid being bankrupted by exorbitant medical bills.

One of America's great failings seems to me the lack of comprehensive medical coverage for its citizens, as they have in Canada and Britain. An estimated 37 million Americans do not have any medical insurance; 26 percent of American women have no maternity coverage; and 18 million American children are not covered by any health insurance plan. In fact, America shares with South Africa the dubious distinction of being the only industrialized countries that do not provide basic health insurance for all their citizens.

The stories I heard and read about every day of Americans selling their possessions to pay medical bills, of parents appealing to public charity for funds to pay for their children's expensive operations, of the poor being denied proper medical care for lack of health insurance, of American children deformed by or dying from preventable diseases, as if they lived in an underdeveloped country, of overcrowded mental hospitals dumping chronically ill patients in the streets—all this made me realize how far America was from the Utopia of my South African dreams. It also made me understand somewhat my impression that average Americans often felt so alone, so insecure, so desperate to safeguard whatever they had for fear that the vicissitudes of fortune could leave them destitute, homeless, uncared for, abandoned by loved ones. Such chronic anxiety bred selfishness and greed and fostered the me-first and me-alone syndrome which smothered the spirit of community.

37

THE INHUMANITY OF CITY LIFE; YUPPIES AND
BUPPIES; FIGHTING SELFISHNESS; FEELING
TRAPPED

Nowhere, it seemed to me, was the lack of community spirit more evident than in New York City. Since I had begun living in the teeming metropolis, every day and everywhere I had seen manifestations of selfishness and scorn for the values which bond people together. Greed and the abuse of power made the rich richer yet more insecure, and the poor poorer and alienated from society. It was a two-tier society with a vengeance. On Wall Street, scandals of insider tradings were breaking out. Racism and residential segregation tore communities like Yonkers and Howard Beach apart. The mayoral elections revealed how divided and polarized the city was. The median income of the poor, mostly blacks and Hispanics, hovered around $11,000 for a family of four, while more white millionaires were added to the list of the rich.

Crime, murder, drugs, and police brutality constantly made headlines on the evening news and in newspapers. The acquittal of Bernhard Goetz, after he had confessed to wanting to kill the four black teenagers he shot in the subway, and the outpouring of white support he received for his vigilantism, led David Dinkins, Manhattan Borough's president, who is black, to label the verdict "a clear and open invitation to vigilantism." Another respected black civic leader, Roscoe Brown, said that "the climate in which this decision [acquitting Goetz] was made, whether it be by white jurors or black jurors, is one of racism and fear of young black men."

I was a young black man. Often when I rode the subway, and happened to stand or sit next to a white woman with a purse, she instinctively shifted the purse to the side away from me. Whenever I hailed a cab, those driven by whites rarely stopped. At many department stores I was watched like a hawk by store clerks, and when I paid by check, I was asked for all sorts of IDs, while a white person wasn't. Whenever I spontaneously greeted or smiled at people when our eyes met, I was stared at.

"Why are New Yorkers so tense, suspicious, and cold?" I asked my agent, Kevin. Even after living in New York for almost three years these attitudes still baffled me.

"It's the city," Kevin said. "When it gets into people's systems it makes them behave strangely."

"I'm often called naïve and a fool for acting like a human being," I said.

"I'm not surprised," Kevin said. "It's a jungle out there."

I could cope with the racism, impersonality, and toughness of life in New York City. But what I found increasingly intolerable and disgusting was the sight of young adults my age—whose counterparts in previous generations had borne the torch of progressive change—transformed into strange creatures called Yuppies and Buppies.

A growing number of my acquaintances from college and I-House had become Yuppies and Buppies. A couple were black South Africans who, after studying business in America, had returned home to work for U.S. companies that followed the Sullivan principles. Articles later appeared in South African publications hailing the emergence of this new species of blacks. One publication, *The Natal Witness* (Natal is a province of South Africa and the stronghold of the Zulu leader Gatsha Buthelezi), stated in a prominent article:

The appearance in South Africa of "buppies" has been greeted with approval by *Time* magazine. In a report in its latest edition, *Time* notes that an increasing number of blacks are able to improve the quality of their lives by entrepreneurship in the private sector. . . . That the operation of free market forces opens avenues of advancement for blacks is undoubted. What is surprising is that notwithstanding their evident knowledge of this fact, liberal Americans continue to press for disinvestment from and sanctions on South Africa, thereby denying blacks the employment opportunities which are prerequisite to economic progress.

American Yuppies and Buppies, like their South African counterparts, were largely conservative. They seemed unaware that our
world—with its senseless wars, racism, starvation, bigotry, selfishness, oppression, sexism, poverty, drugs, exploitation, and numerous
other banes—had very little good to conserve and challenged young
people to be radicals like Jesus Christ. In my view, the young
generation of a society constitutes the liberal wing of progress and
reform, and the older generation the conservative wing of order and
stability. It is the interplay of these two forces which brings about
needed changes and improvements while preserving past improvements. But what sort of progress can come from a society where the
young are more conservative than their elders, and blindly follow
authority and custom?

As long as Yuppies and Buppies had their credit cards, VCRs,
BMWs, elegant apartments, and hefty salaries, as long as they had
their superficial identities and materialistic happiness, it was the
golden age. Caring little about social responsibility, they had transformed the Rotary Club motto of Service Above Self into Self Above
Service.

The harshness of New York City life threatened to transform me
into a Buppie. With each passing day I felt myself becoming
preoccupied, almost against my will, with looking out for number
one. Each time I realized that the little money I possessed would soon
run out and leave me destitute, each time I realized that I was an exile
in a strange land without a family support system, I wondered how
long I could resist the temptation of concentrating on making money.

I began to suspect that people befriended me only because they
thought I had money or because they wanted something from me. I
became greedy and selfish. I considered it a waste of time when
Marianne Kellogg at the Columbia School of Journalism suggested
that I spend part of my weekends helping Habitat for Humanity, an
organization which was building low-income housing for the poor.
Youngsters from Harlem in the I-House tutorial program, whom
earlier I had taught tennis, begged me to continue the free lessons at
the Riverside Park tennis courts but I told them I had no time, instead
of making time. For a while I even stopped sending money home.
Almost without noticing it, I started believing that in order to survive
the rat race I had to become insensitive or indifferent to the pain, the
poverty, and the racism I saw around me.

In South Africa spontaneously helping those in need was considered a necessary part of one's humanity. My own mother would often invite into the house total strangers, including drunkards, lunatics, and the homeless, to share with us our scanty meals and crowded shack. When asked why she did that, she would reply, "We're all God's children and must take care of each other."

But in New York City only my needs, and Gail's, mattered. I came to see the homeless and winos in the subway, the Bowery, on Cooper Square, along Eighth Avenue, and in a dozen other places as part of the New York City landscape, just like Central Park or the Empire State building, and not as human beings like me who needed to be helped. I learned to walk stoically past them, to dine elegantly in a restaurant while they ate out of trash cans and McDonald's dumpsters, to sleep in a cozy bed while they slept on grates and pieces of cardboard, on cold benches, in salt pits, in bus depots, in abandoned cars and dilapidated buildings. I learned to rationalize their suffering.

Each time I became aware of this sinister transformation within me, I was shaken. I felt guilty at the thought that I was attempting to live a lie. I was reluctant to discuss this dilemma with Gail, wondering if she would understand. After several months of such anguish it finally dawned upon me, one morning in the summer of 1986, following a week of soul-searching, that the rat race and decadence of New York City were the principal causes of my woes. The soul-searching was precipitated by an encounter I had with a black panhandler outside a café on the Upper East Side.

"Can you spare a dime, brother?" the black man whined as he accosted me with an extended, withered hand clasping a tin can. He looked no older than thirty, had a dirty beard, wore dreadlocks and a white shirt blackened by grime. I had just parted from a friend, a wealthy, self-made black businessman who lived in Scarsdale, New York. He had treated me to a rather expensive dinner. I reached into my pocket and brought out a bunch of pennies and a nickel, all the change I had. I also had a subway token.

"Sure. Here." I handed the man the change.

He stared at the money and then at me. He spat at me.

"What do you take me for? A beggar?" he railed.

I was speechless.

"I have no more change," I said.

"You just ate in there, didn't you?" he said, pointing to the elegant restaurant.

"Yes."

"And you paid a lot of money, didn't you?"

"No. A friend paid for me." The dinner had cost about fifty dollars.

"I haven't had a decent meal in weeks, yet you give me pennies. What meal costs a penny?"

"I'm sorry, but that's all the change I have."

He swore at me but kept the money. I walked away debating whether or not to continue giving money to destitute people.

I later recounted the episode to my friend from Scarsdale. He was indignant. He replied, "Most of these people use the money for drugs and alcohol anyway. I never bother giving them anything. Just look at yourself. You were born under worse poverty than they, yet you've lifted yourself up by the bootstraps. Why don't they do the same?" he said.

Shocked by such insensitivity, I made no reply. But I wondered if my friend, who himself grew up in a ghetto, knew that there were destitute people who needed help, and that without a pair of boots, such a magnificent acrobatic feat as "pulling yourself up by the bootstraps" is impossible.

These moral dilemmas convinced me that I had to find a way to escape from New York City. I had to flee to a place where once again I could trust and help instead of fear my fellow men.

From my travels I knew that there were still places where the community spirit still bound people to each other. If only I could become financially independent enough to be able to leave New York, I could move to such a place. But *Kaffir Boy* wasn't selling like hot cakes. The articles I wrote were sporadic and paid little. The Macmillan advance was almost gone: to taxes, to supporting my family, to paying debts, rent, and keeping me alive. All things considered, it seemed impossible I would ever leave New York.

If *Kaffir Boy* faded into oblivion, as it seemed to be doing, without opening up other opportunities for earning an honest living, what would I do? How would I live? My work permit was due to expire in a little over a year. Did I have another book in me which would enable me to apply for an extension? Would that extension be granted? Would that book be published? After all, people had said that *Kaffir Boy* was an exception. It was a book which came at the right time, when American public attention was riveted on South Africa. But South Africa, since the state of emergency was imposed and the media heavily censored in its coverage of unrest and protests, had almost disappeared from the front pages of newspapers and television screens. Some Americans even thought that the absence of pictures of violent protests from their TV screens meant that apartheid had been abolished.

38

HELPING A FRIEND; FINANCIAL STRAITS; READER'S DIGEST TO THE RESCUE; SENDING *Kaffir Boy* TO MY FAMILY; A VISIT TO NORTH CAROLINA

Word reached me through Ellie Spiegel that my friend Phistos Stone had graduated from the New York Institute of Technology but was in financial trouble and his student visa due to expire in a few months. The foundation which had brought Phistos to the United States and supported him while he pursued his master's degree had abruptly cut off his funds after he expressed a wish to remain here awhile because of increased repression in South Africa and his legitimate fear of imprisonment. I met with Phistos one afternoon in the cafeteria of I-House. He appeared haggard. Though I was burdened with my own problems I tried not to show it.

"Mark, I have no money left," Phistos said. "I can't pay rent and I can't afford a decent meal."

I was down to about $2,000 in my Pro Serve account. I gave Phistos $200.

"You can repay me whenever you get the money."

He thanked me.

We then discussed what he should do now that he was in danger of becoming an illegal alien.

"The only alternatives you have, Phistos," I said, "are to either find an internship or pursue another degree. Having just graduated you're eligible for a year of practical training."

Phistos's eyes lit up. "Really?" he cried.

"Yes." I explained what practical training entailed: Foreign students who had just earned degrees at American schools were allowed some time in the U.S. to work in their field of study. It turned out that under the new immigration laws the practical training period had been reduced to six months.

Over the next several weeks he applied for jobs at companies with investments in South Africa, and at labor groups around New York. He met with no luck. His practical training allowance period dwindled.

"I think you should definitely apply to graduate schools for a scholarship," I suggested to him the next time we met. "You're a black South African. You're bright. Your need is clear. And many of these schools have publicly pledged to help educate black South Africans, so you should have no problems getting financial assistance." I was mistaken. Phistos later took law exams, passed them, and then applied to law schools at Howard University, Columbia University, and lesser-known schools. He was rejected by some; those who accepted him had no financial assistance to give him.

Phistos's plight and my own desperate situation increased my disillusionment with New York City. There were times when I wished that I had never come to America, that I had chosen another profession—gone to business school, perhaps, and found a job, any job, with some paternalistic company which would have taken care of me and mine in return for blind loyalty—than the risky one of a writer. Yet I never entirely lost hope. Friends like Ned Chase and his wife, Lyn; Stew and Claudia on Long Island; Stan and Margie; Ellie and Hans; Fifi and Kevin; and, most important, Gail's support, kept me afloat.

"Don't worry yourself to death about money, Mark," Gail said one evening.

"But I have to worry," I said. "How will I pay my bills? How will I live?"

"Don't you remember the advice you used to give me before I got my job?" Gail said; she was now employed as an editor at the German Information Center on Third Avenue. "You always told me that if I kept trying, worried less, and took things a day at a time, something was bound to happen to rescue me from disaster."

News from home offered little comfort. My remittances had been exhausted and the family's miseries continued and multiplied. Still no job in sight for my father. My mother's diabetes had worsened. Another sister, Merriam, seventeen years old, was pregnant. Her first sexual encounter with an unemployed menial laborer occurred when black schools had once more been ordered shut by the government because of escalating student protests. My mother worried day and night that it was only a matter of time before Linah and Dianah followed the deadly pattern. She begged me to please find a way to bring Linah and Dianah to America to be under my care.

"Your father no longer has any influence in the house," she said during one telephone conversation. "He's just a shadow of his former self. His own children no longer listen to him. They have little respect for him because he has no respect for himself. Whenever he tells them to straighten their conduct, they retort that he should straighten his own. That in turn makes him more bitter and more abusive. There's no longer any harmony in the house. It's almost as if God were dead. But I know that He lives. You are a sign that He lives. You are our only hope."

George had left the religious cult but was still frustrated at his bleak prospects. He was entering his third year without regular schooling. He had watched a number of his friends brutally killed and others go beserk or turn to crime or become chronic alcoholics out of frustration. I periodically sent him books and urged him to educate himself and master the English language. He still played tennis and had begun coaching some youngsters in the ghetto, and his dream was to go to college. But with each passing day that dream seemed more remote, and he seemed headed for the same fate as most of his peers.

It was in the midst of all my worries that something happened to give me respite. In an unusual move, several months after *Kaffir Boy* was published, Reader's Digest Condensed Books became interested in purchasing the condensation rights. Barbara Morgan, an editor at Reader's Digest Condensed Books and Stan and Margie's friend, brought the book to their attention. For some time there was concern at Reader's Digest that *Kaffir Boy*, though it was an important and gripping story, might be too strong for their audience. But in the end the risk was taken. Macmillan received $35,000 for the condensation rights and I got half the money, minus the agent's fee of 10 percent.

At this time I began thinking seriously of building my family a decent home, with electricity and running water and an indoor toilet. Maybe I could even afford to bring them over to the U.S. for a visit. If we were reunited, would they recognize me? Especially my father: would he still see me as his son, and would I understand what he had been through?

I managed to send the family some money and a hardcover copy of *Kaffir Boy* through Thomas Getman and Ned Bennett, two white

American Christians I had come to know and whose love for the people of South Africa, black and white, inspired them to work tirelessly toward bringing about a peaceful end to apartheid. Tom was employed by Worldvision in Washington, D.C., and Ned worked for an insurance company in Massachusetts. Tom and Ned brought back photos of my family eagerly congregated about the book, faces full of smiles and pride at witnessing a miracle performed by one of their own. I was told that my mother was the proudest. She ululated all day about "her darling son who had become educated and written a book, all for the glory of God." She dearly longed to see me and urged me to reconcile with my father, who, she said, never stopped boasting that "the son who had inherited his smart brain was now a famous man in America."

Shortly after his return from South Africa, Ned Bennett was fired from his job. His crime, as he put it, was "seeking to raise the social consciousness of the company on issues such as apartheid and affirmative action." But the dismissal may have been a blessing in disguise. Ned now works for Franklin Research & Development, a Boston-based investment company which specializes in socially responsible investments for clients who want to ensure that their money doesn't end up in corporations with businesses in South Africa, and in defense and nuclear power companies.

A week before the U.S. Open tennis championships Stan and I were invited to a working lunch with editors of Reader's Digest Condensed Books at their picturesque headquarters in Pleasantville, New York. Stan and I were interviewed on television about how we met, the nature of our relationship, and the role that tennis had played in our lives. After lunch Stan and I played tennis together before television cameras as part of the publicity campaign designed to sell the story of *Kaffir Boy* to a largely white and conservative audience.

As we drove back to New York City I shared with Stan my plans for the future.

"Life in New York City is inhuman," I said. "I have finally decided to leave."

"Where will you relocate?"

"I don't know yet."

After a pause I went on. "I would have left a long time ago. But I couldn't because I had no money. Now things are changing. I have a feeling that this Reader's Digest deal is a precursor of more good fortune. It proves that *Kaffir Boy* has wider appeal. I have a feeling more copies will be sold."

"You may be right," Stan said. "But beware of the danger of unrealistic expectations."

At the heels of the Reader's Digest scoop word reached me through my agent that New American Library had bought the paperback rights to *Kaffir Boy* for a whopping $40,000. Half of it, of course, went to Macmillan, and the agent got his usual commission. I was elated. Here finally was the financial independence I had long sought. I could now afford to leave New York.

But a complication had arisen. My relationship with Gail had become serious and we occasionally discussed marriage. I wondered if we could stand the strain of separation. I had heard of the dismal failure rate of commuter relationships. When we met at Columbia each of us had striven to retain our independence, believing that a strong, lasting, and mutually satisfying friendship was often the result of the two partners' being able to grow individually and have fulfilling careers. We had experienced our share of ups and downs as we adjusted to each other, especially when my career as a writer blossomed while her manuscripts remained unpublished. Just as she had stood by me in troubled times, I now stood by her.

I therefore postponed my intentions to leave New York City. Gail and her friend Michal Shapiro, a student at Union Theological Seminary, rented a spacious and sunny upstairs apartment from a Jamaican family in the Park Slope section of Brooklyn. I urged Gail to continue writing despite the rejection slips. Still employed as an editor at the German Information Center, she wrote from five to seven each morning before work. She continued to submit manuscripts.

"Another rejection slip," she said one day in exasperation. "I don't think I'll ever be a writer. No one cares about what I write."

"I care," I said.

"Yes, you do. But what difference does that make? You're not a publisher," she said. "You know, sometimes I get the feeling that you only praise my work because you don't want to hurt my feelings. Just tell me the truth, am I a writer or not?"

"Only you can answer that question."

"What do you mean?"

"Look, it's obvious you have talent. If you're not convinced that you're a writer, then most likely you aren't one. But if you are convinced you are a writer, and act upon that conviction, no matter what people say to the contrary, you will in the end succeed. That's been my philosophy."

"How come your very first book was published and mine is continually rejected?"

"Stop comparing yourself with me. My case was very unusual. I was just plain lucky. I happened to be at the right place at the right time with the right subject."

Gail had begun writing her first novel, *Chasing Freedom*, while she worked as a journalist for *Die Neue Presse* daily newspaper in Hannover, Germany, in the summer of 1985, shortly after graduating from Columbia. The novel was inspired by her sojourn in Budapest in 1983, and travels through Yugoslavia, Czechoslovakia, Germany, Austria, and the Netherlands. *Chasing Freedom* became a love story about two Hungarian artists who flee the Eastern bloc for the West, searching for freedom, little aware that what they are searching for is already within them.

The novel was submitted to half a dozen publishing houses, including Houghton Mifflin and Random House, and editors said it showed great promise. The editor at Random House even said that *Chasing Freedom* would be published, but not as Gail's first novel. Phyllis Whitney, an astute critic of good writing, gave Gail this encouragement: "You *are* a writer, and a very good one—so you'll get there somehow." Gail was already working on her third book and we both felt that New York was the place to be for aspiring writers, or was it?

My disenchantment with New York kept resurfacing. One day I was invited to High Point, North Carolina, the unofficial furniture capital of the world, by Lyston Peebles, Brenda Williams, and Robert Brown. The three had been inspired by the story *Kaffir Boy* to become directly involved in South Africa. International Concern Foundation (ICF), a nonprofit organization which they had recently founded, sought to help black South Africans help themselves, and to build bridges between black and white South Africans. The foundation was to be funded by donations from other foundations, the public, and major American companies.

Bob Brown, a self-made black businessman, was a former Nixon aide, and founder and president of B & C Associates, a public relations firm which had Sara Lee Corporation, Johnson Wax, and Nabisco Brands among its clients. Bob was an interesting and complex character. Born in a poverty-stricken section of High Point in 1935, at the height of Jim Crow, he grew up wearing thrift-shop clothes, eating scanty meals, walking to school, battling rabid white racism, and working as a shoeshine boy to make ends meet. Thwarted by destitution and lack of opportunity in his dream to become a journalist, Bob, a lover of books and of learning, attended Virginia Union University, and later North Carolina A&T State University, before working for the Federal Bureau of Narcotics. Afterward, he founded his own public relations company. One of six children, he was raised, and profoundly influenced, by his grandmother, Nellie Brown. She died in 1976, yet her spirit still drives Bob.

Nellie's Christian beliefs, her self-reliance (she didn't believe in welfare), and beneficence, her belief in an education as a powerful weapon of hope, merged with Bob's entrepreneurial skills, resourcefulness, and dogged determination to succeed to make him one of the most powerful blacks in North Carolina, a multimillionaire, a philanthropist, and the owner of a lovely home with a swimming pool, and a gallery of African art. An avid golfer, Bob and his wife, Sallie, a high school sweetheart, hobnobbed with movers and shakers in business, education, and politics.

Brenda, a strong-willed black mystic who dressed expensively and drove around in a new BMW, was Bob Brown's confidante and ran the day-to-day operations of B & C Associates. She later became chief of staff for Marion Barry, Jr., Washington, D. C.'s controversial black mayor. Lyston Peebles, thirty-nine, was a short, garrulous, benevolent, born-again white Christian. He had once stayed at Stan's condominium on Hilton Head Island. Before becoming the Executive Director of International Concern Foundation, Lyston had been affiliated with Young-Life Christian groups in the South and had powerful friends in the Reagan administration. I stayed with Lyston in his townhouse in Greensboro, a much different city—progressive, integrated, cosmopolitan, and full of Buppies—from the Greensboro of the civil rights movement.

During meetings at the offices of B & C Associates, I discovered that Bob and Lyston, conservative Republicans, were opposed to sanctions and divestment. Brenda remained an enigma. Bob Brown considered sanctions and divestment self-defeating to the black struggle for economic independence from whites.

"Mark," he said to me one afternoon during a meeting at his office, "during my career in government and in business for myself, I learned a very important lesson: blacks can have all the political rights under the sun, but without economic power, they are doomed. You only have to look at black America to test the truth of that statement. I don't want to see the same thing happen to blacks in South Africa. I don't believe in government handouts. There's no dignity or security in that. What white folks give you, they can always take away. But what you earn, you'll always keep. That's why I believe that American companies which follow the Sullivan principles are doing blacks some good. They're giving your people equal pay for equal work, they're making them managers, supervisors, stockholders, directors, and homeowners. In other words, they're giving you *real* power. People can't eat votes. Don't get me wrong, Mark, I'm not implying that the vote is not important. I mean that while you fight for the vote, people have to eat.''

Bob Brown's arguments were persuasive. They made me take a more critical look at my own arguments for supporting sanctions and divestment, which went this way. The South African economy is based on apartheid, and its main beneficiaries are whites. American companies employ less than one percent of the black labor force. Even according to the most generous trickle-down theory, the majority of blacks remain mired in poverty. Moreover, all American companies would end up doing under the Sullivan principles would be to create a small black middle class, whose interests were interwoven with the apartheid economic fabric. The Pretoria regime could use such a bourgeoisie elite, whose limited economic privileges were likely to make it resist any radical change in the system, as a buffer between the aspirations of the black majority and the interests of the ruling white minority. Only the complete abolition of apartheid, therefore, and the creation of a democratic society where fairness and equal opportunity prevail offer the black masses any hope of improving their lot. But for most whites, apartheid is the source of their power and privileges, and it is naïve to assume they would willingly give both up unless there was a telling cost. And short of an all-out race war, sanctions and divestment were telling costs because they hit whites where it hurts the most: in their pocketbooks.

Theoretically and philosophically, I considered my arguments sound. But Bob Brown's practical approach showed me that the black man's struggle for genuine power, freedom, and independence from whites was more than a matter for theories and philosophical abstraction. He was right in saying that people had to eat while they fought, and that the black community needed to have economic power to safeguard its interests. The Marxist strategy of "emmiseration"—let the people become hungrier and poorer, so much the better for the revolution—was certainly not the aim of the black struggle against apartheid. We wanted a democratic, not a communist, revolution. So if "emmiseration" was not our aim, it made sense to economically empower the black community even while apartheid existed.

I already knew of the importance of economic power to effect political change. During the civil rights struggle in America, it was in part the black boycott of white businesses that forced them to desegregate, employ blacks, and treat them fairly. And in South Africa, black consumer boycotts led cities like Durban, Port Elizabeth, and East London to repeal petty apartheid laws that had kept blacks out of parks, pools, libraries, and other public facilities. And black South Africans have hardly begun to flex their full economic muscle. Particularly when one considers that the black majority of 28 million, though on the average poorer than the country's five million whites, accounts for nearly half the total consumer spending and pays more taxes.

Knowing all this, I came to view sanctions and divestment not as ends in themselves, but rather as means to an end. I also realized that the issue was much more complex, offered no magic solutions, and called for more than the simple litmus test of being for or against divestment and sanctions. It called for a responsible, realistic approach, which weighed equally the advantages and disadvantages of both sides of issue, and kept ever in mind the goal of liberating the black majority economically and politically, and with the minimum amount of suffering and pain.

Despite our philosophical differences on sanctions and divestment, Bob and I found common ground. I agreed with him on the need to help blacks wrest some of the control of the South African economy from the hands of nonblacks. Like he, I knew that the American companies being forced to leave South Africa in the name of black liberation were being taken over not by blacks, but by whites, Afrikaners at that. I also knew that in Alexandra, the ghetto where I grew up, black money enriched mostly Indian and white store owners who lived in exclusive suburbs, leaving the black community wallowing in a miasma of destitution, without even the most basic services like running water, electricity, and sewerage. Most important, I knew that the triumphs of the civil rights struggle in the United States didn't eradicate black poverty, and that in many black-ruled countries, *Uhuru* (independence) didn't usher in a millennium.

ICF's strategy was simple. Encourage the growth of black-owned businesses and entrepreneurs. Ensure that blacks have a stake in any American company forced to leave South Africa by the divestment movement. Identify and educate black youngsters for future leadership in all aspects of South African society. Increase and strengthen the links between blacks in America and in South Africa. In short, further the economic agenda of blacks at the same time as the political agenda.

The advice I gave Bob and Lyston, who were planning a fact-finding visit to South Africa, was on how to best approach an increasingly radical black community without having their motives questioned or impugned, for two reasons: their opposition to divestment and sanctions, which were supported by most blacks; and the growing anti-Americanism caused by the widespread perception among black South Africans that the Reagan administration—through its policy of constructive engagement—was an apologist for the Pretoria regime. It was interesting to note that constructive engagement had led Reagan to be regarded by the majority of white South Africans as the best American President ever, and by blacks as the worst.

While in High Point I read the local papers—the *Greensboro & News Record* and the *High Point Enterprise*—and was surprised to see incentives such as free month's rent, microwaves, and washers and dryers offered for renting beautiful apartments. I asked Lyston to take me to a few. We drove to about half a dozen apartment complexes in the Triad—Greensboro, High Point, and Winston-Salem. Everywhere I was astounded by the reception I got. All the apartment complexes were run by white managers, yet I was eagerly shown the best apartments and offered incentives to rent.

"Isn't this the same Greensboro where the Ku Klux Klan often marches?" I asked Lyston as we drove back home. Back in New York, stories about Ku Klux Klan rallies in Southern cities regularly made headlines.

"It's the same Greensboro," Lyston replied. "But the Ku Klux Klan has a very small following here. Most whites no longer support such hate groups. A lot of progress has been made since the sixties, Mark."

"You know, in New York I was denied various apartments because of my race," I said.

"Well, down here, if you can afford an apartment or a house, you will move in with no hassle. Even in places like Starmount and Irving Park." These places contained some of the most expensive real estate in the Piedmont Triad.

"But the picture of the South we have up North is very different," I said.

"I'm not surprised. For a long time the South has been stereotyped. We always tell Northerners to come down and see for themselves. We Southerners aren't perfect. But we also aren't the monster racists we are said to be."

It turned out that North Carolina was considered the most progressive state in the South, and many of its communities were among the most desirable places to live in America.

I was struck by Lyston's candor. He even related intimate details about the evolution of his own racial views. He admitted that when he was growing up he was prejudiced against blacks. But then came the civil rights movement. At first he and most Southern whites resisted the changes. But when they did change, they changed in a genuine way.

"Once change came," Lyston said, "and we realized that we were wrong, it wasn't hard for us to accept blacks as equals. After all, we had lived side by side for many years and knew each other well. And being a Christian helped."

Upon my return from North Carolina I told Gail that my mind was made up: I was going to leave New York.

"Where to?"

"North Carolina," I said.

"North Carolina! Are you crazy?" she cried. "Don't you know the South?"

Gail reminded me of her childhood in Austin, Texas, when her father was getting his Ph.D. She recounted harrowing stories of the endemic racism there: the race riots that occurred at her junior high school, her friends calling blacks "niggers," and her father being called all sorts of vile names for selling their house to a black family.

"The South has changed, Gail," I said. "Where I was in North Carolina I saw more progress than up here. You won't believe some of the things I saw."

"Like a Ku Klux Klan march full of Confederate flags, rednecks, and racial slurs."

"That's the stereotype, Gail," I said. "I went to North Carolina full of them, but many were dispelled. I felt more at home down there than up here."

"Of course you felt at home," Gail said. "It's probably just like South Africa."

"Gail, you don't understand," I said. "You just have to see things for yourself. I'm not saying the South is a paradise. Far from it. There's still awful poverty, ignorance, and racism in some places. But I've finally realized that the North, with all its liberal professions, hardly practices what it preaches. Up here there's the kind of racism that leaves black people numb with rage and schizophrenic. In the South at least you know who your true friends are. In the North people smile in your face and then stab you in the back. No, Gail, I know racism when I see it.

"For instance, what's the state of race relations in places like New York City, Chicago, Boston, Philadelphia? Yes, in the South the Ku Klux Klan still marches. But up here a Bernhard Goetz shoots you and goes free. An Eleanor Bumpurs gets blasted with a shotgun by white policemen. You know how many times I've been refused an apartment by bigots simply because I'm black? Just to compare, while I was down in High Point, white managers eagerly showed me the best apartments, and offered me incentives to rent."

"But what about us?" she asked. "When I come down to visit you, I don't want people staring at us bug-eyed wherever we go. At least in New York City we just blend in with all the various shades of white, brown, and black."

"I did see several mixed couples around the Triad," I said. "And they elicited the usual stares. Remember, Gail, people will stare at anything different. But what struck me the most is that as a black man I was treated with courtesy. In the stores white people smiled and greeted me as if they knew me. I walked the streets without the tension and fear and suspicion that is so typical of New York. I felt human for once. And the blacks down there are different from blacks in New York City. Even though they are poorer, they have more dignity, pride, a greater sense of community, and are less consumed by hatred. I know this sounds incredible but that is the South I saw. And it wasn't a façade. Yes, I have no doubt that there are places where black people aren't welcome. But that's hardly peculiar to the

South. There are places here in New York where black people aren't welcome."

"That's not the South I know."

"That's the South I didn't know either."

Friends and business associates tried to talk me out of moving South. Ned reminded me of the intellectual stimulation, the culture, the excitement and energy of New York City.

"You'll be so isolated from everything down there," he said. "You'll be stifled as a writer."

"I don't think so," I replied. "There are more than half a dozen fine universities in the area. Besides, a little solitude isn't a bad thing. And I can always hop on a plane and be in New York in a little over an hour." It was during the days of airline price wars. A flight from one of the New York airports to Greensboro cost as little as thirty-nine dollars. Theoretically, I would be nearer to Manhattan living in North Carolina than I would be living on Staten Island. It took me about two hours by ferry and subway to get to the Upper West Side.

"I hope you'll think this thing through," Ned said. "I think you're making a serious mistake."

39   UNEXPECTED PUBLICITY; VISITS TO STAN SMITH AND ARTHUR ASHE

One afternoon Dave Grogan, a white associate editor at *People* magazine, called me with the idea of writing a story about *Kaffir Boy*.

"It's the best book I have ever read on the subject of apartheid," he said. "It's a deeply touching human story."

"Will *People* magazine be of the same opinion?"

"Most likely. But I won't know for sure until I submit the story."

Dave, a tall, angular, sensitive man, came to my Staten Island apartment one Saturday afternoon and for several hours I told him the story of my life. In the process I got to know and like Dave, who was married to a Chinese freelance photographer, Chung Ching Ming. The two had a baby girl named Rae Lyn and lived in Park Slope, Brooklyn, a few blocks from Gail's apartment.

"Your story is amazing, really," Dave said at the conclusion of our interview. "And you tell it so well. It's not the usual *People* magazine story but I hope to convince my senior editors to run it because it's important."

For several weeks it was touch and go whether the story would be published. The editors admitted the story's importance, but as *People* magazine was essentially a photo magazine, they insisted that unless a good set of photographs accompanied the story, it was doomed. They assigned a professional photographer, Nicole Bengiveni, to follow me around for half a day. She took scores of photos of me riding my bike along the quay and posing before bookshelves. She even took photos of me skipping rope on the porch, and of me dripping sweat and holding a tennis racket.

"These are great photos," she beamed. "That's what I've been looking for all day."

"My God, Nicole, don't tell me you'll be using those!" I gasped.

"They're great shots, Mark," she replied. "If these won't make them run the story, I don't know what will."

"But I'm almost nude," I said. I wore only skimpy gym shorts. "Don't you think they'll demean the subject matter?"

"I don't think so," she said.

The photos apparently were not enough to convince the editors to run the story. They also wanted pictures of me with Stan Smith and Arthur Ashe, since both had played an important role in my life. I called Stan and he agreed to help sell my story. I flew to Hilton Head and *People* magazine sent Nicole down for Saturday afternoon, May 31, 1986. Various photos were taken of Stan, myself, Margie, and their three children—Ramsey, Trevor, and Logan. The setting was idyllic, and reinforced traditional family values and the warmth of friendship. Margie was expecting any time, and apparently the excitement and activity surrounding the afternoon-long photo session was enough to induce labor. Late that night she was rushed to the hospital and delivered a bouncing baby girl named Austin.

When I returned to New York I contacted Arthur Ashe and he agreed to be photographed with me. Nicole and I visited his lovely apartment on the Upper East Side where we spent about an hour taking photographs. Ashe, dressed in shorts, a T-shirt, and long sports socks, looked extremely fit, despite having had quadruple bypass surgery for hereditary heart disease in 1979, which prematurely ended his magnificent tennis career. When Ashe became the first black man to win Wimbledon, by upsetting highly favored Jimmy Connors on Center Court in 1975, his stunning victory filled blacks across the world with pride. It inspired me in Alexandra.

The presence of Ashe and Stan made the difference, and the story was approved by the editors. It appeared in the July 7, 1986, issue, under the heading "Memories of a Native Son." To my dismay, the dreaded semi-nude photo of myself dripping sweat and holding a tennis racket led the story. Incredibly, that same photo sold hundreds of copies of *Kaffir Boy,* and brought the book to the attention of readers who would not otherwise have bothered reading the book. That's America for you. In an immense country of 240 million people, only the national media can catch the attention of busy Americans. I didn't complain.

40 A TELEVISION APPEARANCE; GETTING TO KNOW WHITE SOUTHERNERS; MEETING MAYA ANGELOU

I made a second visit to High Point in the middle of August. On the way I stopped in Virginia Beach and appeared on "The 700 Club," a program of the Christian Broadcast Network headed by Pat Robertson. I was graciously received by the network's staff, and was surprised to find many of them reasonable and compassionate individuals, albeit overzealous about their proselytizing. They were eager to hear my point of view. Before I went on the set I exchanged ideas with Michel Janice, an assistant to one of the producers of the show, on a wide range of issues, including poverty, racism, homelessness and illiteracy in America, and religion.

I was interviewed by Ben Kinchlow, a former black militant turned Christian, on growing up black in South Africa and on my mother's faith. At the end of the program Pat Robertson, in an adjacent set, attempted to score political points (he was in the process of laying the groundwork for his 1988 campaign for the Republican Presidential nomination) with my story. His concern for the victims of apartheid was genuine, but his understanding of the South African situation struck me as simplistic. He admitted that apartheid was an abomination and had to go, but suggested that "communist elements of the ANC" might be behind the uprisings in the ghettos.

The truth of the matter is that blacks do not need communists to tell them that it is apartheid that is starving their ragged children, tearing their families apart, uprooting them from their ancestral lands and dumping them on impoverished tribal reservations, teaching them to hate, and denying them basic human rights in the land of their birth. Anyone with a feeling heart will spontaneously resist tyranny.

In High Point I stayed at the home of Dr. William "Butch" Farabow and his wife, Suzanne, a middle-aged Christian white couple. Butch and Suzie were Lyston's friends. They had read and been moved by *Kaffir Boy* and were eager to meet me. When I arrived in town they were vacationing on the coast. I had the entire house to myself for several days. Butch and Suzie were Republicans who cared about social, environmental, and peace issues. Butch, an obstetrician, was a graduate of Davidson College in North Carolina and had attended medical school at Emory University in Atlanta, where in 1988 Bishop Tutu gave the commencement address. Suzie had attended Salem College in Winston-Salem. They had three grown-up sons, Clint, Pres, and Matt. In 1985 Butch and his firstborn, Clint, spent several weeks in Bon Fin, Haiti, assisting Haitian nationals deliver babies and perform surgery. The experience did not make a flaming liberal of Butch, but it increased his sensitivity to the plight of underdeveloped countries.

Butch and I later spent time discussing race relations in the South. He poignantly recalled the world of eastern North Carolina—an area where blacks are the majority but whites hold political power—at the height of Jim Crow. He spoke of children of poor whites and poor blacks growing up together, with no hint of prejudice or hatred of each other. But "as the shades of the prison-house" began "to close/Upon the growing boy," the white youngsters, as part of their rites of passage into manhood and womanhood, often abandoned their human instincts and began to despise, fear, and refer to their former black friends as "niggers." All this in the delusion, he said, that by indulging in such bigotry they belonged to the white gentry.

Again I was struck by the candor of open-minded Southern whites in discussing racial issues and their past. They acknowledged and regretted the mistakes, but were proud of the progress they had made in integrating neighborhoods, schools, and workplaces. Often they thought Northerners unfairly clung to stereotypes about Southerners. Many Southerners, I discovered, still harbored animosities toward "Yankee Northerners" and misunderstood the meaning of the word "liberal."

Butch and Suzie introduced me to several of their friends, among them Frank and Jane Sizemore, Dr. Arnold and Janice Gill, and Dr. Thomas and Jean Stockton. Jane and a friend, Pat Colona, a real estate agent, drove me to various apartment complexes around High Point. In the car they related anecdotes about themselves and the city's history, and gave me pointers on interior decorating and furniture buying.

Dr. Stockton—now a bishop in Richmond, Virginia—was a progressive minister at the local Wesley Memorial Methodist Church. He regularly preached against the arms race, and about the need for social and economic justice in America. In 1963, at the height of the civil rights struggle, as a young minister in Reidsville, North Carolina, he and a black colleague, the Reverend Joe Bathea, now a bishop in South Carolina, went about town integrating eating places. One afternoon Jean took their young children out for ice cream. Finding the ice-cream parlor stripped of chairs, she asked why. She was told "because we don't want niggers eating here." She replied, "If blacks can't eat here, so won't we," and walked out. The Wesley Memorial Methodist Church helped fund ten clinics in Cape Town, including one at the Crossroads squatters camp.

Getting to know Southern whites gave me insights into white America I would otherwise have lacked had I concluded, as many blacks unfortunately do, "What do I have to do with whites, Republicans at that?" Such encounters taught me that all people essentially share a common humanity. Americans, I have observed, have a tendency to perceive their racial and cultural differences as mutually exclusive, rather than see those differences as contributing toward a whole greater than the sum of its parts, from which whole should come the cooperation and strength to tackle intractable problems of racism, poverty, homelessness, drugs, and crime, to name a few.

Toward the end of my visit, Bob Brown and Lyston Peebles took me to Winston-Salem to meet Maya Angelou, the celebrated black author of *I Know Why the Caged Bird Sings* and Reynolds Professor of American Studies at Wake Forest University. Maya Angelou was in every way the sensitive, proud, and eloquent lady I had imagined her to be. In her sitting room, elegantly furnished with African art, she gave me advice on dealing with agents, reminisced about her ties to Africa, and revealed that she was once married to a black South African, a member of the African National Congress, a fact I already knew as an avid reader of her series of autobiographies. I gathered from the visit that she was happy living in the South.

When I returned to New York I spent a week thinking hard about relocating to North Carolina. I knew that I by no means fully knew or understood the South, that I had hardly seen all there was to see in the land of Dixie, that the Ku Klux Klan and other hate groups from time to time roamed the streets of Southern cities, but the little I had seen had convinced me beyond doubt that the experiment of living there was worth making.

41   ANOTHER TELEVISION APPEARANCE; MOVING TO NORTH CAROLINA; LEARNING TO DRIVE

One morning a call came from Gil Noble, the black host of the television program "Like It Is," inviting me to appear on his show, to be taped in New York. I was thrilled by the invitation for I had great respect for Gil's program. In his weekly Sunday program Gil regularly explored in-depth controversial issues confronting black America and the Third World: drugs, the CIA's illegal activities, corruption in public officials, the effects of teen pregnancy and single-parenting on the black community, racism, and police brutality. He had recently done an illuminating series on how crack, the deadly cocaine-derivative drug, was decimating the black community.

Meeting Gil proved rewarding. A tall, imposing, and handsome man, he exuded the confidence of a veteran of many battles for social and racial justice. The walls of his office were decorated with awards, photos, African art, and books about black history from across the world. He was a defiant radical, and made no apologies about that, even though he was in a business where towing the official line was requisite for survival. We both were admirers of Frederick Douglass and other fighters for the black man's liberation: Lumumba, Paul

Robeson, Mandela, Nkrumah, Bob Marley, Malcolm X, Marcus Garvey, to name a few.

I was not surprised to learn that Gil's technique of telling the truth "Like It Is," instead of packaging it as entertainment, as so many in the media did, had earned him the disfavor of the owners of the television station. They tried to sanitize the program, to make it more palatable to conservative America and squeamish advertisers, and to replace its agent provocateur. They failed. "Like It Is" was Gil Noble. He was a hero to a large and vocal audience that no media mogul cared to offend. Many television watchers on Sunday planned their day around "Like It Is." I did, too.

My appearance on the show, on August 23, 1986, brought a deluge of calls into Gil's office from viewers. Some praised the contents and style of the interview, some expressed shock and outrage at what I had revealed about black life in South Africa, and others requested information about how to get in touch with me, how to get me as a speaker, and where to purchase the book. That interview alone sold hundreds of books, and each time it was rebroadcast, the effects were the same.

By the end of August my mind was made up on leaving New York. In September I hired a truck and an Iranian driver and left for North Carolina. My new home in High Point, which Jane Sizemore and Pat Colona helped me find, was a lovely apartment in Eastchester Ridge, a fully integrated complex. It had amenities which in New York would have cost me a fortune: two large, sunny bedrooms; two full baths; a wood-burning fireplace in a spacious living room with a bay window and patio overlooking a cluster of trees; cable television and washer and dryer hookups; full kitchen with dishwasher; thick, well-maintained neutral carpet; around-the-clock maintenance service; and the use of a clubhouse, pool, and all-weather tennis courts—all for $425 a month, one hundred dollars less than what I paid for the basement hovel on Staten Island!

Butch, Suzie, and their friends helped me resettle. With their assistance I had no trouble getting a telephone installed and utilities turned on; finding a personal physician, Dr. Nelson Pollock, who gave me my first physical in years; an accountant, Horton Godwin, who told me all about Keogh plans and IRAs, helped with overseas royalties, and with whom I occasionally played tennis; and William McGuinn, a banker at whose First Citizen Bank I arranged to send money to my family back in South Africa. I also had my teeth checked for the first time by Dr. Harry Culp, who was amazed that I had no cavities.

"Proper diet is the secret, I guess," I said.

Dr. Culp later replaced my missing front tooth, knocked out with a brick when I was fifteen and assaulted by radical black youths who were opposed to my playing tennis with whites.

I had no car, and public transportation in High Point was poor, so Suzie and her friends took turns driving me on various errands. Within a couple of weeks, Suzie had arranged for me to take free driving lessons with a soft-spoken Quaker public-school teacher named Robert Kent, who became a friend. Shortly thereafter I bought a car, a gray Honda Accord LXI. I passed the written exam easily but failed the driver's test a week later, for driving on the wrong side of the road. I guess I thought I was in South Africa!

I failed the test the second time.

"You didn't stop at the stop sign," the white inspector said. I could have sworn I did.

I failed the test a third time.

"You didn't keep to your side of the road," the black inspector said.

I could have sworn I did.

"Driving inspectors in the South are a little crazy," Suzie joked. She had accompanied me to the licensing bureau all three times. "And Butch's Wagoneer is not the easiest car to drive," she added.

"What should I do?" I said. "I've bought a car and I can't drive it. I'm afraid if I take the test the fourth time they'll come up with yet another excuse for not giving me the license."

"Why don't we try Thomasville?" Suzie suggested. Thomasville was an adjacent town.

Before going to Thomasville, I took delivery of my new car. It was the first week of October. I test-drove it a few times. The next day, after smashing my fingers closing the car door, and in exquisite pain, unable to hold the steering wheel firmly, Suzie and I drove to Thomasville and I finally got my driver's license. I returned to the dealership triumphant, and all the salesmen there came out and clapped.

Everywhere I went in the Triad, people black and white were helpful and courteous. Of course part of this had to do with my newly acquired celebrity status as the author of *Kaffir Boy*. But in a large measure people were just being human. Away from the hustle and bustle of big-city life, I set about rebuilding my life and rearranging my priorities. I began thinking of ways of bringing my family to America. I hardly missed New York City.

A VISIT TO LONDON; THE LECTURE CIRCUIT; DEBATING A DEFENDER OF APARTHEID

In the meantime, *Kaffir Boy* was being purchased by publishers in England, Norway, Italy, Germany, Sweden, Denmark, the Netherlands, and France. I was invited to England for a weeklong promotional tour by Bodley Head and Pan Books, my Commonwealth publishers. I was almost denied entrance into the United Kingdom because the travel document I had in lieu of a passport made British custom officials suspect that I might be a refugee. The matter was straightened out after more than an hour of anxious waiting and phone calls.

When I returned to the United States I signed a contract with Greater Talent Network, a lecture agency in New York. Soon I was appearing on college campuses across the country relating my story and occasionally engaging in debates with Stuart Pringle, an eccentric thirteenth-generation white South African, now living in the United States, who insisted that apartheid was a "necessary evolutionary step."

Gaunt and middle-aged, Stuart, a filmmaker and spiritualist, was a direct descendant of Thomas Pringle, the famous Scottish–South African poet and friend of Sir Walter Scott. Thomas Pringle, after whom a South African literary award is named, fought against slavery in the British colonies, including South Africa, where the newspaper and magazine he published were suppressed by colonial administrators for their reform views. It was therefore ironic that his descendant, pursuing with religious zeal a perverted form of Hegel's theory of historical dialectics, had come to regard legalized racism and oppression as necessary evolutionary steps.

During our heated debates Stuart often said, "Most black South Africans, in terms of the progress of civilization, are still living in the

Bronze Age. They are like teenagers. They need a strong, wise, and firm parent to guide them to maturity, to civilize them. The current protests in the ghettos are the equivalent of teenage rebellion." In Stuart's eyes, that "strong, wise, and firm parent" was the white race, which he insisted represented the most advanced civilization toward which all "primitive" societies inevitably tend. According to Stuart, white South Africans had the moral right to use every available means, including force, to wean blacks from "antiquated ways of life, clanism, and rebellious teenage behavior." If unweaned, so went Stuart's preposterous theory, blacks would be eternally embroiled in tribal disputes and wars, ignorant of the marvelous advances achieved by Western civilizations.

"Most European nations too were once rebellious teenagers," Stuart would harangue, with veins bulging in his neck. "Then the Romans came along and ended all the silly behavior." Stuart had previously debated Bobby Seale, the former leader and founder of the Black Panther movement. Their acrimonious confrontations were legend on many a college campus. In debating Stuart I took the calm and reasoned approach. I sought to convince him that his views were wrong, without attacking him personally. But I was unable to change his mind significantly. Whenever my arguments were telling he resorted to personal attacks. Despite our sharp differences, there were a couple of things we agreed on: the need to wipe out illiteracy throughout Africa; the need to end black oppression and one-party rule; and the need to reforest the continent, and import more agricultural technology to help end drought and hunger throughout Sub-Saharan Africa.

One of Stuart's intriguing but wild ideas on how to end hunger in places like Ethiopia and the Sudan involved building a pipeline that would transport fresh water from the North Pole, across Europe and the Strait of Gibraltar, and into the Sahara, and from that arid desert create what he called "the breadbasket of Africa." Incidentally, the Fascist dictator Benito Mussolini first used the expression "breadbasket of Africa" to refer to a lush Ethiopia (then Abyssinia) rich in grain, which Italy was about to invade and occupy during the Second World War. Ethiopia is now, alas, the victim of one of Africa's worst tyrants, the Soviet-backed General Mengistu Haile Mariam.

PART FOUR

REUNITED
WITH
MY
FAMILY

43 PHISTOS GOES UNDERGROUND; REASSESSING MY RELATIONSHIP WITH MY FATHER; A CONVERSATION WITH MY SISTER FLORAH

One afternoon I heard from Ellie Spiegel that Phistos no longer lived at I-House. A vagabond, he now lived in awful places in New Jersey and Harlem and occasionally trudged back to I-House for companionship and sponging. I sent him some money through Ellie. One afternoon during a visit to New York City I met him along a street in Harlem. Desperation, fear, and resignation were now visible in his face. He told me that because of his precarious immigration status, unscrupulous landlords often took advantage of him. Sometimes he found his belongings missing; he was still applying to law schools; he ate what he could find; his family had sent him some money—all of it went to rent, examination fees, and postage—but he hadn't heard from them since; he had no phone in his hovel. I promised Phistos that I would use my contacts to find him a job, but each time an offer came up, his precarious immigration status prevented his being hired. I soon lost touch with Phistos, and at the writing of this book I have still not tracked him down.

The slow pace of life in High Point and the absence of the rat race enabled me, when I was not off lecturing, to focus more attention on several important things in my life. One of these was my family's well-being, especially my father's. The two of us had not spoken to each other since my leaving home almost nine years earlier. I now sought ways of reconciling with him. The passage of time, the distance from South Africa, the maturation I had undergone from living in America—all now made me see him in a different light.

When I was growing up in the ghetto I had hated him for his impotence, for his failure to protect the family in the face of the brutal police raids, for his gambling and alcoholism, for his frequent abuse of my mother and us children. But I now began to see that in a way he had largely been a victim of deadly forces beyond his control. He needed help and understanding, not hate and abandonment.

My mature explanation of my father's problems ran this way. Since apartheid had over the years emasculated him, just as it had emasculated countless black men in his situation, it was inevitable that the more my father's manhood was sapped by white oppression, the more he would, in his desperation to retain a semblance of his dignity as a man—especially since he had been raised under rigid tribal customs which regarded the husband as the provider, master, and lawmaker of his household—tyrannize over those who were helpless to resist: his family. Deprived of control over his life, he had to have control over something. By repeatedly denying him means of earning an honest living, by repeatedly humiliating him in front of his family, by repeatedly arresting him for the crime of being unemployed, the apartheid system inexorably twisted my father's humanity and turned him into a beast. Once transformed, he constantly wore a malignant sneer. He constantly muttered curses. He constantly suppressed, denied, or covered up what pain and joy he deeply felt. His terrifying presence banished all mirth and warmth from the house and created such tension that, at the mere sound of his voice, his children sometimes urinated involuntarily or suffered temporary amnesia.

But there were times when glimpses of his loving true self showed. Occasionally when he was drunk he would give his children pennies to buy candy, or a shilling to buy a book, and on Friday, payday, when he had a steady job as a menial laborer many years ago, he would bring home fish and chips wrapped in newspapers, or exchange rare and loving banter with my mother.

I now realized, at twenty-six, and he nearly sixty, a time when life had already shown me much of its tenderness and meanness, how he must have suffered, how much he had endured, stoically, without flinching, alone. I now realized how, despite the unimaginable pain of his life, he still managed to do something which forever endears him to my heart: he never abandoned his family. That point was driven home the more when I realized that in America, black and white men, but especially black men, in the inner cities among the underclass, were deserting their families left and right, either from sheer irresponsibility, or from realizing that the family would be better off—by being eligible for welfare—without a male in the house.

But I believed that it was more important that the black man stay with his wife and children because the black family structure, like any other family structure, should be sacrosanct. It had to be protected at all costs. It is the fortress of our being. Its disintegration spells doom for the race by destroying its only hope, only salvation, and only future: black children. This disintegration of the black family structure left black children easy prey to the myriad problems facing single-parent households: welfare dependency, illiteracy, lack of positive values, crime, and drugs. This disintegration placed too disproportionate and heavy a burden on the shoulders of the black woman, who more often than not groaned under the yoke of a triple oppression: as a woman, a black, and an illiterate. This disintegration reinforced many of the worst racial stereotypes about black people and gave credence to the bigotry of many white people.

I often wondered how I would have turned out if I had grown up in a single-parent household. Most likely I would have continued defying my mother and scorning education until the streets and gang life claimed me wholly. But my father was always there, drunk or sober, the terror of the house. His presence kept me in line and curbed my excesses. Even his failures served as important warnings.

I now saw that despite the traumas that he had subjected me to when a child, he still served the role as my father. His blood flowed in my veins. In his own different, confused, and sometimes bitter way he loved me. I remembered the tears he had shed, the first time I'd seen them in his life, when be bid me farewell when I left for America.

"Take care of yourself, my son," he had said.

How would I now take care of him? How would I now, given my successes, given my experiences forged in worlds beyond his knowledge and imagination, convince him that I was still his son, his firstborn, his Thanyani? How would I convince him that though apartheid had ruthlessly crushed his dreams and hopes, they continued to live and to bear fruit in me? How would I thank him for staying with the family and ensuring that at least we children, though deprived of much, grew up with a father?

I wrote the family letters in which I requested that he be at the phone whenever I called so that I could talk to him, heart to heart. I was told that for some strange reason he refused to talk to me, that he always absented himself from home when he knew that I would call. At first I was baffled by this. Then it dawned upon me that probably his strange pride—the one thing the system could never destroy—made him act that way. He could not stand the thought that I was now the breadwinner, that I was now supporting the family and him, that I now gave him advice on how to mend his life. I, the son who he had thought would never amount to anything because I refused to follow his example; I, the son he had been ashamed of and had called a wimp for crying when hurt, for loving books, for playing tennis. No, the humiliation for him would be too much. He preferred to wrestle with the demons of his life alone. But I kept trying to talk to him.

"Please ask Papa if there's anything I could do to help him," I said to my sister Florah one day.

"He says you should send him money."

"But I've sent him a lot of money already."

"He drank it all."

"Why won't he personally ask me for the money?"

"I don't know. He just wants you to send him more money, that's all."

"Has he found a job yet?"

"No. His arm still bothers him. From time to time he gets a *skoropo* [a part-time job held a day or so], but that's all."

"Tell him that from now on I'll only send him money if he personally requests it."

Always during these lengthy and costly telephone calls to my family Florah would plead with me to bring the family over to America. Her ambition was to become an American-trained beautician, so she could open her own perming school in the ghetto and make a fortune; the "American look" was sought after.

"Life is so hard over here," she said one time.

"I know," I replied. "And believe me, I would bring you over immediately if I had the money."

"We hear that life for black people in America is very good. You always sound so happy."

"Well, for some it is. But for others it's worse than some of what you're going through." I always tried to sound happy during telephone calls to my family because I did not want to have them worry too much about me; they already had enough problems to worry a lifetime about.

"Worse. In America?" Florah exclaimed. "Don't say. I read in magazines that black Americans are very rich people. I read every day about the fortunes of Michael Jackson, Diana Ross, Bill Cosby, and Lionel Richie."

"There are a few very rich black people in America," I said. "Richer than anything you've ever seen or imagined. But there are millions of very poor black people, too. Some of them are so poor that they're forced to live on the streets, to beg for pennies to buy food, and to eat out of garbage dumps."

"I don't believe it. Are you sure you're talking about *the* America?"

"I'm talking about *the* America. I, too, didn't believe such things happened until I came here."

"Even with that," Florah insisted, "I still want to come to America. I want to see New York and Hollywood, all the movie stars and the bright lights. There is a New York and Hollywood, isn't there?"

"Yes, there is a New York and Hollywood. But I can assure you it's not all as glamorous as you think."

"You know, my boss, who's been to America several times, tells me there's no apartheid there."

"Yes, there's no apartheid as you know it. But there's another form of apartheid, which is also deadly."

"What do you mean?"

"You have to be here to see what I mean."

"Which do you like better, Mark, America or South Africa?"

"America. There's no doubt about that."

"Why?"

"Because even to a black man, America, with all her shortcomings, has something South Africa doesn't have: freedom and hope. Those two things, sister, in my opinion, are priceless. With the right attitude they can be made into formidable weapons."

To Florah, like to many black South Africans, America was a black man's paradise. The magazines, the movies, the lavish appearances by American superstar entertainers and athletes at places like Sun City, in the spurious homeland of Bophuthatswana, bolstered such an image. To her, black Americans were the most glamorous people in the world—wealthy, sophisticated, very intelligent, and sexy. Their hairstyles, leather coats, jewelry, music, cars, accents, and so on were the trend-setters in the ghettos. The only way she could ever believe that America was not the utopia she dreamed of was to see things for herself, just as I had done. I did not want to sully her beatific image of America too much, because I knew that there was some degree of reality in her fantastic dream: there was hope in America, there was freedom, and there was opportunity, but it was no utopia.

How, in all fairness, could I have led my sister to believe that America was a utopia for blacks given the following realities? In 1987, one-third of black families lived below the poverty line. Of those poor black families, 73 percent were headed by single mothers, often unskilled and undereducated. At 18 percent per thousand births the infant mortality rate of blacks was twice that of whites. The jobless rate among black youths, twice that of white teenagers, was around 45 percent and rising. The dropout rate in many inner-city schools was 36 percent and climbing. Child abuse and alcoholism among poor blacks were on the rise, the latter, as in South Africa, often exacerbated by a preponderance of liquor billboards in black neighborhoods. Gang warfare in cities like Los Angeles, Washington, D.C., and Detroit left hundreds killed and maimed. Crack and other deadly drugs were wreaking havoc in many a black community. Homelessness, police brutality, racism . . . the list went on and on.

I began making plans to get my family over to America, but the obstacles seemed formidable. Where would I get the money for the airfare? How would they obtain passports from a regime that had revoked mine? And since my family was so large, and it would be impossible to bring everyone over to America, how would I go about selecting who should come? For the moment the dilemmas seemed insoluble.

44 PONDERING THE NATURE OF FAITH AND RELIGION; CONFRONTING CHRISTIAN FUNDAMENTALISM

Another important issue I now addressed in earnest was religion. Many Americans who had read *Kaffir Boy* and were thus familiar with the circumstances that led to my rejection of Christianity when a youth had written or called me wanting to know what I now thought of it. Did I believe in God? What was the nature of my faith? Others even urged that if I was not yet converted they would be delighted to turn me into a Baptist, a Pentecostal, a Jehovah's Witness, a Transcendentalist, a Mormon, a Muslim, a Seventh-Day Adventist, a Spiritualist, a Hare Krishna, and so forth. That way, I was variously told, I could better understand and appreciate the miracle of my having survived apartheid; not through my own resiliency and willpower, and my parents' sacrifices, but through the sufferance of their all-powerful god.

One black man in High Point, a tinkerer, whom I sometimes met during my daily walks, even suggested that with the kind of life I had led, the obstacles I had overcome, my education, and my verbal skills, I could easily start my own church. The man had seen me on "The 700 Club" and had read *Kaffir Boy.*

"In everything that's happened to you," he said with conviction, "there was clearly the hand of God Almighty at work. You are truly among the elect, brother."

"I honestly don't think God wants me to be a minister," I said.

"How do you know?"

"For one thing, all my life I've been skeptical about this religion business."

"Wasn't Saul? And didn't he become Paul?"

High Point, part of the Bible Belt, had the most churches of any city I had ever lived in. Altogether there were nearly three hundred churches in a town of about 70,000 people. Many of these churches were fundamentalist, white-male dominated, and segregated. Added to all that, there were programs and televangelists of every stripe on almost every television station, seven days a week: Jerry Falwell's "Gospel Hour," Gospel Expo, PTL, Jimmy Swaggart, Coral Ridge Ministries, Oral Roberts, and "Rock Alive," to name a few. Many seemed nothing but "feel good" businesses. They spent most of the time raising money by sending people—particularly the elderly, the lonely, and the spiritually confused—on guilt trips, exploiting their inadequacies and fears, especially the fear of death, "a necessary end, which will come when it will come."

The ignorance and narrow-mindedness of many of these tele-vangelists gave Christianity a bad name. During sermons they uttered such things as "No one can know God without knowing Jesus Christ," "Nothing in the world existed before Jesus," "The Bible should be interpreted literally because it was written by the hand of God Himself," "Man is not descended from apes," "The world did not evolve but was created in seven days by the voice of God," and "Christianity is the only pure religion, and the only true way to salvation and eternal life."

I knew that these claims ignored important facts. Other non-Christian religions had as valid a claim to worshiping the true God. Darwin's theories on evolution were rational, scientific, and indispensable to the proper understanding of biology and botany, even though a recent survey by sociologists at the University of Texas found that 30 percent of biology teachers believed in Creationism. And Christianity, to which the world undoubtedly owes much for its morality and civilization, nevertheless has, like other religions, a checkered history. The religion had not descended from heaven, "clad in its native purity," as fundamentalist zealots maintained. Christianity was founded in the first century A.D. by Jesus of Nazareth, a man whose exemplary life and morality have led millions to worship him as the Son of God. Following Jesus' crucifixion, in 33 A.D., Christianity was almost wiped out by persecution under various Roman emperors. As John Stuart Mill put it, the religion only survived because "the persecutions were only occasional, lasting but a short time, and separated by long intervals of almost undisturbed propagandism.''

That "propagandism" sometimes took brutal form. Under the reign of the emperors Constantine and Theodosius, Christianity, once the despised cult of a tiny sect of Nazarenes, replaced paganism as the dominant religion of the Roman Empire. The fanatical followers of Christ, prompted by the notion that it was their duty to convert the whole world, began persecuting and massacring non-Christians. More persecution and bloodletting in the name of Christ occurred during the Crusades, during the era of the conquistadores, and during the European colonization of Africa and North America.

I went to several white churches in High Point and Greensboro hoping to find at the least an acceptance of these facts. Their being accepted, I thought, could only enrich the Christian experience and underscore the need for toleration. With few exceptions (notably a Quaker meeting in Greensboro, which my driving instructor Robert Kent attended, and the Wesley Memorial Methodist Church in High Point, where Dr. Stockton preached), I discovered that in most white churches the factual history of the evolution of Christianity was unknown or ignored. There was absolutely no room for Darwinism. And the validity of other religions which did not have their basis in the Bible was only grudgingly acknowledged. Most fundamentalists seemed unaware that just as they had a right to regard and worship Christ as their Lord and Savior, millions of other people, in America and around the world, had the same right to pay tribute to Buddha, Confucius, Swikwembus, and Mohammed, and to read as their sacred texts the Koran, the Torah, the Veda and Bhagavad Gita, and the Tripitaka, just as Christians read the Bible.

From time to time I tried to reason with fundamentalists about toleration. I would meet these people—men and women—at the apartment complex where I lived; at the gym, Living Well Fitness Center, where I worked out several times a week; at the various stores where I shopped for furniture, food, and clothes; at barbecues and parties hosted by friends; at book-signing events; on Hilton Head Island whenever I visited Stan and Margie; at churches and schools to which I was invited to speak. I would tell them that toleration wasn't only necessary for religious freedom in America—it was indispensable. I would explain that from my reading of history, the founders of American society, many of them men of deep faith, had the wisdom and foresight to conclude that, since there was no incontestable truth concerning religious matters—in other words, since one man's religion sometimes turned out to be another man's heresy—then everyone, the atheist and the agnostic included, was orthodox to himself.

But most of these people didn't buy such arguments. Others considered my remarks blasphemy. One evening at sunset I was visited by Thomas, a fundamentalist I had met shortly after my move. After seeing me on "The 700 Club" he had read *Kaffir Boy* and been deeply touched. Middle-aged but with youthful features, Thomas was an amiable and decent gentleman. He was well read in Scripture and his faith was genuine. He regularly did works of charity in the Triad community. He was eager for me to visit his church.

As we sat on the patio of my apartment, talking about the South, the situation in South Africa, and life in general, our conversation turned to religion. Thomas asked me if I now accepted Jesus Christ as my Lord and Savior. I said no. He was surprised.

"You mean your position hasn't changed from when you lived in South Africa?"

"It has."

"What then do you believe?" he asked.

"I believe in God."

"But Jesus Christ is God," he said.

"Only according to Christianity," I said.

Thomas was taken aback but he tried not to show it.

"But you've been going to churches down here," he said. "I thought you were a Christian."

"A person doesn't have to be a Christian to go to church, does he?"

"No."

There was a pause.

"What exactly do you have against Christianity?" Thomas asked with a pained look on his face. "Not all Christians are like those racist Afrikaners, you know."

"Of course I know that," I said. "I have nothing against Christians. Some of my closest friends are Christians. I have worked, and continue to work with Christians in the struggle for justice and freedom in South Africa. My own mother is a devout Christian. Part of my moral code is derived from the teachings of Christ. But I've been influenced by and respect other faiths, too, including the faith of an atheist."

He was puzzled. "What is the faith of an atheist?"

"Belief that there is no God."

"Are you suggesting that atheism is the same as Christianity? I'm shocked to hear such things from you, Mark. Especially considering how much God has done for you."

"I'm suggesting no such thing," I said. "But never mind. Do you respect the Constitution of the United States?" I asked.

"I do."

"Do you know what the First Amendment says?" I asked.

Thomas didn't. But he wasn't alone. Most Americans revere the Constitution, as they should, but few have ever taken the time to read critically that magnificent document.

I quoted the First Amendment: "Congress shall make no law respecting the establishment of religion, or the prohibiting the free exercise thereof. . . ." I then explained that with this Amendment the First Congress, during its first session held in the City of New York on September 25, 1789, sought to minimize religious discord, and prevent the majority or one powerful faction from imposing its religious beliefs on minorities or dissenters.

"The First Amendment essentially says that religion is a matter of individual conscience," I said. "And to me the various religious doctrines, including Christianity, contain contradictions which I cannot yet reconcile. Therefore I cannot outwardly profess what I inwardly disbelieve."

"What's contradictory about Christianity?"

"Many things. Take as an example the belief in the miracles of the Bible. If I started believing that they really happened, why shouldn't I believe in the miracles connnected with the tribal beliefs of my parents?"

"I don't see any reason why you shouldn't believe in those miracles, too, if they really happened."

"That would be nice," I said. "Except for one thing. Fundamentalist Christians call my tribal beliefs, which include ancestral worship, heathenism and devil worship."

This explanation left Thomas dumbfounded and a bit embarrassed. He attempted to modify his dogma somewhat. He admitted that toleration was a good thing, and that he and fellow fundamentalists didn't mind coexisting with other faiths. Yet he insisted that America was a Christian nation. "One nation under God, indivisible," was his favorite refrain. He then added that for the good of the country, politicians, teachers, and other keepers of the public good ought to believe in God. He was a fervent admirer and supporter of Pat Robertson, who, as a candidate for the Republican Presidential nomination in 1988, erected his political platform upon such principles.

"You mean you wouldn't vote for a person who didn't believe in God but otherwise was of upright moral character?" I asked Thomas.

"I certainly wouldn't," Thomas replied.

"Why?"

"Because there can be no morality without God, no right and wrong," Thomas said. "Did you know, Mark, that atheists, humanist teachers, and liberal politicians have allowed every type of sin to exist in America?"

"What do you mean by sin?"

"Pornography. Abortion. Homosexuality. Forbidding prayer in the classroom. The humanist curriculum in schools, which says there's no right or wrong and that man wasn't created by God in His own image but came from some ape. The list is endless."

"Come on, Thomas," I said. "Aside from the fact that your definitions of humanism and sin are wrong, it's not humanists, atheists, and liberals who allow all those things to exist. It's the laws of the United States."

"Then the laws must be changed," Thomas declared. "And only men who believe that God is alive have the courage to do that. Even though I dislike some of the things Reagan does, like selling arms to the Ayatollah, I continue to support him because he believes in traditional family values and is determined to put God back into American life. He has promised to appoint more conservative judges to the Supreme Court. Yet I know the liberals and atheists in Congress and the media will fight him all the way. But in the end Reagan will win. He has God on his side. And God is more powerful than all the liberals and communists put together."

Confronting such a mind-set I could argue no further.

I discovered that in their preoccupation with orthodoxy, many white Americans—not only Southern fundamentalists—see no contradictions between their faith in Christ or their particular God and their support, tacit or overt, of the status quo: of government policies which worsen poverty and homelessness; spawn wars, devastation, and suffering; and infringe upon individual liberties. They eagerly spend millions on evangelical foreign missions and very little to help bring about racial, social, and economic justice at home.

In sections of High Point, Greensboro, and Winston-Salem—and in various other parts of America—I encountered poor blacks, whites, Native Americans, and Hispanics living under conditions reminiscent of Soweto and Alexandra. Many of the these areas have no adequate plumbing; some have no running water. Children suffer from neglect and malnutrition. And without adequate health insurance, the poor are often denied proper medical care in hospitals.

During my residency in High Point I also visited several black churches. I was heartened to discover that a good number of black preachers, despite being faced with dwindling congregations and lack of funds, continued to challenge the status quo. One example is the Reverend Paul Perkins, of St. Matthew United Methodist Church in Greensboro, where I went with Ronald and Carole Weatherford, a black couple from High Point. Carole, thirty-two, a talented jazz poet, worked for B & C Associates as a writer, and Ron, thirty-three, worked as a mail carrier while he studied theology. He is now a minister at three small rural black churches in Seagrove, North Carolina.

Another example is the Reverend David Baker, of the St. Stephen A.M.E. Zion Church, who in 1987 ran for the city council in order to better serve the practical needs of the black community, much of which was mired in poverty and hopelessness. Reverend Baker, deeply concerned that the black community was losing its future by raising a generation of illiterates, invited me to speak at a library in the black section of High Point, before a packed audience which included youngsters being honored by the library for having read the most books. I spoke of my love for books, of how I had used education as a powerful weapon of hope, and of the importance of never giving up despite the obstacles.

Recently a nineteen-member delegation representing American black churches visited southern Africa and came up with evidence that the Angolan people were victims of South African terrorism, and that U.S. interests and businesses in Angola were contributing to the aggression. The Reverend John Mendez, pastor of Emmanuel Baptist Church in Winston-Salem, was quoted in the papers as saying that African-American church leaders should become involved in issues of political, economic, and social justice, in America and abroad.

But there were other black preachers who thought otherwise. Their attitude toward religion was similar to that in most fundamentalist white churches. During my travels and sojourns in several Southern towns, I came upon black preachers who, either intimidated by the white power structure or beholden to it for salaries, funding of church activities, and other favors, had become accommodating, conservative petty bureaucrats. In their sermons, laced with religious fatalism, they exhorted their flocks to rivet their attention on the world to come, rather than attempt to solve the practical problems of this world. They ignored or glossed over issues vital to the black community: racism, crime, drugs, teen pregnancy, single-parenting, high dropout rates, alcoholism, child abuse, and gangs. It was hardly surprising that these kinds of black preachers had a vested interest in segregated churches. They saw interracial cooperation in church activities as an attempt to deprive them of their influence and power. Ironically, one of the unfortunate outcomes of this self-imposed segregation was that many progressive-minded young blacks had drifted away from the church. And in turn the church, once the citadel of moral and political black power, was losing influence over its future leaders.

Such a state of affairs convinced me that true faith had very little to do with congregating under a roof each Sunday morning, or with numbing oneself to or withdrawing from the painful realities of this world, or with singing hymns and asking for the remission of sins committed during a week of self-indulgence and conscious disobedience of God's commandments. Instead, true faith, I felt, had everything to do with one's humanity. The best religion, I concluded, is one that helps people become more loving of their brethren, more understanding, more tolerant, more caring, more helpful. It manifests itself in deeds, in earnest attempts to lead a virtuous life, and not in hypocrisy, moral expediency, and power struggles. It certainly is not a prescription given out each Sunday morning to salve uneasy consciences.

And since there were so many religions in the world and, as far as I knew, none had a monopoly on God or salvation, nor possessed irrefutable evidence that its God was the only true God, then it made sense to me to embrace a God above all the various creeds. And to me, given my life experiences and temperament, this all-transcending God has endowed human beings with reason, consciences, feeling hearts, and a free will.

This all-transcending God is the one who, in St. Francis of Assisi's "Letter to the Rulers of the People," admonishes us: "Remember that when you leave this earth, you can take with you nothing that you have received—fading symbols of honor, trappings of power—but only what you have given: a heart enriched with honest service, love, sacrifice, and courage."

Further, people should "imitate his [God's] preference for the poor and powerless. Enter into his plan of liberating all peoples from everything that oppresses them and obstructs their development as human beings. Do not grow tired of working for peace among all people.

"Help remove unjust social structures and patterns of exploitation. Uphold the rights and dignity of the human person. Foster the creation of a society where human life is cherished, and where all people of the planet can enjoy its many gifts, which God created for all in a Spirit of Love and Justice and Equality."

This became my religion.

45

THE MATERIALISM TRAP; SPEAKING OUT AGAINST BLACK RACISM; YOUNG REPUBLICANS; I'M CALLED A COMMUNIST

Such a faith made it easier for me to define the meaning of happiness. I was thankful to be living in America and to have a caring and supportive friend in Gail. I was now earning a comfortable, though precarious, living on sporadic payments from articles, lectures, and royalties from *Kaffir Boy*. I had already begun to write this book, and negotiations were under way with several producers who wanted to purchase the film rights to *Kaffir Boy*. My life-style was not extravagant. I continued to save for the future. And even though I supported the family back in South Africa, paid taxes, and put my siblings through school, I still had enough money left to afford almost anything reasonable I wanted.

The temptation to waste money on frivolities was ever present. The Triad area was full of Buppies with extravagant life-styles. But having grown up in poverty, having had to eat leeches and locusts to still excruciating pangs of hunger, having seen my siblings diapered with rags, and having myself worn repatched hand-me-downs, I knew the importance of wisely using the little money I had. I formulated the following creed, along the lines of Franklin's *Poor Richard's Almanac:* never need something simply because it is there or others have it; everything you possess must be honestly earned; giving is receiving; the world owes you nothing but you owe everything to the world.

I did not want to fall into the trap of worshiping Mammon. I had witnessed, both in America and in South Africa, that money, seen as an end in itself, bought people the miseries of their choice, things like alcohol, drugs, pornography, and illicit sex.

Life in South Africa had taught me that money cannot buy happiness, love, or security. The whites of South Africa are among the wealthiest group of people in the world. Yet every day there are stories in South African newspapers and television of whites plagued by divorce, alcoholism, drug and child abuse, rape, infidelity, fear, neuroses, and suicide. In 1988 alone, over forty Afrikaners killed themselves and their families in what psychologists call "extended suicides," a phenomenon which surfaced in 1985 when black political violence threatened the closely knit Afrikaner community's sense of superiority. Throughout South Africa whites know that only brute force, racism, and a perversion of their consciences perpetuate their power. They wonder when the whole powder keg will blow up.

In speeches before college students, convicts, churches like St. John the Divine, civic groups like the Long Island Human Rights Committee, and companies like Bell Communications Research in New Jersey, I shared these convictions and ideals with blacks and whites. People asked how I could remain so hopeful, given all that was happening in South Africa, and all that my family and I had been through. My reply was:

"The end of hope is the end of life."

"You mean you don't hate white South Africans for having created apartheid?" asked one student at Eastern New Mexico State University.

"I'll be honest with you," I said. "I once hated whites. I hated them so much that my nostrils would dilate at the sight of an Afrikaner. That hatred reached a frightening peak during the Soweto student rebellion of 1976, when hundreds of blacks were murdered by the police. Blind hatred so consumed me that it almost killed me. I knew I had to find a way to rise above hate. It wasn't easy. But I kept working at it. And many white friends, in relating to me as a human being and an equal, helped me tremendously. Now I don't hate white South Africans; I pity them. But I continue to hate the monstrous system of apartheid. White South Africans, in a way, are victims of apartheid, too. And it is the system, not they, that has to be destroyed, just as during the Second World War it was the Hitler regime that had to be extirpated, not the German people."

Some militant blacks took my attitude as an indication that I had become mealymouthed on racism. From time to time they confronted me with angry questions.

"Our brothers and sisters in South Africa have a right to hate those fuckin' white swines," said one militant student at the New York Institute of Technology in Old Westbury, New York, where I met in private with a group of black students before the lecture. He was a tall, thin fellow, in his early twenties, with brown deep-set eyes, a hard face, and short black hair.

"What will hating whites bring us?"

"Satisfaction."

"What kind of satisfaction?" I asked.

"The satisfaction of their knowing we hate them."

"Will such blind hatred change the white man's evil ways?" I asked.

"No. The white man will never change his ways. He is a murdering, exploiting, cheating, and racist son of a bitch by nature. Look at his history. Look at what he's doing to people of color all over the world!"

"If all you say is true, then our future is bleak indeed, because only a change in white people's attitudes can bring about lasting peace and justice, not only in South Africa, but in America as well."

"And how do you propose to change white people's hearts, my educated bow-tied brother?" the student demanded sarcastically. "By constantly turning the other cheek?"

"By showing them that their fears of me as a black man are unjustified," I said. "By refusing to stoop down to their degraded level of bigotry."

"How do you propose to do that?"

"By loving them when they hate me. Because if I hate them for hating me, then I justify their hatred and we get caught in a vicious cycle."

"Are you an Uncle Tom?" the student asked.

"Call me what you will," I said. "I know who I am."

At almost all the colleges and universities where I spoke there was a vocal minority of white students who styled themselves "Young Republicans." Most of them defended constructive engagement, the Reagan doctrine toward South Africa. With their tunnel vision, they saw the struggle in South Africa only in terms of East-West conflict. They kept harping on the importance of keeping the Botha regime in control so as to guarantee that America and its Western allies continued to receive minerals from South Africa and to thwart Soviet advances in the region. They seemed unaware that the apartheid regime, by depriving blacks of freedom and hope, by destabilizing and fomenting civil wars among its neighbors, by continuing its illegal occupation of Namibia, was the greatest champion of communism and the deadliest enemy of Western interests.

Even on the home front, the Young Republicans exhibited a contempt for the democracy they so worshiped. In their heated arguments with me and other liberal students, they unabashedly supported and called "patriots" Oliver North and his fellow lawbreakers in the "Iran-gate" scandal. I sometimes felt that they regarded the Reagan administration as some sort of Leviathan, incapable of doing wrong, to criticize whose policies was tantamount to violating the First, Second, and Third Commandments! They believed that America had a monopoly on freedom and goodness, that she was always right, and that any system of government which was not a replica of America the Beautiful was no good.

These Young Republicans loved calling me a communist, especially when they couldn't refute my arguments. Some of my liberal friends in New York expressed concern at my being thus labeled. One of these friends was Phyllis Reed, a charming, fifty-three-year-old white woman from Northport, Long Island. Phyllis was not only an activist for justice at home, but also a zealous champion for the liberation of South Africa. She was a proud liberal Democrat. Inspired by the words of Dr. Martin Luther King, Phyllis composed the song "I Have a Dream," published by Galaxy Music in 1978.

Phyllis regularly wrote letters to various newspapers condemning bigotry and advocating affirmative action and an end to housing segregation, a pervasive problem in the suburbs of New York and Long Island. One time, after one of her letters supporting open housing on Long Island was published in *Newsday*, she received hate mail, including an anonymous pamphlet from the Ku Klux Klan.

Another time, after suggesting that the Huntington Congregational Church, which she attended, address the issue of apartheid, she received an anonymous call at three o'clock in the morning. The caller, with a foreign accent, threatened to bomb the church if any antiapartheid activities took place. She reported the matter to the Suffolk County police and the FBI, and even contacted Les Payne, the outspoken *Newsday* black columnist and senior editor. The police investigation revealed that a conservative member of her church was responsible for the threats. Apparently he had links with the South African consulate in New York. He was warned but not prosecuted. On February 23, 1986, I did address her church on the apartheid issue.

When Phyllis learned that my work permit expired in less than a year, and that I was often called a communist for criticizing the Reagan administration's bad policies, she asked, "Aren't you afraid that the Reagan administration can make life difficult for you?"

"I'm aware of that. But I love America too much not to speak out when she's wrong."

"But this is not the time to do that. The whole country is reactionary."

"I believe this is the best time to speak out."

46   WEDDING PLANS; A PHONE CALL TO MY MOTHER; BLACK OPPOSITION TO RACE MIXING

In the spring of 1987 Gail and I became engaged. Neither of us had much money, but she was thrilled to receive the ring I gave her, though the diamond was so small one could only see it by holding it a few inches in front of one's face and squinting with one eye shut. She was still in New York, living with a Lebanese-American friend from her days at Brown University, Carol Abizaid, a dancer. The two rented a large third-floor apartment in Brooklyn from Cecilia Lewis, a beautician from Trinidad who lived on Flatbush Avenue. Since I had moved down to North Carolina, Gail and I saw each other every other weekend. Either she would fly down to High Point on one of those

People Express discounted fares, or I would combine a visit to her and my publisher and agents in Manhattan.

Gail and I wanted a quiet wedding. During our two years together we had experienced the usual ups and downs of a couple learning to know, understand, and respect each other. But through it all we had forthrightly confronted the weaknesses and strengths of each other's characters.

Our racial and cultural differences enhanced our relationship and taught us a great deal about tolerance, compromise, and open-mindedness. Gail sometimes wondered why I and other blacks were so preoccupied with the racial issue, and I was surprised that she seemed oblivious to the subtler forms of racism in American society. We regularly compared our backgrounds. I would describe growing up in a large, close-knit family, my dealings with constant hunger and pain, my joy at finding nightly relief from the hard life in the ghetto in my mother's and Granny's stories, the only books I had, and my learning very early in life to take my destiny into my own hands. Gail would describe growing up, protected and loved, in a middle-class nuclear family in the suburbs of the Midwest, the abundance of toys at Christmas, the feasts at Thanksgiving, full meals each day, the security and pride of being an American.

Gail and I had no illusions about what the future held for us as a married, mixed couple in America. The continual source of our strength was our mutual trust and respect.

We wanted to avoid the mistake made by many couples of marrying for the wrong reasons, and only finding out ten, twenty, or thirty years later that they were incompatible, that they hardly took the time to know each other, that they had glossed over serious personality conflicts in the expectation that marriage would miraculously make everything work out right. That point was underscored by the fact that Gail's parents, after thirty-five years of marriage, were going through a bitter and painful divorce, which had devastated Gail and for a time adversely affected our budding relationship.

When Gail broached the news of our wedding plans to her family she met with some resistance. Both her liberal-minded brothers, Paul, a research scientist at Cornell Medical School in Manhattan, and Dan, a psychologist in New York, advised her to wait a little longer before "taking such a big step." Even her mother, Deborah, who all along had been supportive of our relationship, and even joked about when we were going to get married so she could have grandchildren, now counseled Gail to really be sure that she was doing the right thing.

"So it was all right for me to date him, but it's wrong for me to marry him. Is his color the problem, Mom?" Gail later told me she asked her mother.

"No. Color has nothing to do with it. I must admit that at first I had my reservations about a mixed marriage, prejudices you might even call them. But then I realized that as a mother I have to be supportive of whatever or whoever makes you happy. And when I met Mark I found him a charming and intelligent young man. Any mother would be proud to have him for a son-in-law. Yes, my friends talk. Some even express shock at what you're doing. But they live in a different world. So you see, Mark's color is not the problem. My biggest worry is that you may be marrying Mark for the same wrong reasons that I married your father. When we met I saw him as intelligent, charming, and caring. It was all so new, all so exciting, and we both thought, on the surface at least, that ours was an ideal marriage that would last forever. I realized only later that I didn't know your father very well when we married."

"But Mark and I have been together more than two years," Gail replied. "We've been through so much together. We've seen each other at our weakest many times. I'm sure that time will only confirm what we feel deeply about each other."

"You may be right. But I still think that waiting won't hurt. You're only twenty-five."

"But his parents may be coming to the U.S., and wouldn't it be special if we were married during their visit?"

"It would be. Yet I still stick by my opinion. But remember it's your life. And anyone you choose to love I would love, too."

Gail's father, David, whom I had not yet met personally, approached our decision with a father-knows-best attitude. He basically asked the same questions as Gail's mother: Why the haste? Who is this Mark? What's his immigration status? And when he learned of my problems with the immigration department, he immediately suspected that I was marrying his daughter in order to remain in the United States.

"But Dad, that's unfair," Gail said.

"Then why the rush? Buy time, buy time," he chanted.

"Mark has had problems with immigration before and has always taken care of them himself," Gail retorted. "In fact he made it very clear when we were discussing marriage that if I had any doubts about anything, I should not hesitate to cancel our plans."

"Well, that's what they all say. But I still believe everything is happening too fast. Your mother and I are going through hell because of a mistake we made which could have been easily avoided, if we had only waited a year, as we initially talked about doing. But then we changed our minds and decided not to wait that long. That was a mistake. I now think that had we waited, we might have found out things about each other then that would have revealed that we were not meant for each other. I don't want my only daughter to make the same mistake. It would break my heart."

"Dad, Mark and I love each other, even though we may get strange looks as we walk down the street," Gail said. "In society's eyes, we're not a perfect match. But at least I've learned to choose love over social acceptability."

Her father proceeded to quote statistics showing that mixed couples had higher divorce rates than same-race couples and gave examples of mixed couples he had counseled who were having marital difficulties.

"Have you thought about what your children would go through?" he asked.

"Dad, are you a racist?"

"No, of course not. But you have to be realistic."

"Maybe our children will have some problems, but whose children don't? But one thing they'll always have: our love and devotion."

"That's idealistic. People can be very cruel toward biracial children."

"Dad, we'll worry about that when the time comes. If one had to resolve all doubt before one acted, there would be very little done."

"Remember, it's never too late to change your mind."

Other relatives of Gail's voiced similar concerns, but I'm happy to say that none of them were overtly racist. Yes, there were one or two persons who, privately, were appalled that a Daughter of the American Revolution would marry a black man. Gail's mother's mother, Susan Stork Scott, a descendant of Stephen Hopkins, who came to America on the *Mayflower,* had been active in the DAR, a national patriotic society founded in 1890.

In time everyone came to respect our decision.

On my part, I met with no resistance from my family. In fact my mother was delighted at the news and was quick to point out to me once again that under Botha's recent reforms, mixed couples were now legal, and that she had seen a few in Johannesburg.

"But Mama," I said, "Gail is as white as they come. Doesn't that bother you?"

"Why should I be bothered?" my mother asked. "She's a caring and intelligent human being, isn't she? I would be bothered if she drank and smoked and was lazy and disrespectful."

"But Mama," I went on. "What will people say?"

"Who cares what people say? Child, if I had cared what people said, given the many times they have poked their noses into my affairs, I would have done nothing in my life. I learned too late to care only about what my heart and conscience said, but learn I did. Life is too short to waste worrying about what people will say. They will always say what suits their fancy, and what satisfies their prejudices."

"Won't you have hang-ups caring for light-skinned grand-children?"

"I have been caring for white children all my life. A child is a child, whether black or white. It needs loving, hugging, and kissing."

My mother's reaction was in sharp contrast to the attitudes of some black mothers I had met during my travels across the country. One time I was at the University of Alabama at Huntsville on a lecture arranged by a charming and defiant black woman who had done wonders for her children in the Deep South. One son now attended Yale University, another was enrolled at a prestigious private school in Tennessee. She eloquently talked about racism in America, the need for black people to stand up for their rights, to cherish their African roots and not be deluded into thinking that the American culture was their only culture. She was dismayed at what was happening to black youths across the country. She was proud to have raised her children to withstand the influences of drugs, peer pressure, and inferiority complexes.

"It was never easy," she said with the confidence of a veteran. She had just picked me up from the hotel and we were headed for the lecture hall. "But I knew I had to do it, alone if need be. Fortunately my husband was around, even though it was often I who made the gutsy decisions like which school they should go to. Every day of their lives I sought to prepare them for the reality out there. I told them that though their mama pampered them, they would get no pampering

from the world out there because it was built for the benefit and
pampering of white children. Black children had to learn how to
fight for the little they got. Often they had to fight twice as hard.
Many times they would fail. But they owed it to themselves never to
give up."

"You know," I said. "That's what my own mother used to tell
me."

"That's what my own mama used to tell me, too," she said with a
laugh. "We had nothing when I was growing up. We wore rags, we
were denied an education, our men were lynched, we had no vote, we
feared the white man like he was the devil incarnate. But we had
something the white man, devil or no devil, could never take away
from us: our dignity. We were a proud people. We were a caring
people. We were a loving people. We took care of each other. And we
did survive and we did accomplish things that have made us proud.
But that spirit is gone from today's black folks."

I agreed with her. By degrees we fell into talking about interracial
relationships.

"I encourage my sons to know white people as individuals and to
have friendships with them if possible," she said. "But I warn them
never to forget where they come from."

"I have many white friends," I said.

"Lucky for you."

"What would you say if your favorite son, the darling of your life,
came home one day and said, 'Mama, I've met this white girl and
we're going to get married'?"

"I would be very disappointed."

"Why?"

"I'm not racist. I don't mind my sons dating white girls. I know
that black men, for some inexplicable reason, need to do that
sometimes. But if my son married a white woman, I would be very
disappointed."

I wasn't too surprised by this statement. I had encountered it
before: at Limestone, Quincy, and Dowling, in books, and in many
black communities where I had lived. This statement, and variations
of it, even from intelligent and reasonable blacks, showed me how
much of the black man's identity in America was predicated on race.
It was not only bigoted whites who opposed race mixing, but some
blacks also, out of a strange sense of pride, strange because it seemed
to accomplish the very thing that white racists wanted. The black

opposition to interracial relationships and marriages rarely is as rigid or has the potential for violence as white opposition has exhibited.

I knew that by marrying Gail I would once again be opening myself up to accusations of betrayal from black militants. Some friends had already warned me that marrying a white woman would undermine my credibility as a black writer and spokesperson against apartheid. But my mind was already made up. I had the blessing of my family, and even if they had opposed my intentions, I would have gone ahead anyway because I understood that in the final analysis I had to do what I thought was right.

I informed Stan and Margie of my decision. They were taken aback, more it seemed to me by the suddenness of it than by the fact that Gail was white.

"We didn't even think you had a girlfriend," Margie said.

"Well, I seldom trumpet such personal matters," I replied. "But I have known Gail for some time and we had both agreed to keep a low profile. Moreover, our careers kept us very busy."

"She must be a very lucky girl," Margie said with typical warmth and generosity.

"I'm a very lucky boy," I replied.

47 A FELLOWSHIP AT CORNELL; TRYING TO GET THE FAMILY TO THE UNITED STATES; AN AFRIKANER HELPS THEM GET PASSPORTS

While wedding preparations were under way, through the urging of Ned Chase, I applied for a fellowship in the Humanities Department at Cornell University, where his son-in-law, Jonathan Culler, was director, and daughter Cynthia a professor of English literature. I was accepted. The fellowship was for the academic year 1987–88. I was promised a stipend of about $24,000 to teach a course comparing the black experience in South Africa and America. The position would leave me ample time to complete the sequel to *Kaffir Boy*. Further, Gail and I would get a chance to enjoy the beautiful countryside surrounding the renowned university, and be in the midst of intellectual and artistic ferment. The opportunity seemed alluring. Gail and I began making preparations to relocate to Ithaca. She still had her job in New York. We both had fallen in love with North Carolina and intended to return to High Point after my year at Cornell.

Meanwhile, I persisted in attempts to get my family over to the United States. The wedding date was set for August 1, 1987. I kept hoping for a miracle to bring my family to this important event of my life. It so happened that Lyston Peebles, who had just returned from his first visit to South Africa as executive director of International Concern Foundation, had gone to see my family in Alexandra. Accompanying him on the trip was a Christian Afrikaner named Gary Beukes, who acted as his escort. When Lyston returned to the United States and told me that this Gary Beukes had become a close friend of the family, I immediately became suspicious.

"First of all," I said to Lyston, "he shares the same name with the South African ambassador to the U.S. Are they related?"

"I don't know. But Gary is truly a man of God," Lyston said.

"Most Afrikaners will tell you that," I replied. "After all, the Dutch Reformed Church says that apartheid is God's will."

"But Gary is different. Give him a chance to prove himself."

Lyston was right. It had been my experience that all Afrikaners are often blamed for all the ills in South Africa, and regarded without exception as racists and killers. In truth, there are many English-speaking whites, and blacks, who are equally tools of apartheid.

"I'll talk to this Gary," I said. "But remember, I won't be blackmailed."

"Given the kind of life you've led," Lyston said, "your suspicions are understandable. But I assure you that you'll find Gary to be a forthright, honest, caring, and loving human being. He's already talking about getting together whites from the suburbs to join blacks in a campaign to clean up Alexandra."

Under apartheid, with the government's deliberate neglect of basic services for black communities, Alexandra had been transformed into a sort of Augean stables. I wondered how the whites, most of whom had never set foot in a ghetto, and lived secluded in suburbs which were paradisian by comparison, would react to the inhuman conditions under which blacks lived. Would the sight change their attitudes?

"That should be mighty interesting," I said to Lyston. "I hope they clean the ghetto so well that they wouldn't mind spending a night there, or swapping places with blacks."

Lyston laughed. "Gary is part of the new generation of Afri-kaners who reject apartheid and are reaching out to their black brethren," he said.

"The same thing was said about Prime Minister Botha," I said. When Botha came to power in 1978, following the black student revolts, of 1976 and 1977 which radicalized the black majority and galvanized the international community into demanding a speedy end to apart-heid, he promised to usher in a new era of justice and freedom for all in South Africa. "Adapt or die," he told his fellow whites. Black leaders hailed the bold declaration, only to be cruelly disappointed when Botha, despite his promises and limited reforms, turned out to be to some, a variation of the old guard, and to others, a forward-looking leader without the political courage to make a complete break with a discredited past for fear of the unknown.

Lyston changed the topic.

"Well, I took the liberty to ask Gary to help your family obtain passports," he said.

At first I thought this presumptuous; but knowing Lyston, I realized that he meant well. "Thanks for the effort," I said. "But I can assure you nothing will come of it."

Lyston later quit ICF out of frustration. His departure came at a time when the issue of sanctions and divestment had polarized the American public, and ICF, despite Lyston's indefatigable attempts, was unable to raise the necessary funds to carry out its mission. The foundation became dormant. But Bob Brown's involvement with South Africa continued and deepened. In 1986 he was poised to become the first black U.S. ambassador to South Africa, but a storm of controversy derailed his nomination by President Reagan. Allega-tions circulated in the media of his involvement, early in his business career, in questionable loans and union-busting, and of his association with Umaro Dikko, a former Nigerian cabinet minister who, follow-ing a military coup in 1983, absconded to Britain, charged with corruption and theft of millions of dollars from Nigeria.

Throughout the ordeal, Bob Brown maintained his innocence. He subsequently made several trips to South Africa, often alone, sometimes in the company of black American leaders like Coretta King, ministers, business executives, and presidents of predom-inantly black colleges. He was still doggedly pursuing the goal of economically empowering blacks, of helping them help themselves, of building bridges between South Africans of all races. He spent thousands of dollars of his own money providing bursaries for black youngsters studying in South Africa and in the U.S.; he bought some land in Alexandra for the construction of a home for the elderly; he provided books and clothing to black schoolchildren, many of them orphans; and at the writing of this book, he was educating and supporting one of the Mandela daughters, Princess Zenzani Mandela Dlamini, her husband, Prince Zinhle, and their family, who are studying at Boston University. His generosity led him, in 1987, to become the first American to speak with Nelson Mandela at Pollsmoor prison, spending almost two hours with him.

Yes, I continue to have sharp differences with Bob Brown; yes, some of my friends have warned me that associating with him will tarnish my "image as an uncompromising foe of apartheid"; but I continue to believe that anyone is innocent until proven guilty, and that a person who does something to keep hope alive, to alleviate human suffering, deserves some respect, if not praise. My respect for Bob Brown remains undiminished.

48

AN INVITATION TO APPEAR ON "The Oprah Winfrey Show"; ARRANGEMENTS ARE MADE TO BRING MY FAMILY TO AMERICA

One morning at about eleven the phone rang. I had just finished breakfast and was getting ready to run some errands.

"Mark?" the caller asked. It was a female voice.

"Yes, this is Mark speaking."

"Hi, Mark, this is Oprah," the caller returned. "Am I glad I finally tracked you down!"

"Oprah who?" I asked, thinking it was another fan of *Kaffir Boy*. I had been receiving many such calls lately.

"Oprah Winfrey," came the reply, followed by a pause.

My heart skipped a beat. Was I really speaking to *the* Oprah Winfrey, the famous talk-show host and one of the stars of *The Color Purple* and *Native Son*? Then I recalled that Kevin, my agent, had sometime ago told me that someone from "The OprahWinfrey Show" might be calling about *Kaffir Boy*.

"She was deeply affected by the book," Kevin had said. "She definitely wants you on her show."

"Hi, Oprah," I replied. "I'm delighted to hear from you. Thanks for your interest in the book."

"Interest!" Oprah cried excitedly. "That's an understatement. This is about the most moving, most interesting book I've read in my life. It has enriched my life in ways I can't begin to describe. Thank you for writing it."

"Thank you for reading it."

Oprah proceeded to relate how she had chanced upon *Kaffir Boy*. She and her boyfriend, Stedman Graham, were walking down a Chicago street one evening. The two saw the book displayed in a store window. At the time Oprah was reading black authors and on the lookout for new material. The jacket of *Kaffir Boy*, showing the determined and defiant face of a black South African youth, arrested their attention. I had been told by many people that the book jacket of *Kaffir Boy* was powerful and made the book stand out.

"I immediately bought the book," Oprah went on with mounting enthusiasm. "And once I began reading it, I just couldn't put it down. I've made it a part of my special collection in my home. I've bought over a dozen copies and given them out to friends. Wherever I go I tell people about it. I arrived at the studio the following morning with an armful of *Kaffir Boy*s, and I told my whole staff about your incredible story. I urged everyone to read the book."

It turned out that the producers of "The Oprah Winfrey Show" had been sent a copy of *Kaffir Boy* by Macmillan about a year ago and had rejected the subject without reading the book, probably as too controversial. One thing they forgot was the magnetism and intelligence of Oprah the individual, her amazing facility to get even the most squeamish, narrow-minded, or bigoted audience to listen, to learn, and to care. If Beelzebub himself appeared on "The Oprah Winfrey Show," I believe Oprah could persuade an audience of fundamentalists to listen intently to his case against God.

"I want you to come on my show," Oprah said. "I believe your story ought to be heard by every man and woman and child in this country. Not only black people, but white people as well. Yours is not a black man's story, it's a human story."

We went on to discuss with passion the problems confronting black youths in America, and dwelt particularly on the defeatist attitude adopted by many.

"You know, Oprah, many of our people don't believe they are equals with anybody. It's about time we started believing it and acting accordingly to defend our rights because no one will do it for us. Yes, there is racism in America. Yes, we are not getting our fair share. And yes, many of us are confined to terrible ghettos. But we can and must fight. We have already survived the worst. But the tragedy is that many black youths have simply stopped trying."

We talked for almost an hour. In that time I came to know what makes Oprah so lovable. She is a woman of conviction, compassion, and deep faith. She doesn't hide behind a façade or put on airs. She has known pain. She is not the least afraid to tell you what is on her mind and in her capacious heart. She cries, she cares, she laughs, she is vulnerable, she admits her imperfections, she tries to understand, she's willing to learn, and she's very giving. She recently gave $750,000 to her alma mater, Tennessee State University, a predominantly black college, for the establishment of ten scholarships to help create opportunity for others. These qualities—which many talk-show hosts lack—have endeared her to millions of television viewers across the nation: blacks, whites, liberals, conservatives, old and young, city dwellers and country folks. These qualities account for her meteoric rise as a leading daytime talk-show host.

I agreed to appear on "The Oprah Winfrey Show." Over several days, on the phone with Oprah and her executive producer, Debra DiMaio, we worked out the details of my appearance. Oprah and her producer happened to have scheduled a show on South African music, featuring Paul Simon and several black South African musicians who were part of the controversial "Graceland" album. It was felt that as the author of *Kaffir Boy*, I could describe the world, the milieu, in which the music of "Graceland" was forged so successfully.

For many people apartheid remained an abstraction, a black-and-white issue. When *Kaffir Boy* came along it made people see that trapped within the ghettos of apartheid were men, women, and children whose aspirations were the same as those of people everywhere.

One of the weaknesses of the protest movements against apartheid is that they have failed to portray the struggle in human terms. Instead, they have allowed the debate to remain on the abstract level of politics and ideology. Theoretical argumentation is on a level at which the Pretoria regime is most formidable. The regime has worked out an elaborate propaganda which can "make the worse appear/The better reason, to perplex and dash/Maturest counsels." How many times have we heard so-called experts on South Africa, including officials of the Reagan administration and members of Congress, characterize the rebellion by the black majority as "communist inspired," and praise the Botha regime for "reforming apartheid," forgetting that apartheid, like slavery, is inherently evil and cannot be reformed but must be completely abolished? If Abraham Lincoln had reformed slavery rather than abolished it, there would still be plantations all over these United States.

I was excited about appearing on "The Oprah Winfrey Show" but in the back of my mind lingered several misgivings. Would my message be heard on a stage with Paul Simon, the superstar? Wouldn't people be more interested in posing questions to him about his album and the controversy it had generated? Would they really care to hear about suffering, about heroic struggles, about children contemplating suicide or prostituting themselves for food, about the resiliency of the human spirit? I would be lucky to get in as much as a sentence.

I wished that the entire show would be devoted to the story of *Kaffir Boy*. But that was wishful thinking, I thought. With "The Oprah Winfrey Show" involved in a fierce battle for ratings against "Donahue," would her producers risk devoting the show to an issue such as apartheid and thus possibly alienate a large segment of her audience? Still, other talk shows, like "People Are Talking" in San Francisco and "Like It Is" in New York, had featured me in hour-long programs. But those shows were different. Both were local and their audiences mainly liberal.

The feeling that my story should be told by itself, in its own context, kept nagging me. I conferred with my agent, Kevin, and he basically agreed with me but said, "It's Oprah's show. She calls the shots and she chooses the angles. Just be glad you will be on it. And Paul Simon isn't bad company, you know."

"I know," I said.

Several weeks passed. As the date of the show, June 25, approached, word reached me through Kevin that the show had been postponed because Paul Simon could not make it. Was this a prelude to its being canceled? I wondered.

One weekday Debra DiMaio called me.

"Paul Simon is unable to appear on the show because of concert commitments," she said.

"Is the show canceled then?" I asked anxiously.

"No, not at all," Debra hastened to reassure me. "We intend to go on with it. What's changed is that you will be Oprah's only guest."

I could hardly believe what I was hearing. Now I had center stage.

"You will be on for half an hour," Debra continued. "I hope you have enough to talk about in all that time."

Enough to talk about! I had enough to talk about for a century of television time.

"I've just started reading your book," Debra said. "I hope to finish it by the weekend, and then I'll be in touch with you early next week with further details."

A week passed without word from Debra. I naïvely began suspecting that maybe she had found the book too strong, had advised Oprah of the danger of going ahead with the show, and that Oprah had heeded her counsel. I called Kevin in New York and asked him to follow up on the matter and find out exactly what was going on.

Kevin came back with the reply that the show was still on, the date was being set, and Debra would be contacting me shortly. A day or so later I received a call from Oprah. She wanted to know how my family was faring back in South Africa. I seized the opportunity to tell Oprah that for some time I had been attempting to get my family over to the U.S.

"Really!" she exclaimed. "Are they coming?"

"There's a possibility they may come," I said. "But I have one big problem. I can only afford to bring one or two members because the airplane tickets are expensive. But whom do I choose? I was thinking of bringing over my parents. But they're illiterate and traveling alone may be dangerous. What if they got lost in Europe? Also, I would very much love to see by siblings. We've been separated for almost nine years, you know."

"That's no problem," Oprah said. "Why don't you have the whole family come over?"

"The whole family!" I exclaimed. "You know how much that would cost? Almost twenty thousand dollars. I haven't got that kind of money."

"Don't worry. I'll take care of the money issue," Oprah said.

I was speechless.

"Give me their names and I'll get my travel agent to buy them tickets," she said.

"Oprah, you don't have to do this," I said.

"I want to," she said. "I feel like I know them so well from the book that they've become my family, too."

"This is all unbelievable," I muttered. "Let me think about things awhile."

"Okay," she said. "You know where to reach me."

I spent the afternoon in a daze. Was all this real? The next day I called Gary Beukes in South Africa. Recently, whenever I was unable to communicate with my family in the ghetto, I had been getting word to and from them through Gary. We had been in touch several times since Lyston told me about him, and I was now comfortable with him, having concluded that he was worth the risk. Since he was a white man and lived in Johannesburg it was easy to reach him because the authorities seldom interfered with my calls to white suburbs. It was only the ones to my family and friends in the ghetto which were tapped, closely monitored, or sometimes cut off.

"Gary," I said, "I have wonderful news for you. But first give me a progress report on my family and their passport applications."

"Well," Gary said in his thick Afrikaner accent. "The family is fine. Your father is still drinking too much and causing trouble for the rest of the family. Just the other day he got into a fight with your sister Florah, but I have talked to him about it. And I gave him that letter you sent and your brother read it to him. I have wonderful news for you, too. Your mother, Granny, and George have received their passports—"

"Have they really!" I cried. "My gosh! I never thought they would receive them."

"But your father refuses to sign the papers. So I can't complete the application for his," Gary went on. "And you know Granny may be unable to travel because she is very sick."

"I pray she gets better," I said. "I very much want to see her. She's getting old and I'm afraid if we don't see each other soon it may be too late. She must see America and what's become of her favorite grandchild because she and my mother made it possible for me to become what I am today."

"I hope she gets better, too," Gary said. "She's such a lovely human being. Very witty and forever hopeful."

"Gary, are you ready for this?" I said. "I want the entire family to come to America."

There was a pause. I had shocked Gary.

"The whole family," he repeated slowly.

"Yes," I said. "I want to see every one of them. I want them to see America."

"Will they come back?" Gary asked.

It crossed my mind that Gary's phone might be tapped after all. On occasions I had heard strange noises during our conversations.

"Of course they will go back," I said matter-of-factly. "South Africa is our home. I, too, would come back if I wasn't considered an enemy of the regime."

"Well, time is running out," Gary said. "I don't know if I can get the rest of your family passports on time. When do you think they will be coming over?"

"How about in a week?"

"In a week!" he exclaimed. "That's too soon. I'll do my best. But I make no promises."

The same day I informed Oprah that three members of my family had already been granted passports, but that with the rest it was a race against time. Gary called a few days later.

"I've done the best I can," he said, "and it's impossible to get everyone a passport. Your mother, Granny, George, Florah, Linah, and Dianah have received theirs and will be able to make the trip. Maria and Merriam and your father will not come, unfortunately."

Aware of strange noises on the phone, suggesting that our conversation was probably being listened to, I decided not to go too much into details. I simply said, "You've done your best. I'm deeply grateful."

The next day I called him about the plane tickets. He suggested that it would be better if they were purchased in South Africa as he knew of a way to get very low fares. Gary had an account in the United States and he requested that I send the money for the tickets to that account, through Lyston. Gary would use his own money to buy the tickets back home. I conveyed to Oprah the arrangements and her response was "Do you trust this man?"

I replied that based on what I knew about Gary I trusted him.

"Okay," Oprah said. "I'll wire the money to his account." The next day about $8,000 of Oprah's money was in Gary's bank account.

49 MY FAMILY ARRIVES; THEIR VIEW OF AMERICA

Granny, seventy-six; my mother, forty-seven; Florah, twenty-five; George, twenty-two; Linah, fourteen; and Dianah, eleven, left South Africa on the twenty-sixth of June, 1987, aboard a Lufthansa jumbo jet headed for Frankfurt, West Germany, where they were to connect for a flight to the United States. None of them had ever been aboard a plane before. Their excitement, I was later told, knew no bounds. As the plane cruised above the clouds, Granny and my mother were in awe and adamant that they were flying through heaven, and any minute expected to see God in His resplendent glory, surrounded by angels and cherubims hymning hosannahs and hallelujahs.

The parting from other family members was most painful. My father, I was told, regretted his stubbornness, which made him refuse to sign his application form when Gary applied for passports in behalf of the family. A day before the family left South Africa, my father pleaded with Gary.

"I want to go. I want to see my son."

"You can't go without a passport, Jackson," Gary replied. "You shouldn't have been so stubborn. You brought this upon yourself, you know."

Meanwhile, Oprah had come to New York to host the Emmy Awards. She proposed that instead of having my family fly down to High Point, North Carolina, I should come up to New York and together we could meet them at JFK. That way they could spend a few days sightseeing in New York City.

"Won't New York be too much of a shock for them?" I said.

"Mark, all visitors to this country love to see New York."

But my family were no ordinary visitors. They were literally coming from another world. I wondered how they would deal with the sights, the freedom, and the madness of New York City. Granny had never been in an elevator or ridden a subway, let alone stayed at a hotel. Oprah had reserved the family suites at the Sheraton Hotel on Fifty-second Street and Seventh Avenue, where she was staying with her entourage.

I flew to New York Saturday morning and arrived just in time to join Oprah, Stedman, Debra, and Beverley Coleman, her personal assistant, and we headed for JFK to await the arrival of Lufthansa flight 404 from Frankfurt at 1:30 P.M. Gail had traveled from Brooklyn and Phyllis Reed, Hans and Ellie Spiegel, and some friends from my days in New York were also present. Oprah was mobbed at the airport. The minutes ticked away. We bit our fingernails and clung to each other in anticipation. The flight landed. The tired passengers came streaming out of customs. The ABC affiliate in New York was present and cameras were rolling. The interviewer asked me several questions which I answered dreamily. All the time I was asking myself, What will my family look like? How much have they changed? Is all this true?

Then I saw them. Florah was the first to recognize me, and we rushed toward each other and embraced. Within minutes I was hugging and kissing Granny, George, Linah, and Dianah. They resembled visitors from another world. They were heavily dressed in winter clothes, including thick woolen hats, as it was winter in South Africa. My mother kept saying in Tsonga, "Oh, my child, oh, my child, is it truly you? God is alive, God is alive indeed."

Oprah introduced herself.

"Hi, I'm Oprah," she said, shaking hands with each family member.

My family simply stared at her, uncomprehending. They took her for another well-wisher. I had not explained to them who Oprah was because it wouldn't have been understood. When my mother and Gail saw each other they embraced so naturally that even I was surprised. I had sent my mother a photo of Gail.

"Hullo, *skwiza* [my son's wife]," my mother said to Gail, then spoke rapidly in Tsonga.

"She says you're very beautiful," Florah translated.

"You're very beautiful, too," Gail warmly told my mother.

Everyone packed into long black limousines with tinted glass and we drove back to Manhattan. When we alighted before the hotel my family was in awe. The tall buildings that almost touched the sky, the bustling crowds, the maddening din of cabs and pedestrians—all seemed overwhelming. White porters came and politely offered to carry my family's heavy bags. I could detect that my family was uneasy, especially Granny and my mother, at the thought of being served by a white person. They locked hands and guided each other through the throng entering and leaving the busy Sheraton. Granny almost got trapped in the revolving door.

The suites were heaven to them. None of them had ever slept in a hotel. What was most remarkable was the ease and friendliness with which they related to everyone, despite churning stomachs and the confusion that whirled in their heads. I finally tried explaining to them who Oprah Winfrey was, and that she was the one responsible for their visit to America.

"God bless you, my child," my mother said to Oprah.

"I'm the one who is blessed in meeting you," Oprah replied.

Florah and George spoke fluent English. Granny and my mother, having worked for English-speaking whites most of their lives, understood basic expressions but had a hard time responding. But their faces and emotions spoke volumes. That evening the family appeared on the local news. Oprah gave her credit card to Beverley, who then took the family shopping for summer clothes at Alexander's. The following day, Sunday, Gail and I took them for a walk through Central Park and to museums. We rode the subway, an adventure.

On Tuesday we flew to North Carolina. Since my apartment had only two bedrooms, I rented, with Oprah's help, another apartment, where some of my family stayed. My friends in High Point made the family most welcome. They were driven around, taken here and there, and pampered with affection and attention. Pat Hutcherson, a charming, gregarious Southern lady who was the office manager at the medical practice where Butch was a partner, invited the family to her home for a barbecue and homemade ice cream. On the way home my mother compared her treatment by whites in South Africa and by whites in America.

"I have encountered many whites in my life, child," she said in Tsonga. "Yet few had what I see in abundance in the hearts of the white Americans I have met: *rirhandzu* [love, charity]." To underscore her point, she proceeded to quote verbatim her favorite Scriptures,

Corinthians 13. She ended with verses 12 and 13: *"Sweswi hi vona hi ripfume exivonini; kambe enkarhini wolowo, hi ta langutana hi mahlo; sweswi vutivi bya mina a byi hetisekanga, kambe enkarhini wolowo ndzi ta tiva hi ku hetiseka, tani hi leswi Xikwembu na xona xi ndzi tiveke hi ku hetiseka. Sweswi, ku tiyile swilo swinharhu leswi: ku pfumela, ku langutela, ni rirhandzu; kambe lexikulu ngopfu eka swona i rirhandzu."*

Shortly after arriving in North Carolina, Granny and my mother formed an important friendship with Edmonious "Eddie" Torrence, a motherly and very giving black woman whose only son died in the Korean War. Eddie, a widow, was very artistic. She taught Granny and my mother how to paint ceramic Christmas ornaments, and she feted the family with a dazzling array of Southern dishes. My mother called Eddie "sister," and Granny called her "my American daughter."

One of the first things my mother wanted to know was if there were any churches in High Point she could attend. She went to black churches and white churches and loved them all. I was struck by how nonjudgmental she was. I had expected her to ask me all sorts of questions about why the churches were segregated. All she said was "Americans are very friendly people. They truly have God in their hearts."

One afternoon following brunch at a local black church my mother said to me, "Child, this is Canaan. This is the land of milk and honey. This is the land of the living God."

With those expressions of innocent, all-embracing love my mother, I believe, captured the essence of America. As days went by I heard from my family examples of why they regarded America as a Promised Land.

"We aren't required to carry passes."

"We can go anywhere we want."

"White people are very friendly here."

"We can ride in the same buses and use the same toilets as anyone."

"We can talk and have dinner with anyone we wish."

"We can attend church with anyone."

"There are no police raids."

"In America all people are equal."

I knew that there was more to America than what my family saw, heard, or was exposed to, but I did not want to lessen their sense of joy and liberation. After all, their visit to America was only supposed to last a month. If they had to go back to South Africa, I wanted them to know that somewhere they could breathe free and life could be lived differently, that somewhere they were regarded as full human beings and treated as such.

Through Butch and Suzie Farabow, I succeeded in getting each member of my family a complete physical examination. Various High Point physicians performed the invaluable services for free. My mother's chronic diabetes was fully diagnosed and prompt and extensive treatment begun under the supervision of Dr. Richard Orr at the High Point Regional Hospital. Dr. Edwin Auman found Granny to be in remarkably good health for her age and background. It seemed that several of her illnesses had been caused by anxiety that she would die without ever seeing me again. George, examined by Dr. Thomas Jarrett, and Linah and Dianah, by Dr. Thomas Goldston, were also given clean bills of health. Dr. Eldora Terrell, who examined Florah, recommended further tests to determine the nature of a suspicious growth in her cervix.

"I don't think it's cancerous," Dr. Terrell said. "But we'd better be sure."

Before further tests could be carried out, the family flew to Chicago to appear on "The Oprah Winfrey Show" on July 6. We were treated like dignitaries. Oprah put the family in suites at the luxurious Hilton Hotel on South Michigan Avenue. She and her staff went out of the way to make my family feel at home. The show was deeply moving. People in the audience, including whites, wept when they heard me recount my life story. Toward the end of the program my family joined Oprah and me on the stage. It was a poignant, memorable moment. Granny and my mother hardly understood what was happening but they carried themselves magnificently, like the African queens they were. Unfortunately the show was preempted in many parts of the country because Oliver North was taking his famous stance before the congressional committee investigating the sordid Iran-Contra affair. Our appearance on "The Oprah Winfrey Show" made *Kaffir Boy* a nationwide best-seller. It reached third place on *The New York Times* best-sellers list, and was number one on *The Washington Post* best-sellers list. To date it has sold more than 200,000 copies. The book also won a Christopher Award in 1986 and was one of the finalists for the 1987 Robert Kennedy Memorial Award.

The family was interviewed by *Jet* magazine and wire services, and the story of our reunion appeared in papers across the country.

This led to more interviews and another appearance on "The 700 Club," where my mother was given a literary kit which she began using immediately. One afternoon we had lunch with Oprah in a famous black-owned restaurant on the South Side of Chicago.

"This is how many black people across America live," I said to my family as the limousine cruised down streets of ghetto havoc.

"Is this America, too?" George asked, astonished.

"Yes, this is still America," I said.

"My God, some of these houses are as bad as those back home," he said.

"In other places they are worse," I said.

"How come?"

"That's the same question I constantly ask myself," I said. "And I have yet to come up with a satisfactory answer."

"But there's supposed to be freedom and the good life for everybody in America."

"There's supposed to be," I said. "But sometimes there isn't."

"Oprah is black. Why is she so rich and powerful?" Florah asked.

"She worked hard to get where she is. She always believed in herself. She never gave up, despite the obstacles which litter the black man's way to anywhere. And she was lucky."

"I'm confused."

"Let me put it this way. If you work hard in America, it's possible to achieve your dream."

I proceeded to tell them briefly about Oprah's inauspicious beginnings in Mississippi thirty-four years ago, the struggles she endured and finally overcame, and her rise to fame, fortune, and power. I drew the analogy between her successes and mine.

"Only in America could this have happened to both of us," I said.

My mother's diabetes responded well to insulin treatment and a modified diet. The family spent the evenings catching up on what had happened in our lives during the long separation. Many of the gaps in the letters we had sent each other were filled, and the picture that emerged was one of dogged survival, of violence and repression, of unbreakable bonds of family. Through it all, my mother saw the almighty hand of God at work, preserving, sustaining, strengthening. When the family had attended the Fourth of July celebrations at a local church, my mother, as she saw the joy and pride in the hearts of Americans, again said, "This is truly the land of God."

Preparations for the August first wedding went ahead as planned. Gail was about to leave her job at the German Information Center and move to North Carolina. It took her little time to adjust to the family. She was struck by the closeness of everyone.

"Are families in South Africa always so large and this close?" she asked.

"Yes. By the way, family for blacks in South Africa means everybody: grandparents, aunts, uncles, cousins, nephews, nieces, the lot. The concept of the nuclear family is foreign to us. We believe in taking care of each other. Maybe that's how we survive all that oppression."

Gail was embraced by everyone as part of the family. Her color was never an issue.

50 THE WEDDING; FLORAH'S CANCER; THE FAMILY RETURNS TO SOUTH AFRICA

The wedding was to take place on Long Island. The family drove to New York the week before, and Alice and Ziggie were kind enough to let us use their home for the duration. They moved in next door with their son Eddie and his wife, Nancy, and their children. The wedding was planned as a private affair. Stan Smith was best man. Joanne Matzen, Gail's friend from high school and a law student at the University of Minnesota, was her maid of honor. Gail's parents, grandparents, and several relatives came. All my friends from my days on Long Island attended, as did those from New York. Gail's father, after walking Gail down the aisle to my side, stepped into the pulpit and, after quoting some verses from Genesis, said the following words:

Dear Gail and Mark,
The verses I just read contain some thoughts about what a man and a woman can bring to each other that may be instructive for us all. In receiving Eve as God's gift to his loneliness, Adam receives back a missing part of his undiscovered self, his feminine

soul. . . . According to our Genesis narrative, we are made in God's image. But that image is neither male nor female: it is man and woman in a relation of interdependence that ideally mirrors the divine. . . . What I hope and pray for is that the greater completeness you can bring to each other will make your relationship truly fruitful, fruitful in the lives of the children you may raise, fruitful in the words you may write collaboratively, fruitful in other ways beyond our present imagining. May the promises you now will make further what is most promising in you both, in the remarkable gifts God already gave each of you before he gave you each other.

The last words brought tears to Gail's eyes.

The reception was held at the Unitarian Fellowship in Bellport where *Kaffir Boy* had been discovered and my life changed. It was an idyllic day, sunny with crystalline skies and a light breeze which wafted across the estuary. On that memorable day, Granny danced to Madonna, *Mbaqanga* (South African township music), Paul Simon, and Bob Marley.

"How I wish your father and your other siblings were here," my mother said. "They would have been very proud."

Gail and I had our honeymoon—a gift from the Chases—at the quaint American Hotel in Sag Harbor, Long Island. The day neared when my family would have to return to South Africa. They had all fallen in love with America and wished to remain in this country, but there were several obstacles in the way of that dream. For one, half my family still remained in South Africa; two, they had come to America on visitors' visas; three, money was needed to relocate them; four, Gail and I were due to move to Cornell in September.

Every one of my friends wanted the family to remain here permanently. Oprah and I discussed the issue several times, and she promised to help in whatever way necessary. Gail and I also discussed the issue since we knew that our life together and plans for the future would be affected.

In the middle of all that talk word came that the results of Florah's tests for cervical cancer were positive. A biopsy was recommended to determine the extent of the malignancy. The family was stunned, and their departure was postponed indefinitely. Butch offered to perform the operation for free; Dr. Virgil Robertson, the anesthesiologist at High Point Regional Hospital, also demanded no payment: all in all the family was saved bills amounting to thousands of dollars by the kindness of friends. Gloom settled over the family but my mother dispelled it with constant prayer and an upbeat spirit.

"God will make Florah well," she would say. "He didn't bring us all this way for her to die."

In the meantime, concerned as I was about Florah's health, I continued efforts to get George a scholarship to the local private school, Westchester Academy, so he could remain in the United States and continue his studies. I also spoke to Marty Van Lith and Anita Cohen, a white couple, friends of Gail and me, who lived in Brookhaven, Long Island, and had offered Linah and Dianah a home and to put them through school. I worked around the clock to help Anita and Marty prepare applications and affidavits for guardianship. Linah and Dianah, only fourteen and eleven and having grown up so close to the family back in South Africa, wanted to return home, but my mother insisted that they remain in the U.S. and go to school.

"What future do you have back home?" she said in Tsonga. "Don't you know how lucky you are to get this opportunity to stay in America and go to school? Do you want to be like your sisters Florah, Maria, and Merriam, who became pregnant because of the disruption of black schooling? You *will* stay here with your brother, so stop the nonsense."

We all kept praying that things would work out. And they did. Florah's operation was a success. The biopsy turned out to be a cure in itself, as the cancer was in its very early stages. But she needed at least a week of follow-up treatment to ensure that there were no complications.

George was accepted at Westchester Academy and given a full-tuition scholarship. Dr. William Hovenden, the headmaster and a former Peace Corps member stationed in Cameroon, was instrumental in George's receiving the award. I had to pay only for his meals, fees, and transportation, and find him housing. But since Gail and I were planning to move to Ithaca, where would he stay? I discussed the matter with several friends, including Richard Payne, owner of a local furniture store. Richard, a middle-aged white Christian, was a mod-erate Democrat who opposed the death penalty and ran a prison ministry. With profits from his furniture store, he operated a halfway house for ex-convicts, black and white, being rehabilitated prior to reentering society.

"I'd be glad for George to stay at the halfway house," Richard said. "He can help run the place. He'll have his own room and privacy."

I had misgivings about having my brother stay with ex-convicts, particularly because he was still new to America. I spoke to George about the arrangement and he said, "Don't worry, I can take care of myself. My main goal is to get that education."

"If he experiences any problems," I told Richard, "inform me immediately."

"Don't worry," Richard said. "If he doesn't like it at the house, he can move in with me and my wife."

I applied to the INS for George's tourist visa to be changed to a student visa. It would be months before I heard from them, and I hoped there would be no complications under the recently overhauled immigration laws. Meantime, Marty and Anita had filed the applications of guardianship for Linah and Dianah. After several bureaucratic delays, having to do with obtaining my father's signature, Marty and Anita were given a conditional go-ahead to enroll the two girls at the Bellport Middle School while the applications were being processed. Plans were made to have Linah and Dianah fly to New York before the fall school term began. But first we had to see Granny, my mother, and Florah off.

It was a tearful sendoff. Granny's last words to Gail and me before she boarded the plane were "Take care of each other." And my mother said to Gail, "Take care of my son, your husband. And God watch over both of you."

Linah and Dianah wept. The plane took off. We returned home, and Gail and I started packing for Ithaca. Linah and Dianah left for their new home in New York a few days later and George moved into the halfway house. But I continued being anguished about the way my siblings were being farmed out all over the place. Was it the right thing to do? Shouldn't we be together, at least for the first few months? Finally I told Gail that I was having second thoughts about going to Cornell.

"I think we should remain in High Point and help everyone adjust," I said.

"But Mark," she said, "think of what this fellowship means for your career. Besides, they're expecting you at Cornell and your class is ready."

"There will be other teaching posts," I said. "I'll explain to Jonathan Culler and I'm sure he'll understand. At this point being here close to my family means more to me. I just don't feel right farming them out to different places while I go my own selfish way."

"But Mark, you have your own life to live," she said.

"Yes, but I must be there to help them adjust," I said. "I know how terrible things can be without that support, understanding, and reassurance. You know, too. You've read the first chapters of *Kaffir Boy in America*. You've lived in a foreign country. My siblings need me more than I need Cornell, Gail."

"But we'll be able to see them during holidays," she said. "Also, your appointment is only for a year. After that we can come back and gather everyone together."

"A year can be an eternity to someone in a strange land," I said.

"What do you plan to do?"

"I don't know yet."

I explained to Ned my predicament and he advised me to go to Cornell.

"It's a fine break," he said. "Cornell is a prestigious school and your having taught there will mean a great deal in your background." But he understood my problem.

Gail and I flew to Ithaca, found an apartment, and paid the deposit and a month's rent. The day came for us to leave. We rented a U-Haul truck but it broke down as we drove it home from the rental shop. We rented another and it, too, broke down. Was this some sort of omen? Finally we rented a Hertz Penze, loaded our belongings, and parked it outside the empty apartment for the night intending to start on the long drive to Ithaca at the crack of dawn. During the night, after much reflection, I made up my mind that, much as I wanted to, I would not go to Cornell.

In the morning I told Gail of my decision. She concurred and we both went out looking for another apartment. Pat Colona, who helped me find my first apartment, told us of a three-bedroom townhouse which had just become available at Guilwood North in High Point. We moved in the same afternoon. A few days later I went and fetched George, who had already begun having problems living with ex-convicts. A month or so later Linah and Dianah began having problems adjusting to their new home. Marty and Anita, though they showered the girls with attention and love, found themselves stymied by the cultural differences. Gail and I brought Linah and Dianah to North Carolina to live with us. We enrolled them at the local public school while we applied for their student visas.

Epilogue

It has been over a year since my family came to America. George had a rough start at Westchester Academy. At twenty-two he was the oldest student in all his classes. When he was tested for placement—his ghetto grades were inconclusive—it was discovered that, though intelligent, he was totally unprepared for twelfth-grade work. Pat Sams, Westchester's guidance counselor, recommended that he begin in tenth grade so he could master the fundamentals of subjects like algebra and English. The Bantu education system in South Africa hardly prepared George for the rigors of an American private school, with its emphasis on the liberal arts. While in South Africa I had managed to mitigate Bantu education's noxious effects on my intellect by reading everything I could lay my hands on, including books meant only for white schools, given to me by the Smiths, Granny's employers.

When George learned that he had to begin in tenth grade he was naturally disappointed. But he was also grateful for the opportunity to get the best education, and was determined to overcome whatever obstacle lay in his way. He told me one afternoon, in Tsonga: "Even if they had said I should begin in first grade, I would have done it. Getting that education is the most important goal in my life."

The improvement George has made in a year has been remarkable. His English is better, his comprehension has improved, he is able to distinguish fact from opinion (a problem that plagued me during my first year in America), he has adjusted well to the American culture, and according to his teachers he is an exemplary student. Part of the credit for George's rapid progress belongs to his teachers. They were patient with him, they were nonjudgmental, and they saw beyond the poor grades a curious, eager, disciplined young man determined to succeed.

286

Most of the credit belongs to George himself, his diligence and single-mindedness. On the average he spends about five hours every day doing homework. He is constantly checking books out of the library. He does not abuse television. He is undeterred by failure. He began with F's and is now getting C+'s, B's, and occasional A's. And he is not taking easy courses, either; some of the things he is learning I did not learn until after I had left college.

Knowing that he lost over four years of schooling due to the violent protests in the ghettos; that he has been handicapped by an inferior Bantu education and destitute childhood; that English is his fifth language, behind Tsonga, Venda, Zulu, Afrikaans, and Sotho; and that he has an older brother whose successes put so much pressure on him, I admire his courage, level-headedness, and resolve. I am confident that he will succeed in life. He has begun to. During the summer of 1988 he was selected from a nationwide pool of promising minority high school students to participate in the LEAD (Leadership Education and Development) program at the University of Virginia. He successfully completed the month-long program and was awarded a certificate. His dream is to acquire a university degree and return home to help and inspire others less fortunate. He always tells me that he cannot believe that American students, black and white, take for granted such incredible educational opportunities as libraries, good schools, and fine teachers. He remembers how many of his friends were killed for only dreaming of such opportunities.

Linah and Dianah's experiences have been somewhat different. There is little doubt they are intelligent and capable students. In their first year at public school they were near the top of their respective classes. But every day they complained about how "easy" the subjects were, about how disrespectful students were toward teachers, and how education was taken for granted by most American students, many of whom seemed to have come to school mainly to have a good time. Feeling the constant pressure to fit in, they began emulating the conduct of their peers.

To please their friends in public school Linah and Dianah would come home and ignore their homework. They wasted time "hanging out" with friends, many with characters who left a lot to be desired. They spent hours memorizing frivolous MTV lyrics instead of scientific formulas or poetry. They stopped listening to advice and occasionally joined in the general disrespect of teachers by their classmates.

When Gail and I saw the heady days of public school begin to make them forget where they had come from, we decided to move them to a school where student irresponsibility and laziness were not tolerated. It was a difficult decision to make. Their public school had some fine teachers and more cultural diversity, and the girls had more black friends there. And, of course, public school was less expensive. But the environment there was hardly conducive to learning, especially for two impressionable little girls from Africa enamored by some of the worst things in American culture: watching television, singing songs from MTV, cultivating the Diana Ross look, talking in slang—in short, doing their best to be part of the in-crowd. Linah and Dianah did not really know the hardships that George, Florah, and I did. When they were growing up, my mother's toil and Florah's occasional jobs had already begun to make a difference in the family. The family ate regular meals and dressed in clothes better than rags. And there was often money to send them to school and to celebrate Christmas.

Having concluded that the quality of Linah's and Dianah's education, and their overall development as human beings, was most important, even if it cost me thousands of dollars, I discussed their situation with Dr. Hovenden, the headmaster at Westchester Academy. A renowned educator, and someone who knew firsthand the deplorable condition of many a public school, Dr. Hovenden understood my concerns and was eager to help. He offered Linah and Dianah partial scholarships to Westchester Academy. The two had made A's and B's during their year at public school, but unfamiliar with the California Achievement Test, Linah failed it twice (Dianah barely passed it the second time) and would have had to repeat eighth grade unless she went to summer school. Some of these tests, I believe, have a built-in bias against minorities and students who are not trained test takers. I doubt if I would have scored well on standard achievement tests had I been required to take them upon arrival in the U.S., straight from the ghetto.

It turned out that Linah's eighth-grade work in public school on the average equaled that of sixth grade in private school, and Dianah's seventh equaled fifth grade. Several basic skills tests the two took confirmed the point. I explained to Pat Sams, Westchester's guidance counselor, that the tests alone should not be used as a measure of the girls' intelligence and capability. She agreed and a compromise was reached under which Linah enrolled in eighth grade and Dianah in seventh. In those classes they are learning things I did not learn until I was at college. For instance, in history they are learning about the political, social, and cultural environment of countries around the world, and doing comparative studies of African countries, including South Africa. In the process they are acquiring valuable skills like interpreting points of view, developing a global perspective, detecting bias, hypothesizing, and recognizing fallacies in a line of reasoning. In English they are studying the poetry of writers like Eliot, Poe, and Tennyson; Roman literature; and analyzing and appreciating art.

Linah and Dianah could not believe the amount of homework they had each day and the toughness of the subjects they were learning. They also could not believe that while they were among the top students at public school, and got A's with little effort, in private school they are guaranteed F's if they goof around. It has been a rude awakening, to say the least. But they are now working hard and are improving. They have even begun to get A's on their homework and on quizzes. They still have time for sports, their friends, and helping with chores around the house. They no longer snicker at George for spending five hours a day doing homework; they're doing the same. Linah and Dianah became honors students in 1988. In May, 1989, George was awarded a full four-year scholarship to Guilford College in North Carolina, one of the top small liberal arts colleges in the country.

As for the family back in Alexandra, my mother's diabetes is finally under control. She is also making great improvements in learning how to read and write. Granny is well. Uncle Piet is still without a regular job and still addicted to horse-racing. His wife, I'm told, has left him. I am trying to help him learn a new skill—construction—so that he and my dad, a self-taught carpenter, can go into business together. My dad is still struggling with alcohol but there is some hope that the disease can be controlled. Merriam, nineteen, heeded my advice and returned to school after her baby, Sibusiso (Gift) was born. She is now in tenth grade. While Merriam is at school, her baby is being cared for by my mother, who works at night, or by my other sister, Maria, twenty-two. I paid Maria's way through sewing school, and bought her a sewing machine. Until recently, she was working from home: knitting socks, jerseys, scarfs, and so on. But she has written me a letter in which she expressed a desire to return to school and matriculate (she dropped out in seventh grade); I have promised to assist. Florah works as a receptionist for Gary Beukes while I am arranging for her to come to America to study to be a beautician, her dream. She is determined to import the American look—"Oprah's look," she calls it—to Alexandra.

The family is eagerly awaiting the completion of their new home, being built with the aid of Habitat for Humanity, which recently opened a branch in Alexandra. Habitat for Humanity, a nonprofit group headquartered in Americus, Georgia, has helped hundreds of low-income people across the U.S. and around the world build their own homes. Former President Jimmy Carter is its spokesperson. Habitat for Humanity in Alexandra serves an even more important function. As a multiracial organization it is bringing Indians, Coloureds, whites, and blacks together in a common cause. Many barriers are falling as a result.

Mr. Linda Twala, a member of Habitat in Alexandra, visited the United States in October 1987. The authorities almost refused him a passport. In 1985, because of his leadership role in Alexandra and the support he enjoys among the Comrades (radical young blacks), his house was fire-bombed by Vigilantes (conservative blacks supported by the government). During his U.S. visit, Linda told me of the desperate need in the ghetto for books, medical supplies, and help for the elderly. In my lectures across the country I have urged students and other Americans eager to help to organize book and clothing drives and send the items to Alexandra and other ghettos. To date, thousands of books have been sent by such diverse institutions as St. Mark's School in Massachusetts, Guilford College in North Carolina, Skidmore College in upstate New York, and MacMurray College in Illinois. Some individuals have even sent money to Friends of Alexandra, a group headed by Linda Twala, Gary Beukes, and Dorothy Steele, an Englishwoman. A black sorority at Drake University in Iowa recently held a male beauty pageant and raised $200. The sorority is planning similar fund-raising events in the future. I am also working on raising money for the construction of a library in Alexandra; in *Kaffir Boy* I recounted the burning of the only library in 1976.

In 1988, Oprah's production company, Harpo Productions Inc., purchased the movie rights to *Kaffir Boy*. I'm confident that Oprah's sensitivity will do the story justice. Oprah has also donated $7,000 to provide free lunches for the elderly in Alexandra for a whole year. The lunches are distributed through International Concern Foundation, of which Stedman Graham, Oprah's boyfriend, is now president. Stedman is also president of the Graham-Williams Group, a public relations firm in High Point, North Carolina, and has traveled extensively throughout South Africa and seen firsthand the desperate plight of the black majority. He heads the same International Concern Foundation that first brought me to North Carolina. The only difference, aside from a new staff, is that the foundation's mission has broadened beyond South Africa, and now involves helping the needy throughout America and in various developing countries.

One of my greatest joys has been in sharing with young Americans my life story and convictions, and acting as a role model. I was particularly proud when "Teen Express," a television program, and two national magazines, *Black Teen* and *Scholastic Voice*—the three have an audience of millions of teenagers and high school students—interviewed me and ran excerpts of *Kaffir Boy* in 1988. I know that somewhere there is a young black or white child to whom my life story will act as an inspiration. I know this because the life stories of Arthur Ashe and Richard Wright acted as inspirations to me, and strengthened my faith that I could succeed in life despite obstacles of bigotry and poverty. Unfortunately, *Kaffir Boy* is banned from being published in South Africa. But as is often the case, tyrants cannot entirely suppress ideas and literature. A few months ago *Kaffir Boy* received a remarkable review in one of South Africa's defiant liberal papers, the *Cape Times*. The white reviewer, Robin Hallett, apparently managed to get hold of a commonwealth edition of *Kaffir Boy*, published by Bodley Head, London. In the review, Robin deplores the ignorance people often have of the societies in which they live. He writes:

> We are all to some extent trapped behind the invisible walls of our personal ghettos—ghettos of profession or class, generation or ethnic group. But we ought constantly to be making an effort to break down these walls, to enhance our own understanding of society as a whole. Hence the importance of reading.
>
> . . . He [Mark Mathabane] has made it easier for the rest of the world to understand what it is like to grow up black under apartheid.
>
> His book could easily have been searingly abrasive. But he has the temperament to recollect emotions in tranquillity, the balance to convey both the decency and the cruelty of South African life, the meanness and the generosity.
>
> These qualities make him into a notably humane interpreter for his white compatriots. Interpreters need to be listened to very carefully indeed.

It is one of my dearest wishes that *Kaffir Boy* be published in South Africa, the one country where the book's message most needs to be heard.

I also take pride in helping young black South Africans come over to America to study. A free South Africa will sorely need educated blacks. When George was still in Alexandra, I used to send him information about American prep schools and colleges where I had spoken and solicited scholarships in behalf of black South African students. One such school was Northfield Mount Hermon in Massachusetts. The admissions coordinator at Mount Hermon sent George a package of application forms from New England prep schools willing to consider admitting qualified black South African students and providing them with full scholarships. He shared the information with his peers in the ghetto, many of whom had reached the limit of frustration and were in danger of giving up. They in turn wrote impassioned application letters to the schools.

One of these young fighters made it. Noah Jiyani, twenty, a soft-spoken tennis player with a huge Afro, wrote a letter to Phillips Exeter Academy. People told him that the chance of his being accepted at such an elite preparatory school was remote. Noah was undeterred. Phillips Exeter sent him application forms. He completed them, kept up a steady correspondence with the school, and was finally accepted and given a full scholarship for the 1987–88 academic year. He has now graduated and been awarded another full scholarship to Carleton College in Minnesota.

The initiative and determination of George and Noah—and many of their peers in Alexandra and other ghettos throughout South Africa who are determined to acquire a decent education—remind me of my own attitude almost ten years ago, when I believed in the impossible: that I would someday come to America and succeed as a human being. That dream, despite intervening hardships and disappointments, has in many ways been realized. I'm happily married, I own a lovely house, I'm supporting my family and putting my siblings through school, I can write and talk freely, and my human and civil rights are protected under American law.

But the struggle continues. And it will not end until all God's children in South Africa, in the ghettos of America, and in countries around the world are freed from suffering and everything that oppresses their development as human beings. And I thank America for giving me, through an education, a second chance in life—a life I have dedicated to the struggle for justice.

Index

ABOUT THE AUTHOR

Mark Mathabane lives with his wife, Gail, and their
three children in Portland,
Oregon